Under the Bed,
Creeping

Under the Bed, Creeping

Psychoanalyzing the Gothic in Children's Literature

MICHAEL HOWARTH

McFarland & Company, Inc., Publishers
Jefferson, North Carolina

LIBRARY OF CONGRESS CATALOGUING-IN-PUBLICATION DATA

Howarth, Michael, 1977–
    Under the bed, creeping : psychoanalyzing the Gothic in children's
literature / Michael Howarth.
        p.   cm.
    Includes bibliographical references and index.

    ISBN 978-0-7864-7843-9 (softcover : acid free paper) ∞
    ISBN 978-1-4766-1598-1 (ebook)

    1. Children's stories—History and criticism.   2. Children's stories—
Psychological aspects.   3. Psychoanalysis and literature.   4. Gothic
revival (Literature)   5. Terror in literature.   I. Title.
PN1009.A1H69 2014
809'.89282—dc23   2014014781

BRITISH LIBRARY CATALOGUING DATA ARE AVAILABLE

Front cover image © idal/iStock/Thinkstock

Printed in the United States of America

McFarland & Company, Inc., Publishers
  Box 611, Jefferson, North Carolina 28640
  www.mcfarlandpub.com

For Robert, my father

Contents

Acknowledgments

I learned to be fearless from my father. When I was five years old he rented *Jaws* and we watched it at my grandparents' house, eating hot fudge sundaes he'd bought us at Carvel. Lights turned off, we sat in silence and watched a killer shark wreak havoc on a small seaside town. From the opening credits, when the famous score builds to a crescendo, I was mesmerized. The director, Steven Spielberg, shot many scenes underwater, others from high up in the air, and still others from the shark's perspective to heighten the suspense. Each point of view drew me further into that other world and showed me that life could be seen and experienced through different sets of eyes. My imagination exploded. What would it be like to swim through the ocean? To bite a person in half and follow a blood slick two miles down the coast?

I wondered how it would feel to be the victim of a shark attack, or to be the fisherman who gutted the shark for food. My mind reeled and rocked like one of the fishing boats onscreen, and for two hours I lost myself in another world. By the time our voyage was over, my hands hurt from gripping the worn-out seat cushions on my grandmother's sofa. I had never seen or experienced anything quite like *Jaws*, and I wanted more.

While other kids my age were learning that it was bad to eat glue, I was wrapped in a blanket on the couch watching *The Fog, Don't Look in the Basement, Critters*, and *Night of the Creeps*. Having watched *Halloween II*, I was the only kid in my fourth-grade class who knew that doctors consult dental records when the body is unrecognizable. How that topic even came up in an elementary classroom I have no idea.

Whenever Dad drove to the video store I would run straight to the Horror section and gaze up at the titles, entranced by gory and creative box covers I can still remember with fondness: the bloody shopping bag for *Chopping Mall*; Leatherface and his chainsaw for *The Texas Chainsaw*

Massacre; and the manhole cover being lifted by a monster for *C.H.U.D.* I wasn't allowed to watch those movies on my own, and my father made me hide under a blanket during certain scenes, but they ignited my imagination. They made me want to write and read as much as I could.

Thanks, Dad, for trusting me to explore the darkness on my own, even if I did ask way too many questions during the movie.

And thank you, Mom, for being cautious and concerned, yet being brave enough to let go of my hand, knowing this journey would prove worthwhile in the end. Being a nurse, I know you're accustomed to seeing blood, so perhaps that gave me an edge in convincing you not to turn off the TV. If Dad supplied the visual motivation with all those VHS tapes, then you certainly supplied the verbal incentives by championing my twisted ideas as they led me down a dark path toward literature and the arts.

I'd also like to thank two friends from my graduate days at the University of Louisiana at Lafayette: Dr. Jennifer Geer, my graduate mentor who read numerous drafts of each chapter and offered invaluable feedback on children's literature, and Dr. Joseph Andriano, who supplied me with many notes and books on Gothicism that proved crucial in establishing the positive connection between the gothic and children's literature.

At no point during the writing process did I need therapy, although I did make many phone calls to Dr. Carolyn Dennett, one of my favorite psychologists. I appreciate her taking the time to read excerpts and drafts. Her input on behaviorism and cognitive development helped to deepen the many issues and ideas presented in this book.

While this book is academic in nature, it is my hope that many parents will find it informative and enlightening. They can use it as a bridge to communicate with their children, to understand better the various ways in which literature is a catalyst for personal growth and identity formation. As children rely more and more on visual stimuli, absorbed in iPads and Kindles and movie magic, it becomes even more important to surround them with piles of books they must climb over and fall into every day on their path to maturity.

I look forward to the day when I can sit down with my niece and nephew to talk about Peter Pan and Little Red Riding Hood, nudging them to peer into the woods and to take that daring first step that might be the most difficult, but that is certainly the most memorable. My sister and brother-in-law might be hesitant to let me read them bedtime stories, but I promise to leave a light on.

Finally, I'd like to thank my wife, Dr. Joey Brown, for putting aside her grading to read through this entire book and to suggest improvements. I know you don't like horror, but I appreciate you making the effort to indulge my collection of movies, even if you'll only watch classic ones from the 1930s and 1940s. I'm glad you've developed a certain affection for Boris Karloff and Val Lewton. More than anything, though, I'm grateful that you're always there waiting for me when I find my way back out of the woods.

Preface: Appreciating the Big Bad Wolf

I wrote my first scary story in Miss Lawton's English class when I was in seventh grade. She was mildly amused and commented on my vivid imagination. The second story raised an eyebrow, and she suggested I write something happy and uplifting. In December, five stories later, Miss Lawton gave my Christmas assignment an F, blazed across the front page in bright red ink, and made an animated phone call to my parents, no doubt branding me a future serial killer who needed to be stopped immediately. She was upset over my treatment of a major holiday, which I had clearly mangled with my graphic descriptions of a crazed Santa Claus who murdered people with the help of his demonic elves.[1]

I was not mentally unbalanced, nor did I require psychiatric care. I was simply guilty of being a horror fanatic, enamored by the constant ability of films and books to pump my body with fear while their narratives transported me to another world. I was jealous of such power, and I desperately wanted to harness it like Stephen King or H.P. Lovecraft. Indulging in the horror genre helped fuel my imagination at a time when I was still transitioning into a new town and a new school. I was trying to fit in and make friends, and any stress or anxiety I felt was channeled onto reams of notebook paper. Like some grotesque alien hidden away in a decrepit basement, the horror genre was my fun little secret, and it stirred my creativity with an intensity that I could not credit solely to my left-handedness.

Late one night, after I'd already gone to bed, I heard my parents arguing over my literary masterpiece. My mother expressed concern that perhaps I was watching too many horror films. My father defended me, no doubt feeling partly responsible for having introduced me to *Jaws*, *Halloween* and *Aliens* while I was still learning addition and subtraction. While Mom vented her concerns, Dad shrugged off the incident as though I'd done nothing more than to shove one of my classmates into a locker.

Looking back on all those seventh-grade horror stories, I realize that I needed to lean on my burgeoning imagination; it helped to process my conflicted feelings about school and home. What I've learned since is that there's a darker edge to the luminous boundaries that encircle our comfortable lives, and I needed to venture into it to deal with my oscillating emotions. This journey is one that all children will take at some point during their formative years, especially given the fact that children seem to have a greater connection to gothic elements on account of their penchant for frequent emotional displays. Added to this romantic notion of sentiment over reason is a child's heightened sense of imagination, which arises from a naïve perspective regarding how the world functions.

Now, twenty-four years later, I'm a college professor teaching children's literature. And I'm still fascinated with the dark side of human nature. When I'm not writing lectures, or grading papers, I'm reading gothic novels and short stories; when I'm not attending administrative meetings, I'm watching horror movies with the volume cranked to ten. I look forward to chilly, overcast days with strong winds and dark clouds, and I become giddy during a violent thunderstorm. Every October I set up a Halloween tree and spend my nights ensconced in the den, surrounded by ghoulish candles and elaborate jack-o'-lanterns while bloodcurdling screams emanate from my plasma TV.

I'm not morbid or pessimistic. I'm just fascinated by the way happiness tends to keel over when fear creeps up behind it and screams, "Boo!" I admire how gothic literature illuminates the way we view the world, and how it forces us to interpret our ever-changing roles in it. I'm intrigued by the idea that we are not born with an innate sense of our own limitations, but discover them gradually as we learn basic skills and explore our surroundings. And it is only by investigating these surroundings, by crawling through the darkness, that we encounter gothic elements, which expose our limitations while also becoming them.

Then again, perhaps I'm just defensive of my morbid curiosities. Having studied gothic literature in graduate school, I understand the ways in which Gothicism contributes to our social development and identity formation. When we interact with gothic elements, we learn what frightens us, and what we find fascinating. We learn that we are not always in control of our own imaginations. And we learn that domestic spaces can be just as terrifying as a centuries-old graveyard or a crumbling house in the middle of the woods.

These theories and ideas didn't resonate with me until I read the Brothers Grimm version of "Snow White" while taking a graduate class titled The History of Children's Literature. The tale revolves around the theme of female jealousy, specifically an older woman's vicious jealousy toward the youth and beauty of a younger one. It's a woman's story that reflects female fears, the major one being that a woman's worth is based on her beauty and appearance.

Even while reading the tale I knew that Snow White didn't have a choice. She had to leave home and flee into the forest. I knew she could never mature properly while her evil stepmother loomed over her and sent huntsmen to carve out her lungs and liver. I was scared for her because she has nowhere to go. She has no one to rely on and trust. She is moving from the light into the darkness, into the strange and unfamiliar. This is an important journey that every one of us must take at some point in our lives. Like Snow White, we must brave our way forward no matter how scared and confused we might become.

The unknown can be frightening because it often represents change. To embark on a journey alone, whether it is physical or emotional, requires courage and dedication. For a girl like Snow White, who spends her days in a safe and secure world, and who is oblivious to evil, this idea of growth and maturity can seem hostile and unattractive. Once she is inside the forest, Snow White will have to think for herself.

She doesn't realize that the tale's gothic elements (the deep, dark forest; the hunter intending to murder her; the old witch; the poisoned comb and apple) are gateways to autonomy and self-reliance. To suffer is to learn, and Snow White must therefore suffer before she can escape the comfort and security to which she once clung at home. She must rely on herself and assert her independence if she hopes to survive a tumultuous period that clearly symbolizes her own adolescence. Basically, she must find the courage to leave behind all that is familiar so she can grow up.

In the original fairy tale, the dwarfs continually chide Snow White for falling prey to the queen's plots. They warn her of impending danger, and they must constantly save her from death. Unlike the 1937 Disney movie, in which the dwarfs are given silly names such as Dopey and Sneezy and stumble around as comic relief, the dwarfs in the Brothers Grimm version are protectors. They understand Snow White is only a child, and they try to keep her safe. They lecture her on rules and act as moral and intellectual guides, trying to help her develop emotionally so she can feel confident in her own abilities and eventually leave the woods as a wiser and more mature woman.

Prior to taking this graduate class, I had read hundreds of fairy tales, and I found them to be violent and entertaining. But once I began to examine them from a social, historical, cultural, and psychological standpoint, I began to see how the Gothicism in these tales often initiates a thought process in the story's characters, as well as in its readers. For most people, the word "gothic" suggests moonlit forests, crumbling castles, and voluptuous maidens fleeing dank dungeons and sexual harassment. One often associates "gothic" with "terror" and "horror," imagining werewolves and vampires and zombies rising from the muddy ground to gorge on human brains. But for me the gothic is more than a haunted house on Halloween, or strange, lingering sounds that pull me awake in the middle of the night. For me, the gothic suggests our deepest fears and desires, bruising our egos with its sublime power. It's a subtle reminder that life is not always the fairy tale we hope it will be.

Because of my specific tastes, which have often been labeled "creative" and "sordid," I've enjoyed incorporating gothic literature into my classroom lessons, specifically in my children's literature classes. I've taught *The Graveyard Book* and *Boris and Bella*, sometimes *The Secret Garden* and the *Harry Potter* series. I've taught fairy tales like "Snow White" and "The Warlock's Hairy Heart," as well as selections from Jack Prelutsky's *Nightmares: Poems to Trouble Your Sleep*. Over the years, as my students and I have discussed the themes and lessons embedded in these various texts, I've become extremely interested in examining further the importance of Gothicism when placed within the context of children's literature.

While recent years have shown a steady increase, in both publication and sales, of gothic novels for children, it's important to know that Gothicism has always been an integral part of children's literature. During the Middle Ages children read medieval epics like *Beowulf* (AD 850) and *Song of Roland* (1150), works brimming with pages and pages of bloodshed and violent imagery. Later, in the seventeenth century, Michael Wigglesworth's poem "Day of Doom" (1662) and James Janeway's book of moral instruction *A Token for Children* (1671) symbolized the Puritan desire for children to improve their souls and tend to their own salvation. With imagery of babies burning in hell and raging rivers of fire, these texts certainly scared children into living the pious lives expected of them. In these cases, the writers employed Gothicism as a means to curb behavioral issues, to educate through fear rather than through experience.

By the beginning of the eighteenth century, books for children became gentler in both tone and subject matter. Themes such as death and damnation were still preached, especially in texts such as Isaac Watts's *Divine and*

Moral Songs for the Use of Children (1715), but the emphasis was more focused on listening to one's parents and fulfilling one's familial obligations rather than on the pain and torment derived from one's misbehavior.

Throughout the nineteenth century, gothic elements continued to find their way into children's literature, such as Christina Rossetti's poem "Goblin Market" (1862), George MacDonald's novel *The Princess and the Goblin* (1872), and select fairy tales by both Charles Perrault and the Brothers Grimm, to name just a few. Many of these authors used gothic elements to help children understand the differences between what society viewed as proper etiquette and bad etiquette. The gothic imagery acted as a supplement to the story's main purpose (which was to supply pleasurable, yet didactic, reading) instead of setting a somber tone that instilled in children a natural fear of authority and God, as was typical during the seventeenth century.

In the early twentieth century, novels such as Frances Hodgson Burnett's *The Secret Garden* (1909) and J.M. Barrie's *Peter and Wendy* (1911) incorporated gothic elements, but it was only in the latter half of the twentieth century, specifically the past thirty years, that Gothicism in children's literature became the central focus in many children's books. The settings in many children's stories also shifted during this period from pastoral landscapes to urban and suburban locales. This shift reflected cultural ideas about children and their relationships with their environments; it suggested that adults began to feel comfortable in allowing children to encounter themes typically thought to be more associated with urban locales, such as murder, thievery, sex, and industrialization.

It's interesting to note that after World War II, amid a growing distrust of authority, psychoanalysis became more integrated in children's literature. This integration helped further explore the relationships children develop between themselves and their environments. One of the first books to successfully integrate psychoanalysis and Gothicism was Maurice Sendak's picture book *Where the Wild Things Are* (1963), which allowed children the freedom to become angry, translate their emotions into physical creatures that symbolize their frustrations, and then sort through those conflicting emotions at their own pace.

As I pondered a connection among Gothicism, psychoanalysis and children's literature, I sat down in my office and wrote one question: How can gothic elements help children deal with conflicts in their lives, and, in doing so, contribute to the formation of their self-identities?

My first thought was that, while Gothicism and children's literature both deal with universal issues such as trauma and maturity and punishment, there are many parents who believe gothic elements are too scary for children; they believe that reading scary stories will scar their children for life and send them straight to the mental institution like a misguided heroine in some creepy Victorian novel. These parents, who can't help but think from an adult point of view, believe that Gothicism subverts the didactic role that children's literature is expected to play in the growth and development of its young readers. After all, Gothicism is famous for shocking us with heightened acts of sex and violence, two elements typically not found within the seemingly innocent pages of a children's book.

But where do we begin to distinguish between helpful gothic elements and harmful levels of sex and violence?

How dark is too dark?

People have always been captivated and entranced by morbid details, grotesque characters, and disturbing plots, which is one of the reasons why horror sells. It feels good to have an outlet for the emotions we experience in our own lives, emotions we might want to repress or deny. Gothic stories entertain because they allow us the opportunity to lose ourselves in another character's anguish and distress. At the same time, these stories produce Schadenfreude, creating a sense of comfort and pleasure by reminding us that, at least for the moment, we ourselves might be free of such pain and emotional duress. Gothic stories provide an unconscious outlet for our own pain rather than force us to acknowledge our own personal feelings of anger, aggression, and hate.

One of the strengths of gothic literature, then, is that it teaches us things are not always what they seem. To come into contact with monsters and ghosts is vital and necessary to our mental and physical growth because as we grow older we discover that these strange shapes and intense situations often embody our individual fears and anxieties. Just as the characters in a given story succeed in defeating their own individual problems, so, too, can child and adult readers conquer similar problems in their own lives. We might identify with a given story, which unconsciously provides an outlet for how we feel. And when we reflect on that specific story, we are actually attributing our feelings to the book's characters. By going on an imaginary journey with these characters, and through witnessing their rewards and mistakes, we learn how to deal with similar conflicts in reality. While a child is certain not to encounter a troll or a werewolf, he or she might feel threatened or oppressed by other people or events in his or her life. In these cases, gothic literature aids the child in abandoning childish impulses so as to engage in mature reflections.

This process of self-reflection assures us that while struggling with difficult events is an unavoidable part of human existence, the journey it provides will only strengthen our growth, thus helping resolve conflicts so we can advance to the next stage of development. On a simpler level, Gothicism allows us to realize we won't be crushed by our own emotions, but will, instead, survive and prevail. At some point in our lives we will all encounter the Big Bad Wolf, but how we manage the fears he elicits will depend on our psychological development and the lessons we have already learned. As well, such emotional encounters can provide a potential opportunity to re-learn those lessons that we might have learned wrong, but now have another opportunity to correct.

The more I considered Gothicism as a teaching tool for children, the more interested I became in exploring various theoretical models of the gothic. My reading list ran the gamut: *The History of the Gothic Novel, The Gothic Body, The Rise of the Gothic Novel, The Haunted Castle, The Gothic Romance, The Female Gothic, The Madwoman in the Attic,* and *The Gothic Flame.* I read about vampires and female empowerment, about class struggles and male oppression. One particular passage that interested me was Fred Botting's assertion that gothic literature "becomes a fiction of unconscious desire, a release of repressed energies and antisocial fantasies," meaning that gothic stories tend to concentrate on imagination and emotion instead of reason and logic.[2] These characteristics mirror children themselves, who often act on emotions because they are developmentally unable to reason, especially in their early years. Their decisions are usually based on immediate feelings rather than a careful assessment of information.

Spanish writer Carlos Ruiz Zafón wrote that "one of the pitfalls of childhood is that one doesn't have to understand something to feel it."[3] His statement emphasizes one of the main differences between children and adults. Because children have not yet mastered their rational faculties, they often indulge in epic fantasies that mirror their conflicts in the real world. They travel to imaginary places in which they possess unlimited power and everything makes perfect sense. In a fantasy world, a child reigns supreme, no longer controlled by adults. And that's precisely what makes literature such an intimate experience. A book will never yell at a child; it will never accuse a child of being stupid or lazy, or state that a child is worthless. A book doesn't judge; it simply invites the reader to participate in an experience. And if there are pitfalls, if there are bumps and bruises and buckets of tears, then let us remember that pitfalls are often learning experiences, and some of our most rewarding times are those uncomfortable moments when we suffer the effects of a horrible decision, but then use the pain to better ourselves.

Learning to conquer our fears and establish our independence is what makes Gothicism an effective teaching tool for children. Children desire consistency and security. They want to indulge their curiosity and explore the world. They crave independence and want to assert their autonomy, yet crave stability for fear they'll be neglected or abandoned. These characteristics of childhood echo elements found in gothic literature, which is preoccupied "with an atmosphere of oppression and innocence in danger, the development of situations based on persecution and a constant fleeing from pursuit."[4] The stories children read, especially the ones with gothic elements, help them learn how to manage their own distressing emotions, as well as how to survive interpersonal and intrapersonal relationships. These constant attempts at securing stability and ensuring survival thus seem to reflect a child's primal need for self-preservation.

The bottom line is that Gothicism is just as applicable to children as it is to adults. There is no emotion specific to adults and, as renowned psychologist Erik Erikson has suggested, "every basic conflict of childhood lives on, in some form, in the adult."[5] Basically, then, children and adults possess the same fears, but those fears take on different forms depending on one's age and maturity. Children are fully capable of feeling anger, pain, terror jealousy, betrayal, and fear. In childhood, the fears just manifest themselves in different forms. Typically, if we fear something in childhood, then we usually continue to fear it in adulthood. This idea suggests that if children learn to grapple with their fears, then they are learning the necessary tools for adulthood. For example, as a child one might fear the dark because he or she fears being alone. As an adult, however, one might fear relationships because of the potential for a breakup, which will then result in being alone.

Psychoanalytic theory suggests that adults, like children, also fear aggression, death, and abandonment, but these fears get played out in other situations such as money, marriage, and relationships. Without this introduction to fear, children may enter adolescence unprepared to resolve intrapersonal and interpersonal conflicts like puberty, sex, relationships, or peer-pressure. Thus, Gothicism in children's literature, besides being a source of entertainment, achieves a didactic purpose by supplying the emotional training wheels we all need to mature.

Because children's literature is a relatively new field in academia, however, an analysis of its relationship to Gothicism has been marginalized up until now. Yes, there have been studies of psychoanalysis in children's literature, such as Bruno Bettelheim's text *The Uses of Enchantment*, but such analyses do not focus their attention squarely on the gothic. And while other texts, such as *The Gothic in Children's Literature*, do focus their attention on the connection between Gothicism and children's literature, they lack the psychological analysis necessary to show how gothic elements help children resolve individual crises and advance toward future stages of development.[6]

In the subsequent chapters, I hope to show that Gothicism is a noteworthy and necessary contributor to a child's growth and development, as well as to the critical study of children's literature. Children's literature pairs well with Gothicism because the best children's literature is able to "reveal both our greatest pleasures and our deepest fears or concerns. Understanding what pleases or frightens us the most is absolutely key to understanding what it means to be human and how human beings relate to and treat one another."[7] My research is more relevant now than it has ever been because, in the past twenty years, fear has become a prized marketing tool for selling books to young readers. In today's literary marketplace, gothic stories for children cram the bookshelves, from the *Harry Potter* series and the *Spiderwick Chronicles* to R.L. Stine's *Goosebumps* series and *Lemony Snicket's Series of Unfortunate Events*. This popularity is yet another reminder that children, like adults, need a bit of horror in their lives, especially considering that as they move through childhood they suffer mistakes and hardships, often learning life lessons by trial and error. They often feel attacked by parents and significant relations, and that they must defend themselves because no one else will. Children relate to characters in a gothic story because they feel a kinship with someone who is confused and scared, often wandering alone, both physically and emotionally, in a vast world that they don't understand and, perhaps more important, that does not seem to understand them.

By focusing on internal feelings, gothic stories analyze what it means to be a human being, which is especially important in children's literature because children consistently try to rediscover their own identities. The stories they read, whether poetry or novels or picture books, can supply small clues that, over many years, will help to define their own individuality. If childhood is a journey, then Gothicism is just one of the roads we'll have to travel, sometimes frightened, and sometimes wounded, but almost always alone. To be sure, this is a gloomy path, but one that all children should be allowed to explore on their own, for how can children appreciate the light if they have never played in the dark?

Introduction:
Lurking in the Shadows

Children have many fears. Two of the most common are the fear of being abandoned and the fear of being overpowered. Certainly, the two are connected. The first arises from an instinctual need to rely on caregivers for food, clothes, shelter, and protection; the second arises from the self-realization that children are basically weak and helpless, dependent on adults to survive in the world until they're mature enough, both physically and emotionally, to cut the cord and function on their own.

The best children's books address both of these natural fears. Rather than simply scaring children and making them feel foolish and ashamed, these books respect children enough to validate their anxieties, and they present absorbing stories that engage children's attention and give them new ideas and viewpoints to consider. For example, Beatrix Potter's *The Tale of Peter Rabbit* is a story that adults do not find particularly frightening, yet there are many children who can all too easily relate to Peter's fright at being lost in the garden, unable to find his way back home and pursued by an angry farmer who wants to kill him and eat him. While most scholars would not label *The Tale of Peter Rabbit* a gothic story, the story's themes, namely helplessness and abandonment, appeal to children's fears and create in young readers a stronger connection to the narrative, especially because Peter's trauma occurs when he disobeys his mother and leaves the safety of his home. The threat of death teaches children the dangers inherent in not listening to one's parents; it also shows Peter's mother as caring and concerned rather than as nagging and angry, which is how many children view their parents when being lectured and disciplined.

Another example that deals with these fears is Frances Hodgson Burnett's *The Secret Garden*. Unlike *The Tale of Peter Rabbit*, there has been much critical attention paid to the gothic elements in Burnett's novel. Articles such as "Re-reading *The Secret Garden*" by Madelon S. Gohlke and "*Wuthering Heights* for Children: Frances Hodgson Burnett's *The Secret Garden*" by Susan James touch on ways in which the novel's pervading darkness and gloominess affect its child characters. From the English moors to the eerie wailing heard late at night, the novel's gothic atmosphere mirrors the emotional stages of its two main protagonists, Mary Lennox and Colin Craven. A child can understand the isolation experienced by Colin, as well as his anger at being abandoned by his father and the subsequent paranoia he develops while being confined inside the mansion. His self-hatred and fear of sickness renders him sympathetic to children who have few friends, are ignored by parents, or are stricken with a debilitating illness.

Likewise, children can relate to Mary, whose parents have died and who now finds herself living in the mansion without any friends. Her parents were too wrapped up in their own lives to pay her any attention, and at Misselthwaite Manor she continues to be pushed to the side and expected to amuse herself. The gothic atmosphere echoes her anger and rudeness; indeed she seems to feed off the negative energy at Misselthwaite Manor. Child readers understand that it is this dark and depressing atmosphere that fuels the characters' loneliness and eventually brings them together, thus allowing them to mature and develop their self-identities.

When discussing *The Secret Garden* or *The Tale of Peter Rabbit* with children, it's clear the gothic elements help connect children to the novels' characters and themes. These connections occur on an emotional level that spark self-reflection and help children progress through various stages of psychosocial development. For most people, the word "stages" implies finality, an ending that precedes a new beginning. And though children navigate through many stages, it's important to remember that childhood is not a skin that one sheds and then forgets. We need to remember that childhood is not a stage that has to end before adulthood can begin. As adults we navigate through many stages, as well, searching and learning as we rely on information and experiences we've cultivated in our past. Every stage supplies new conflicts and crises, building upon one another to produce different emotions that ultimately form the basis for a child's eventual identity and personality.

Gothicism is the perfect genre to explore because it's one that deals predominantly with emotions and feelings, recognized for promoting psychoanalytic readings and discussions. This focus works well when studying children's literature because children themselves often display heightened levels of emotions as they try to figure out who they are and their place in the world. A connection between children and Gothicism also makes more sense when we consider that "the Gothic landscapes and conventions remain familiar to us because they are, to some extent, inside us."[1] My aim, then, is not only to examine the gothic in children's literature, but to do so from a psychoanalytic perspective.

While there are many worthwhile psychologists to study, I've chosen to focus my analysis on Erik Erikson's studies. In his landmark texts, *Childhood and Society* (1950) and *Identity: Youth and Crisis* (1968), Erikson expanded on Sigmund Freud's theories, though in a very different way with which Freud did not agree. While Erikson accepted many of Freud's theories, such as the idea of the id, ego, and superego, he refused to accept Freud's attempts to describe one's personality strictly on the basis of sexuality. And unlike Freud, Erikson believed that one's personality continues to grow and develop past the age of five. Erikson also believed that sexual *and* social factors were crucial in the development of one's identity and personality. Put simply, Erikson represents a psychosocial approach to personality development while Freud represents a psychosexual approach. While both approaches are crucial to a person's growth and development, I believe a psychosocial approach will help to illuminate the role Gothicism plays in a child's struggle for meaning and self-identity. I also favor Erikson's theories because they have yet to be examined in the context of children's literature and Gothicism.

Erikson divided the human life cycle into nine stages of psychosocial development, each involving warring emotions, as well as a specific crisis that must be solved before one can move on to the next stage. He emphasizes that the word "crisis" is used "in a developmental sense to connote not a threat of catastrophe, but a turning point, a crucial period of increased vulnerability and heightened potential."[2] Each stage contains its own set of crises, both inner and outer, that, through their actions and resolutions, will allow us to mature, develop our personality, and progress forward to the next phase of identity formation. Each of these stages "employs a process of simultaneous reflection and observation" that, when combined with Gothicism, provides a healthy stimulus for readers.[3] Subconsciously, children may perceive a story's gothic tone, recognize the emotions manufactured by the mood or characters or setting, and begin to cogitate on why they are responding to the literature.

Erikson explains each of his stages in a clear, logical manner, while also illustrating a visible connection between the stages themselves, thus showing how each stage unfolds organically based on the stages preceding and succeeding it. His theories connect with the psychological angle of the gothic because in each stage he relates the individual's inner conflicts with social relations. In gothic stories, these relations often break down and need to be put back together. By immersing themselves in gothic tales, children can learn how to deal with family and social issues that affect them in everyday life. As fictional characters take steps to mend these fractured relationships, so, too, can child readers gain a deeper sense of self-confidence by realizing they also have the strength and ability to restore any chaos or trauma that might surface in their own lives.

Like many gothic stories, Erikson's theories examine intrusions in the maturation process, focusing their attention on such themes as healing, loss, and survival, as well as the steps we all must take to learn from our mistakes and mature. All these key moments are links in the chain of identity crisis, a process affected as much by personal growth as it is by the communities in which we live. Surely, children cannot undergo an identity crisis all by themselves, and in each stage of development Erikson suggests a radius of significant relations, such as parents, friends, or significant others, that impact the child and contribute to his or her psychological growth. He stresses the importance of the community on each stage of development, believing that "the environment feels called upon to convey to him [the individual] its particular ideas and concepts of autonomy in ways decisively contributing to his personal character, his relative efficiency, and the strength of his vitality. It is this encounter, together with the resulting crisis, that characterizes each stage."[4] Using these inner and outer conflicts, as well as the radius of significant relations, Erikson's psychosocial approach will provide a fresh and exciting way of examining children's literature, specifically the conflicts that arise in the maturation process and the ways in which Gothicism aids in the discovery and resolution of each fundamental crisis.

I have chosen to focus on only five of Erikson's nine stages because these five stages are the ones that relate most closely to children and young adults. I have omitted the first stage, infancy, because the cognitive skills acquired during this stage do not involve the types of literature I wish to analyze. The crisis during this first stage is trust versus mistrust, the word "trust" being equated with confidence. The child needs to learn to function independently of the mother and begin to see him or herself as a fully functioning individual. The infancy stage is integral to future reading skills because during this period "the eyes, first ready to accept impressions as they come along, are learning to focus, to isolate, and to 'grasp' objects from the vaguer background—and to follow them."[5] These sensory advances prepare a child for reading words on a page. As the child is praised by her parents, and gains confidence in her reading ability, she builds up to sentences and paragraphs and chapters until she is finally able to read and understand an entire book.

A child must enjoy the act of reading before she can be expected to master the act of reading. Finding pleasure in reading allows children to develop analytical skills that are necessary to follow a sequence of main events and construct a narrative, which is crucial to one's emotional and intellectual growth. Narrative is not simply the means by which we understand and analyze literature, but also the means by which we structure our lives and create meaning from our daily actions.

The stages of development on which I will focus my attention are as follows:

- *Stage 2*: Autonomy versus Shame and Doubt (early childhood—toddler, 2–3) *Strengths: Will, Determination. Antipathy: Compulsion.* Radius of Significant Relations: Parental Persons.
- *Stage 3*: Initiative versus Guilt (play age—preschooler, 3–6) *Strengths: Purpose, Courage. Antipathy: Inhibition.* Radius of Significant Relations: Basic Family.
- *Stage 4*: Industry versus Inferiority (school age, 7–12) *Strength: Competence. Antipathy: Inertia.* Radius of Significant Relations: "Neighborhood," School.
- *Stage 5*: Identity versus Role Confusion (adolescence, 12–20) *Strengths: Fidelity, Loyalty. Antipathy: Repudiation.* Radius of Significant Relations: Peer Groups and Outgroups; Models of Leadership.
- *Stage 6*: Intimacy versus Isolation (early adulthood, 20–40) *Strength: Love. Antipathy: Exclusivity.* Radius of Significant Relations: Partners in Friendship, Sex, Competition, Cooperation.

Not everyone who shares the same age is automatically going through the same crises and conflicts, or sharing a similar radius of significant relations. The progression from one stage to the next is based on maturity, environment, and each stage's accompanying strengths and antipathies, thus two eight-year-olds might find themselves in different stages. Regardless of age, though, we learn the most from a specific text when it connects most closely to our current stage. Erikson sums it up best when he suggests that "children, at different stages of their development, identify with those part aspects of people by which they themselves are most immediately affected, whether in reality or fantasy."[6] As readers, we latch onto certain characters, themes, or settings that remind us of personal experiences or feelings. This connection between the real world and the literary world then initiates the crises that Erikson believes are crucial for each stage of identity development.

Basically, the resolved crisis has allowed the individual to move on to the next stage, having now provided him with the growth and identity formation he needs in order to continue developing his personality. This maturation process also relates to adults, however, which is one of the reasons why the last stage I'll investigate concerns early adulthood. Clearly, some individuals in this age range may still be stuck in stage five while others may have already completed stage six and moved on to stage seven. Either way, I will analyze how this group still clings to traces of its childhood, as well as the various ways in which children's literature mirrors this group's trials and tribulations.

I've roamed the canon of children's literature and selected texts that not only best exemplify the characteristics of Erikson's stages, but also illustrate ways in which Gothicism acts as a learning tool by triggering an emotional response, escalating the necessary crisis, and producing self-reflections that shape a child's identity. In exploring the connections among Gothicism and children's literature and psychosocial development, I hope to champion Maria Tatar's idea that "the very real feeling of the fictional world makes it just as critical to the formation of identity as what is encountered in life."[7] Beginning with stage two, I will analyze Christina Rossetti's poem "Goblin Market," followed by Carlo Collodi's novel *Pinocchio* and Neil Gaiman's *Coraline*. For stage five, I will examine three different versions of *Little Red Riding Hood*. Finally, I will conclude my discussion with J.M. Barrie's novel *Peter and Wendy*.

Ellen Raskin's picture book *Goblin Market* is based on the poem of the same name by Christina Rossetti. The poem's themes, coupled with the illustrations, echo the main crisis that typically occurs during stage two, namely the will to be independent. Although some might argue that toddlers cannot understand many of the poem's themes and ideas, I believe they can still understand the main ideas involving desire and impulsivity, especially when helped along by the illustrations. Like many toddlers, Laura suffers from compulsion; in the poem, she possesses an irresistible desire to venture beyond the boundaries of her home and gorge on the goblin fruit. She doesn't listen when her sister, Lizzie, cautions her not to leave home, and the result is that she becomes ill and almost dies. For child readers, Lizzie symbolizes an adult presence in the book, a strong reminder that children cannot function in the world without the aid and guidance of an authority figure who loves and cares for them. Laura's near-death experience, as well as the shame and doubt she experiences after returning home, escalates the poem to a cautionary tale that preaches the merits of behavior.

There have been numerous studies on "Goblin Market," many discussing the idea of fallen women, eroticism, and male dominance. Few scholars, however, have analyzed this Victorian fairy tale as a children's poem and those who have, such as Roderick McGillis in his article "Christina Rossetti: The Patience of Style," do not discuss the poem's gothic elements. The poem's sing-song quality, which is derived from the lyrical rhyming patterns and captivating meter, entices children, as do Rossetti's depictions of the goblin men and the wide assortment of delicious fruits. "Goblin Market" is an important contribution to children's literature because, through its incorporation of the gothic, it advises children to listen to their parents and not yield to temptation. More importantly, it illustrates the idea that children who misbehave can be saved, and it assures children that although they will certainly make mistakes during the course of their lives, there exists the potential to benefit from those mistakes and, as a result, mature into respectable adults.

Carlo Collodi's novel *Pinocchio* is one not many people would consider when discussing Gothicism and children's literature, yet there are many gothic elements that children latch onto while reading the story: Pinocchio's hanging, his near burning to death, his imprisonment in a metal trap, his near drowning, and two threats of being cooked and eaten. These scary and intense scenes help children progress through stage three of Erikson's developmental cycle. As a wooden puppet, Pinocchio must earn the right to be a real boy. Like any child, he wants to take independent steps and make his own decisions, yet he must also master the guilt that accompanies wrong steps and the harm they often produce. These disastrous consequences affect not only Pinocchio, but those around him, such as Geppetto and the Blue-Haired Fairy.

I want to analyze the ways in which courage and inhibition affect Pinocchio's character, and also how Collodi incorporates these themes into his novel, stressing his belief that children's characters and personalities are shaped by gloomy experiences and harsh lessons. While some adults might find the novel to be extreme in its various depictions of how children learn through misbehavior and punishment, it is important to remember that Pinocchio's misfortunes are symbolic and representative of childhood incidents, and while children are afraid for Pinocchio, that fear is lessened by the realization that he is only a wooden puppet. Children between the ages of three and six can relate to Pinocchio's plight, namely the act of being shaped and molded by one's family into a model child who, at the same time, strives to achieve an identity by understanding the differences between right and wrong.

Neil Gaiman's novel *Coraline* deals with the conflicts children experience when they feel the natural desire to pursue their own habits and idiosyncrasies. This pursuit initiates a separation from parents, which gives rise to feelings of inadequacy and weakness that keep children lingering close to home. Coraline grows bored with her parents and what she sees as their mundane lifestyle, yet it's only when confronted with the possibility of having anything and everything she wants (but without parental love and compassion) that she becomes a stronger individual and maneuvers through stage four. This stage centers on school age children, and it accents the importance of placing one's trust and emotions not only in basic family relations, but also in those of neighbors and fellow classmates. Only with the help of Coraline's neighbors is she able to defeat her fake parents and return to the real world where she understands that she belongs with parents who love her for who she is, and not for what she symbolizes.

I'm fascinated with the various ways in which Coraline exhibits the strengths and weaknesses characteristic of this fourth stage, namely competence and inertia. She displays competence throughout the novel as she discovers the ability within herself to fight the fake mother with the button eyes. With the help of the community around her, Coraline becomes more confident in her decisions. But Coraline also displays inertia in the novel when she questions her own abilities, wondering whether or not she has the strength and the intelligence to save her entire family. For many children, inertia occurs because they rely too often on adults to solve their problems and guide them through troublesome situations. Because she must rely on herself throughout the novel, Coraline is able to overcome this sense of inertia and develop a sense of productivity, a pride that results from having accomplished something once thought unattainable, namely the ability to think and act like an adult.

For my discussion of Erikson's fifth stage, I want to examine three versions of *Little Red Riding Hood*: Charles Perrault's "Little Red Riding Hood," Jacob and Wilhelm Grimm's "Little Red Cap," and the folk tale "The Story of Grandmother." I'll analyze them as a trilogy of stories that present various methods for coping with sexual discovery and confronting the dark side of human nature. I chose to include these tales in the adolescent stage because their main characteristics are identity and role confusion, two issues that plague teenagers as they teeter between childhood and adulthood. Many scholars, admittedly, have chosen to focus on the tales' more child-friendly message that children should listen to their parents and not talk to strangers. However, some scholars have interpreted the tale as a story about sexual predation and sexual discovery, such as Angela Carter in her short story "The Company of Wolves." I'll expand upon this theme by linking it with the story's gothic elements and then analyzing the various results that arise when this connection affects adolescents. In my examination of the tale, I also hope to illustrate how the gothic elements function to remind both parents and children that sexual awakening is a normal part of life and should not be repressed by adults who want to seal children in a padded box and keep them safe from nothing more than natural curiosity and physical desires.

Of particular importance during this fifth stage of development are peer groups and models of leadership. These relations exist outside the family unit because adolescents are beginning to search beyond the home for acceptance and friendship. They continually refuse to have anything to do with their parents, often out of embarrassment or anger, yet they also struggle to maintain a sense of loyalty to those adults who have supported and cared for them throughout the years. Certainly, these themes surface in the tales of *Little Red Riding Hood*, presenting a girl on the verge of puberty whose parents have not instructed her on sexual matters. In the wolf's stalking of Little Red Riding Hood, as well as his devouring of Grandma (which, in some tales, symbolizes the girl's usurpation of the parental figure and her expected transition into adulthood), the tale's gothic elements emphasize the conflicts many adolescents possess regarding the urge to cling to their parents and family, yet also those urges to cast their parents aside so they can drift away into an adult world, free to embrace their own distinct roles.

The last stage I'll explore centers on early adulthood, and its themes include intimacy and isolation. I've selected J.M. Barrie's novel *Peter and Wendy*, which is a blending of two children's genres, the fairy tale and the adventure tale. Although the age range for this stage is considerably longer than the previous four, I believe the emotions associated with stage six remain constant throughout its duration. Even past the age of forty these emotions continue to resonate depending on the strengths and weaknesses of each person's individual relationships. Undoubtedly, *Peter and Wendy* deals with the issue of growing up, relinquishing playtime, and having to assume adult responsibilities. Yet few critics have addressed the novel's gothic elements, namely pirates, poisonings, alligator attacks, and decapitations, and how they influence the sexual undertones that permeate the story and develop the relationships among Peter Pan, Wendy Darling, and

Captain Hook. The novel raises many questions that young adults consider:

1. Is it easier to morph into adulthood as an isolated individual, or should we rely on companionship?
2. Does being in a marriage or a relationship signify a loss of identity that can never again be reclaimed?
3. Is it better to live in the present and remain blissful, unable to learn from past experiences, or should we embrace the past, present and future all at once, reflecting on life's merits and pitfalls as we formulate our own choices?

For older readers, these questions entice us into probing the story's themes, examining the characters' thoughts and actions, and then reflecting on our own personal relationships.

The conflict during this sixth stage of development is having the desire to express love, yet hesitating for fear of being too open and vulnerable. Each of the main characters in *Peter and Wendy* yearns for some form of intimacy; they crave a stable relationship, whether it is one based on friendship or love. Neverland, then, becomes a microcosm of society in which Barrie presents and develops many different types of relationships, each one revealing the warring emotions that young adults encounter as they balance the identity they have assumed and now try to maintain, as well as societal pressures to become intimate, marry, and then share that identity with another person.

The gothic elements in *Peter and Wendy* symbolize the fears inherent in growing up and being in a sexual relationship, including the violent feelings and tendencies that often accompany a loss of identity. They're an important reminder that relationships often involve competition and cooperation, a constant struggle not just between people and their identities, but also between people and their significant others. At the same time, the gothic elements symbolize our perpetual fear of being alone, of being unable to share personal experiences, and of living a life devoid of romance and affection, much like the novel's main character, Peter Pan.

Certainly, many other children's books could be used to explore each of these stages, and many texts themselves can be applied to more than one stage. *The Tale of Peter Rabbit* certainly suits stage two, while *The Secret Garden* reflects some of the themes and ideas inherent in stages three and four. Likewise, J.K. Rowling's *Harry Potter* series would be a good collection to analyze for stages four, five, or six, and a novel like Roald Dahl's *The Witches* contains many of the same conflicts as those suggested by Erikson in stage four. The important thing to remember is that while children continue to read the same novel over and over again, developing physically and emotionally, each subsequent reading will yield different results based on their particular stages of development. Children can then use their newly-acquired strengths, which up until that point had not been established and integrated into their personalities, to help guide them through successive stages of psychosocial development.

I have personal affinity for the five texts I've chosen. I believe the memories and ideas these texts ignited in me, as both a child and an adult, will aid in my analysis and further clarify the points and observations I make. Perhaps Bruno Bettelheim explained it best when he argued the following in *The Uses of Enchantment*: "Gaining a secure understanding of what the meaning of one's life may or ought to be—this is what constitutes having attained psychological maturity. At each age we must seek, and must be able to find, some modicum of meaning congruent with how our minds and understanding have already developed."[8] In many ways, the quest for self-identity is similar to the arduous journeys undertaken by the heroes and heroines who populate the pages of countless children's books. Every child deserves to feel the surge of confidence that accompanies victory, and the literature we choose to share with our children can help them complete this important process.

When we examine characters in a story we are staring into a mirror, viewing pieces and remnants of ourselves, aware that traces of these characters linger inside all of us. When I feel bossed around I identify with Pinocchio, and when I feel inadequate I'm heartened by Coraline's productivity. Little Red Riding Hood emboldens me to embrace commitment, Laura and Lizzie help me reflect on the importance of family, and in times of stress and anxiety I retreat to the safety and solace that only Neverland can provide. If all these young, naïve characters can journey alone across gothic landscapes and return home as refined individuals, then shouldn't we allow children experiencing similar crises to share the same rewards?

Children should gain comfort in knowing they're not alone in harboring their fears and anxieties, that there are others out there suffering the same doubts and frustrations, and in the following pages I hope to prove my point by educating, enlightening, and perhaps even terrorizing. So let's unlock that secret door and tiptoe into the darkness. Let's seek out those dark, hidden recesses in the mind, understanding that children often find themselves by losing themselves in Gothicism. Only in the darkness do life's realities come to light with kind of sheer intensity that produces self-realization, as well as a deeper respect for how the greater world functions. And let's remember that such realities are always lurking in the shadows, always creeping under the bed and skulking down a midnight hallway, lying in wait until children are ready to open their minds and unleash the power of their growing imaginations, nervously pulling the horrors out of the back closet, one literary nightmare at a time.

1

Behavior and Boundaries: Autonomy and Doubt in *Goblin Market*

Monsters from the Freudian Night

It wasn't until my senior year of high school that I first read Christina Rossetti's infamous Victorian poem, "Goblin Market" (1862). As a reading assignment, I had initially approached it with trepidation and hatred, immediately disliking the fact that it was longer than a page and began with a long list of fruit. All I could envision was a goblin leaning over the counter to inquire, "Paper or plastic?" If I'd wanted to hear a story about two women who traveled to a market and wandered the aisles, I would have talked with my mother and sister. As far as I was concerned, "Goblin Market" was a poem about two innocent girls who succumb to mass advertising because they lack a shopper's finesse.

Over the years, "Goblin Market" has been examined critically from many different perspectives: gothic, feminist, queer theory, religious, consumerist, sexual, Victorian, Romantic, and childhood, to name just a few. Rossetti herself claimed "Goblin Market" was not intended for children, but then later declared it was written for children. Given that Rossetti penned many children's poems such as "A Frisky Lamb," "What Does the Bee Do," and "What are Heavy?," it's not difficult to read "Goblin Market" as a dark, yet ultimately optimistic, commentary on childhood.

Leafing through critical perspectives on Rossetti, I discovered in the September 1973 issue of *Playboy* that one anonymous editorial voice, in an article titled "Goblin Market: A Ribald Classic," wrote that "hiding between the lines of this nice Victorian nursery tale lurk monsters from the Freudian night. 'Goblin Market' might be called the all time hard-core pornographic classic for tiny tots." Those who've read the poem know it's not X-rated material. Nor is it risqué, at least not by contemporary American standards. And while the poem certainly elicits strong sexual vibes, and explores the Victorian concept of the fallen woman, few critics have commented on it as a gothic nursery rhyme used to enforce discipline. "Goblin Market" succeeds as a contribution to the children's literature canon because it's a warning to children about the price of indulgence and the consequences of yielding to temptation. It's a tantalizing seduction of death and despair, a tortured fairy tale about two young girls confronted with supernatural evils.

Many readers are attracted to "Goblin Market" because of the fine balance between terror and eroticism; they are entranced by countless images of raspberries and peaches and apricots, and hypnotized by the goblins' incessant taunts of "Come buy, come buy." The poem is also an interesting meditation on death and sickness. However, death is not a theme that many children understand, and so they tend to skim over that particular theme and focus, instead, on the issues and conflicts with which they're familiar. For many children, "Goblin Market" is captivating because the girls live alone without parental guidance. They are beholden to none as they make their own decisions, for better or for worse, and suffer the consequences of reaching for freedom before they've learned how to reason.

At its most base level, "Goblin Market" functions as a cautionary tale, and it delivers a simple message that every child must learn: *If you misbehave, then something bad will happen to you.* This message is one most often learned through pain rather than pleasure, an idea that places special importance on the poem's gothic elements. These elements, ranging from the goblin men and the sickly Laura to the dreamy and sublime landscape, appeal to child readers and make them more receptive to the lessons and morals. Essentially, these gothic elements produce a heightened sense of fear and anxiety in child readers that allow them to share in the young girls' traumatic experience. These emotions spark a questioning and self-reflection process that helps to guide children through various psychological landscapes as they attempt to resolve their own individual crises.

Autonomy versus Shame and Doubt

Many of the themes in "Goblin Market," specifically temptation, correspond with Erikson's second stage of psychosocial development, which he refers to as "Autonomy versus Shame and Doubt." This stage comprises the toddler ages of two and three. The strengths in this stage are will and determination, the antipathy being compulsion. According to Erikson, this second stage, also known as the "anal stage," is characterized "by the tendencies of '*holding on*' and '*letting go*.' In this and in many other ways, the still highly dependent child begins to experience her autonomous will."[1] This surge of determination is often seen through the child's constant use of the word "No." Here is one of the first words we learn to speak and understand as children, and with this short, simple word comes a sense of power that maturing children find particularly empowering. Because children are often told "no," which adults employ to help them learn their limitations and boundaries, children enjoy shouting "no" right back at adults, reaching for the control and responsibility they're not yet prepared to assume.

The second stage becomes, then, a war for autonomy as the child begins to understand the concepts of "I" and "You," and begins to see herself as separate from the mother. This separation allows the child to grow more self-assured and confident as she tests the boundaries of her world. One can see this behavior in "Goblin market" as Laura does not run home with her sister, but chooses to remain in the glen to eat the goblin fruit. Like a toddler, Laura feels conflicted in that she understands she shouldn't eat the fruit or associate with the goblin men, but compulsion, as well as the desire to make her own decisions, compels her to misbehave and suffer the consequences.

Clearly, this second stage is crucial in developing not only a child's individuality and self-worth, but also a child's understanding of how to control her compulsions, as well as how to resolve the constant desire to collect items and then discard them at a moment's whim.[2] These conflicting impulses define the anal stage in which children battle between retention and elimination. Erikson emphasizes this aspect of stage two by explaining that "[children] will to do, and they demonstrate that they can. The stronger the will, the more they undertake .... But there are limits; when these are overstepped and things get out of control, there may be a reversion to insecurity and a lack of self-confidence that ends in shame and doubt in their capacities."[3] What happens here is that children believe they can move out of their comfort zone, sometimes with trepidation and sometimes with reckless abandon, but unless they are physically and emotionally ready, they will experience fear and hesitation, which can result in embarrassment. Although parents don't want to see their child ashamed and upset, these conflicting emotions during stage two are important for a child to experience because they help teach the child what is acceptable to *say* and *do* within her radius of significant relations.

The toddler, who by this time is speaking and walking, also believes she is entitled to say or do anything she wants, and that she's entitled to give or receive anything she wants. This is why children will often pick up a random object and hand it to someone, or why they sometimes gather a bunch of objects to hide in their bedroom or present to adults. They don't understand the concept of ownership and believe everything is all about them. But this false sense of entitlement must be curbed in order for the child to understand the limits of her capability. While parents can guide the child through this period, by functioning as teachers and disciplinarians, it is also the child's constant feelings of compulsion, and people's responses to them, that educate her in a basic sense of right and wrong.

Confronting all these emotions can help children grasp the concept of ownership and responsibility, two skills they will need during future stages of development. For example, when they develop personal relationships with a significant other, or land a part-time job. For children, Laura's experience with the goblin men is a warning against greediness and compulsion, but her eventual recovery is also a testament to the power of learning from one's mistakes. This healing and resurgence is crucial because it shows children they can bounce back, emotionally and physically, from poor decisions. What this learning process also does is to foster in children a critical awareness of what society expects from them in terms of role and responsibility.

These societal expectations often reflect gender differences that box children into pre-constructed corners in which they're presumed to be complacent and unquestioning. From a historical and psychological standpoint, boys love the outdoors and girls love the indoors. Girls are expected to be clean and demure while boys get dirty and act rowdy. Erikson comments that "they see their respective roles assigned to the indoors of houses and to the great outdoors of adventure, to tranquil feminine love for family and children and to high masculine aspiration."[4] These dichotomies can also be seen in "Goblin Market" with Laura and Lizzie nestled safe inside their house while the goblin men roam the countryside. The implication is that women are safe inside the home where they belong, and that trying to muscle their way into male-dominated territory is dangerous.

Clearly, Rossetti makes use of masculine and feminine spaces in "Goblin Market" to suggest ideas of aggressive male behavior and passive female behavior. These spaces reflect the poem's gothic elements, as well. And while it's always energizing to witness a fallen woman recover from her troubles and then integrate herself back into society, the poem stresses to children the dangers in traveling beyond their accepted spaces. Laura only becomes sick when she ventures beyond her feminine borders to satisfy her compulsion and curiosity about the masculine spaces in which she isn't permitted to enter. As everyone knows, telling children they cannot do something only provokes them into attempting it further. This is why some critics critique the poem as a cautionary tale that scares women into remaining at home where they are safe from the constant actions and aggressions that exist within the realm of masculinity.

But Laura survives her encounter with the goblin men; and Lizzie survives by thinking rationally and not caving in to those same impulses that propelled her sister toward the forbidden fruit. Perhaps by having both girls survive, Rossetti implies that women may share "spaces" with men so long as they don't acquiesce to society's traditional views of how women should behave, which translates to being silent and subservient to men. Lizzie survives because she doesn't give in to the goblin men's incessant taunts and eat the fruit; she restrains her compulsion and refuses to be meek and submissive, as was often expected of a proper Victorian woman. And while Laura does linger near death, her eventual recovery suggests that feminine power is ultimately stronger than masculine power. This idea is suggested by the fact that the two sisters share a deep bond of love and devotion whereas the goblin men are constantly leering at each other and competing to sell their assortment of poisoned fruit.

Children are some of the most careful and attentive readers, always questioning and never afraid to show their true emotions. Like adults, they bring their own personal experiences to everything they read, imprinting their hopes and dreams and anxieties onto each specific character and situation. That is why Laura's traumatic experience resonates with children. Rather than examine "Goblin Market" through a gender lens, as many critics do, children are more likely to view the battle between Laura and Lizzie and the goblins as just a typical fight among siblings in which mean older brothers tease and antagonize their naïve younger sisters. Or they're likely to view Laura and Lizzie as children and the goblins as adults, which sets up a classic power struggle with which they are familiar and can understand.

Regardless of how one analyzes "Goblin Market," the poem functions as a gothic and erotic fairy tale in which a young girl ventures away from home, encounters trouble and sickness, and must then rely on familial love to save her life. All of these elements combine to create a thought-provoking lesson on compulsion and misbehavior that can aid children in navigating through stage two of Erikson's psychosocial development. Admittedly, many people may be surprised at my choosing "Goblin Market" as a poem to assist toddlers in resolving their individual crises during stage two. After all, most children cannot read at two or three. Furthermore, there are few toddlers who can remain quiet and behaved during an entire reading of Rossetti's lengthy Victorian poem. But the poem's storyline, emotions, and child characters will resonate with toddlers in a constructive manner that allows them to process their own conflicted emotions of *"holding on"* and *"letting go."* And because most toddlers cannot read during this particular stage, I will refer to them throughout this chapter as "child listeners" rather than "child readers."

Poetry is especially important to children because it's often the first form of literature they are introduced to, even before they begin to understand and master their native language. Long before they start reading novels, and long before they begin flipping through picture books, children are exposed to the rhythm of poetry. Parents recite nursery rhymes like "Row, Row, Row Your Boat" and "Hey Diddle Diddle" while babies lie in their cribs; they sing limericks by Edward Lear, and read silly poems by Ogden Nash and Dr. Seuss. In fact, many parents will help their children memorize addresses and telephone numbers by creating a poem out of the necessary information. Consider how many children learn their ABCs by singing them aloud, or remember how many days are in each month by singing, "Thirty days has September...April, June, and November." The sing-song quality, bundled together with imagery, rhyme, and alliteration, is what makes poetry so accessible to children; its lyricism makes it easy to memorize and retell. And being able to sit down and tell someone a story not only shapes a child's understanding and mastery of narrative, but also reinforces the child's passion for reading.

The story of "Goblin Market" is told by an omniscient narrator whose tone and point of view lend the poem a storybook feel not unlike one of Grimms' fairy tales. In fact, the poem's opening line, "Morning and evening / Maids heard the goblins cry," suggests the same timeless quality and mood that children associate with those famous words, "Once upon a time." The short lines and rhyming iambs present throughout the story also give the poem a musical quality. Coupled with the opening lines, which entice one into the story with long, beautiful descriptions of luscious and sensuous fruit, this sing-song quality captivates child listeners and draws them into the poem. These elements are important contributors to the reading experience because children read with much more than their eyes. They read with all of their other senses, often talking to a book or singing to a book.

Sometimes they even act out the book. I've even seen children hug books and lick books.

After reading "Goblin Market" to children it becomes clear that the musical tone of the poem mesmerizes them with its nursery rhyme style and reinforces the theme of temptation that pervades the story and stems from its Gothicism. When children hear an adult read the poem in a way that captures its rhythm and cadence, it becomes much easier for them to understand why the goblins' incessant calls of "Come buy, come buy" are so alluring and hypnotic. Likewise, children can live vicariously through Laura or Lizzie, questioning their choices and decisions. In doing so, children must also ask themselves how they would respond if confronted with similar situations.

While "Goblin Market" can be influential as a haunting poem read directly to children, one of the best versions for child listeners is Ellen Raskin's 1970 picture book of the same name. Unfortunately, Raskin's adaptation is out of print and extremely difficult to find, which is a shame given the book's colorful pictures that are illustrated by Raskin herself. One can only hope for a reprint sometime in the near future. Nevertheless, Raskin's adaptation of "Goblin Market" is available on the Kindle, and it is a wonderful tool that parents can use to introduce their children not only to poetry, but also to picture books.

Therefore, along with Rossetti's poem, I'll refer to Ellen Raskin's adaptation throughout this chapter. Her updated version is faithful to the original "Goblin Market" and respectful enough not to alter Rossetti's Victorian themes and ideas. In the book's afterword, Raskin does admit that she "eliminated 197 lines, mostly self-contained units consisting of two minor themes: the death of Jeanie and the planting of the kernel stone."[5] These omissions do not affect an analysis of the poem when it's applied to children and their emotional struggles during the second stage of psychosocial development. On the contrary, eliminating these two minor themes actually brings some of Erikson's theories into a sharper focus because children have fewer subplots to distract them from the main storyline. In Raskin's adaptation, the poem is now centered squarely on Laura and Lizzie. This creative decision allows children to concentrate their attention on characters that parallel their own individual crises and conflicts, a task that might prove difficult if the goblin men had played a more central role by actively pursuing the two young ladies. "Goblin Market" presents a unique story where the females leave the safety of the home instead of staying inside it for protection.

Raskin's *Goblin Market* is the definitive version for children because it's brief enough, at only thirty-one pages, to sustain their short attention spans. The drawings complement the text and lure children into the story by providing strong visuals; with their round edges and mostly bright colors, the drawings also help to soften some of the darker themes. Toddlers are very much visual learners, watching and absorbing their environment as they attempt to form their own identities, and Raskin's use of color, shape, and object placement all provide a visual narrative that allows child listeners to better comprehend the textual narrative.

The illustrations convey a fantasy world that children will find fascinating. Raskin has combined Rossetti's words with illustrations of chubby-faced goblins that somehow succeed in looking both menacing and harmless. She remarks that "they had always been drawn as frightening creatures. I tried to make them appealing (rendering Laura's temptation more plausible), while still complying to Christina's descriptions."[6] Raskin uses her pictures to represent those very same emotions that children might experience while listening to the poem: for instance, terror and uncertainty when following Laura and Lizzie, or mischievousness and cunning when the goblin men dominate the pages to sell their fruits. Raskin also uses green and blue backgrounds to differentiate between safe and unsafe spaces. Green, which often symbolizes life and growth, surrounds Lizzie because she behaves and makes positive choices; blue, which often symbolizes coldness and death, surrounds Laura because she misbehaves and makes negative choices.

As the story progresses and the illustrations fill most of each page, children have plenty of time to let their eyes rove over the colors and characters while they listen to the words being spoken, or perhaps even sung, by an adult reader. Therefore, by compressing the poem into a storybook filled with vivid illustrations that fascinate children, Raskin is able to intensify the fairy-tale aspect of "Goblin Market." This appeals to children because it helps them develop and maintain an interest in not only the poem's gothic elements, but also in the crises experienced by Laura and Lizzie that perhaps parallel similar crises in their own individual lives.

"Come buy, come buy"

While "Goblin Market" presents many fairy-tale aspects to which children can relate, the poem also adheres strongly to the typical gothic situation, which Fred Botting tells us "involves the pursuit of innocence, usually in an idealized female form, by evil, usually in a villainous male form. In the gothic novel, female innocence is typically the victor."[7] Clearly, Laura and Lizzie function as damsels in distress while the goblins represent the male oppressors. However, unlike most gothic stories, "Goblin Market" reverses this plot element by having Laura and Lizzie leave the security of their home to interact with the goblin men. Rather than presenting a standard gothic situation in which evil men initiate the conflict, it is two young girls who move the story forward. True, the goblins approach Laura at the beginning of the story, but she had the choice to leave with her sister and decided to remain. She voluntarily put herself in danger.

A child will understand Laura's desire to seek out a new experience without regard for the potential consequences. Children often climb trees and on top of the kitchen counter without thinking about their own safety. They run around the house without worrying about banging into the edges of bookcases and coffee tables. Yet, like a child faced with a brand new experience, Laura is apprehensive. True, she does not return home with Lizzie, but she does not approach the goblin men either. Instead, she stands still, unsure of herself and second-guessing whether or not she should interact with the goblin men. Laura's actions define the toddler during Erikson's second stage of development. The child wants to expand her boundaries and be more independent, but hesitates because she knows she is small and weak and still dependent on her parents for survival.

The setting of "Goblin Market" is also gothic, at least from a child's perspective. In most gothic stories the landscape tends to be isolated, alienating, and full of danger; it creates feelings of uneasiness and instills in readers a mounting dread and apprehension. In "Goblin Market," the atmosphere stems in part from the eerie mood that arises as the goblins caravan across the glen. That the goblin men only appear at morning and evening suggests a connection with the darkness, especially since they're often associated with the color blue, which again can symbolize coldness and death. Many people, especially children, have a fear of the darkness because it represents the unknown and "gives free reign to imagination's unnatural and marvelous creatures."[8] The goblin men appearing during these shadowy times of day explains one reason why Laura and Lizzie are so curious about them and their wares. The goblins represent the dark side of humanity, that inner self which feeds us bad thoughts and pushes us toward negative actions. Many of us restrain our dark side because we understand the difference between right and wrong, as well as our responsibility to follow accepted codes of behavior.

This duality in human nature also translates to the natural landscape of "Goblin Market," which often pays homage to the sublime, another staple of Gothicism. Although the sublime is typically linked with mountains and oceans, it refers to any natural landscape that stirs conflicted feelings in its observer, such as joy, wonder, terror or awe. For example, when looking up at a towering, majestic mountain, we might feel an overpowering sense of reverence and amazement; but dwarfed in its shadow, we might also feel a sense of weakness and inferiority. Associated with grandeur and magnificence, the sublime evokes excessive emotions, much like those often expressed by children who have not yet learned to think rationally and, instead, act more on their vacillating emotions.

In "Goblin Market" the glen assumes an entirely new appearance when darkness arrives and the goblin men tramp through the landscape with their shrill cries of "Come buy, come buy." The background becomes cluttered and claustrophobic, and dark blues drive away the bright greens of the natural world. Indeed, the goblin men themselves become extensions of the sublime. On one hand they are ghastly to view, with their wrinkled features, shrunken faces, and shrill cries, yet they're so different from anything children have ever seen that there also exists a grotesque joy in confronting them and witnessing the unknown. Children may want to look away, but find themselves unable to because of their curiosity. Ultimately, these same conflicted feelings of terror and awe entice Laura to let the goblins approach her, whereupon she sacrifices a lock of her hair and eats the wicked fruit.

We must remember that children are voyeurs. They are always watching, always analyzing. Suzy Waldman connects this theme of voyeurism to the poem by explaining how "the narrator of 'Goblin Market' takes obvious delight in looking licentiously at a brightly colored scene; the poem's original manuscript title, 'A Peep at the Goblins,' emphasized the theme of forbidden vision."[9] Laura and Lizzie, who live together in their small cottage, have never come in contact with the goblin merchants. They've only heard the peddlers' eerie chants in the mornings and evenings. Rossetti begins her poem with the lines, "Morning and evening / Maids heard the goblins cry: / "'Come buy our orchard fruits, / Come buy, come buy.'"[10] For child listeners, this seemingly innocent invitation creates a natural curiosity to explore and watch as events unfold. When Lizzie covers her own eyes and tells Laura not to look, this only piques children's interest by hinting at the potential for misbehavior as well as a strong desire to get their own look at the goblin men.

Raskin fills the first few pages of the book with piles and piles of colorful fruit, which provide a visual stimulus for child listeners and helps them comprehend why Laura and Lizzie find the goblin chant so alluring.

In this way, the goblin men tempt child listeners, as well as Laura and Lizzie, by fueling their insatiable desire to understand the unknown. Most children would love to meet a goblin or a ghoul and bring to life the crazy creatures that reside in their imagination, so it makes sense that an audience of children would naturally want to explore the glen and peep at the goblins, too. By trailing Lizzie and Laura, at a safe aesthetic distance from outside the boundaries of the story, child listeners can still watch the consequences that unfold but feel completely safe. From a comfortable vantage point in their own familiar world, children can then experience the effects of the goblins' mischief and the grotesque imagery associated with their peddling behavior.

Although Ellen Raskin's illustrations are bright and colorful, her use of spacing furthers the sense of dread that begins when Laura ignores her sister and allows the goblin men to give her the fruit. The goblins blend into each other and fill many of the pages. They are crammed together and tucked into remote corners. For children, this placement of the goblin men presents the creatures as overbearing and intrusive, two traits that many children abhor in adults because such traits often conflict with their desire to be autonomous. When Laura meets the goblin men, she sits down with them as if lowering herself to their level. They surround her, and it is clear she no longer has control of the situation. First, Laura faces left, which is often seen as negative. Historically, because the Bible references "the right hand of God," left-handedness has been associated with the devil. Facing left implies moving backwards and falling behind, as opposed to facing right which implies moving forward and advancing. Laura's positioning on the page highlights her poor decision-making and foreshadows the illness that will soon befall her.

Other markers of Laura's naiveté and immaturity are the colors associated with her. She wears a drab, off-white dress that echoes the pale gray and ashen blue she later experiences while wasting away after eating the fruit. She also chooses to sit down with the goblin men, and this action suggests a comfort and ease with the situation, a child's desire to be part of a larger group and participate in an experience, whether or not that experience is safe and acceptable. During these scenes, Laura does not stand out among the numerous goblin men who close in on her, thereby illustrating their dominance over her. That Laura does not stand out also alludes to her decision to be a voluntary partaker in the goblins' revelry, to shun her sister's good advice and risk her well-being.

When Laura becomes ill, Raskin depicts the girl in entirely gray and blue tones, symbolizing her lack of energy and proximity to death; her haggard face and inability to even stand up, coupled with the absence of bright colors, enhance the severity of her situation. Seeing Laura lying helpless in Lizzie's arms, her once blonde hair now a tangled mess of blues and purples and grays, helps illustrate to children the negative consequences that can happen when they don't listen to reason and seek too much freedom.

Lizzie, in contrast, wears a gold dress that symbolizes her warm, caring nature. When Lizzie meets with the goblin men, she does not sit down with them as her sister did, but chooses to stand. Her placement on the page, towering above goblin men that must now look up to her, illustrates her autonomy and power. While children don't always understand the concept of death, the difference in color between Laura and Lizzie, and their different placements on specific pages, alert children to the fact that Laura's decision to interact with the goblin men and eat their fruit was a bad choice that put both her and Laura in danger. Children can definitely relate to Laura feeling sick and uncomfortable, and also to the idea that because she made a poor decision she feels shamed and can no longer play with her sister or enjoy spending time outside.

Laura's encounter with the goblin men heightens the gothic mood that pervades "Goblin Market" and imbues the pastoral landscape with fear and paranoia. This dark and gloomy atmosphere in the poem also evolves from the inherent danger in common, everyday things, as Leonard Wolf suggests:

> The poem's imagery is lascivious to the last degree and yet what are we looking at, after all? Peaches, pears, grapes, cherries, apples, and "Plums on their twigs." And that's where the horror lies. In denial. In the passionate denial of passion the evasive mind can be frightened of almost everything, but especially of round fruit, fragrant and juicy.[11]

Rossetti's use of fruit as a luring mechanism reminds children that looks can be deceiving. Beautiful objects may be dangerous, and that which pleases us can quickly become a source of pain. The fruit becomes a symbol of the gothic given that it functions as an extension of the goblins themselves; it is owned and distributed by them and offered with evil intent. Thus, these ripe and exotic fruits, such as dates, pomegranates, and quinces, represent temptation and death. Here, Rossetti suggests that it is not a sense of the familiar that makes one safe. After all, most children understand fruit to be healthy and nourishing, and they see various types of fruit in their kitchens on a daily basis. The fruit in "Goblin Market" is unhealthy because it has been infected by the evil, misbehaving goblins. In this sense, Rossetti implies that it is the execution of good choices that helps to create a safe and familiar environment. This idea resonates further when one considers that Laura does not become sicker when she sucks and licks the juices off her sister's face at the end of the poem. Instead, she becomes well again. The fruit, now associated with Lizzie's love and willingness to help her dying sister, contains rejuvenating powers.

The fruit also links "Goblin Market" to other fairy tales by presenting themes of greed and gluttony. Children, especially toddlers, are constantly putting objects in their mouth. They're obsessed with tasting and gorging themselves on food, and they often suffer punishment before learning to control their impulses. Let children eat as many pieces of candy as they want, and they will often devour them until they become sick and throw up. Laura becomes a victim of these desires just like Hansel and Gretel who feast on the witch's gingerbread house and end up being captured, or Snow White who takes a bite out of the Queen's poisoned apple and must spend her formative years in a glass coffin. In each of these cases, the child's bad decisions lead to a period of inactivity that separates him or her from family and friends.

By venturing outside her familiar landscape, and by changing from voyeur to participant, Laura becomes the example all parents use when lecturing children on why they should behave. In Rossetti's original poem the character of Jeanie functions as this example, but Raskin omits Jeanie from the picture book, which seems to put Laura more firmly in the "bad example" category. By omitting Jeanie from her own version of "Goblin Market," Raskin forces children to concentrate solely on two sisters who represent both halves of the divided self. She enforces this idea on the opening page of the book by placing the two girls side by side, but facing opposite directions as if they're two sides of the proverbial coin. This idea of duality is further enhanced by Laura's blonde hair and Lizzie's brunette hair. Their long, wavy locks are similar enough in appearance to connect them as sisters, but clearly distinguish one girl from the other.

From a gothic standpoint, Laura's illness and her ghost-like appearance portray her as a doppelgänger, often defined as the spectral double of a living person. In literature, the doppelgänger brings bad luck and is often considered an omen of death. The suggestion, of course, is that Laura's selfish actions might harm Lizzie, either directly or indirectly, especially when Lizzie risks her life to save her sister. Children, who don't like being scolded for something they didn't do, can relate easily to the thought of an innocent person being punished, and this scenario fuels their compassion and anxiety for Lizzie. So while child listeners may be attracted to Laura's impulsive behavior, they also connect with Lizzie's struggle to remain safe and healthy amid the danger and sickness that surround her. In presenting these images and ideas, Ellen Raskin guides children toward a deeper comprehension of the actions and consequences that befall "good" Lizzie and "bad" Laura when the goblin fruit becomes too tempting.

Because the fruit functions as an extension of the goblins' personalities, perhaps Rossetti is making a claim that the goblin men did not make wise choices when they were children, and that now they are suffering the consequences of their own impulsive acts. This scenario generates even more concern for Laura because without having someone to help her and love her, she might indeed become a goblin and then find herself corrupting others. Children who consider this thought will understand the suggestion that misbehavior stunts the maturation process. Raskin elaborates on this idea by drawing the goblin men as short creatures whose smiles contain hints of malice and spite. Throughout the story they tug and pull at the two girls, acting like children often do when they want attention. The goblins are grotesque and misshapen because they do not behave themselves; as a result they are isolated from normal people and forced to wander the countryside as a group. For children seeking independence, the lesson seems to be that misbehavior also prevents individuality.

The fruit itself suggests ideas about growth, and the goblins' bad behavior emphasizes the parallel that Rossetti wants children to understand: good decisions (rich soil) produce healthy growth, whereas bad decisions (arid soil) may cause one to wither and die like a neglected crop. Although children can't always comprehend the meaning of death, they do understand that people who die leave their friends and family and never return. And they certainly understand concepts like pain and suffering. For toddlers, this idea of death echoes themes of abandonment, which is a natural fear that every child possesses as a result of being completely dependent on adults for their safety and survival. Thus, child listeners understand that Laura's inability to resist compulsion leads directly to the possibility of her being estranged from Lizzie, abandoned, in a sense, by those poor and stubborn decisions that define the anal stage of a child's development.

By revealing the consequences of the goblin fruit, Rossetti enhances the gothic atmosphere by instilling more suspense into the poem. Laura's indulgence has become both an addiction and an obsession, which is a common result when children cross physical and emotional borders to explore their dark side and escape their monotonous world. Although the effect is heightened in Rossetti's poem, the fact remains that there is nothing for Laura, Lizzie, and a captivated child listener to do except wait for the inevitable outcome as the power of the fruit exacts a terrible penalty for

Laura's misbehavior. The waiting and helplessness associated with this situation evokes apprehension and panic, which, in turn, reinforces the belief that young children should not only remain close to their parents for safety and protection, but they should also pay attention to the heeding of their parents and loved ones rather than surrender to vice and temptation.

Children who listen to and read "Goblin Market" understand that while the possibilities of the unknown might be exciting and exotic, they function as such only because children are in control of the stories and characters that flutter through their imaginations on a daily basis. At any point the child can close the book and run outside, or dump out their toy chest to play with dolls or action figures. Using their imagination affords children a sense of power they do not and cannot obtain while they are still young and dependent upon adults. And it's important to remember that children have an affinity for fantastic stories because their entire way of looking at the world is fantastic. They don't understand cars and vacuum cleaners and computers. To children, those objects are magical and mysterious and full of wonder.

While children are aware of the importance that fantasy plays in their lives, they can still distinguish between make believe and the real world. They are conscious of the fact that inherent in "Goblin Market," as Antony Harrison explains, "is an exemplary instance of betrayed expectations that the sensual delights of this world can be enjoyed with impunity. In fact, indulgence in them is shown to be dangerous and sometimes fatal."[12] At the end of the day, children understand that the fruit represents daily temptations and the goblins symbolize bad decisions. Children also realize that the "goblins" will remain distant and unthreatening as long as children make good choices, resist the urge to misbehave, and don't overindulge like Laura. Eventually, as children resolve their individual crises and progress to the next stage of psychosocial development, they learn that books and movies, along with their own imaginations, can be fun and safe avenues to indulge in their individual fantasies. Doing so provides children with opportunities for growth because they can regulate and control those environments without reaping any of the horrors and consequences that the fictional characters often experience.

The creepy atmosphere in "Goblin Market" entrances children while also reminding them that boundaries exist for a good reason. What tips the balance from pleasure to pain is when children attempt to construct reality out of fantasy, when they act on inappropriate impulses instead of using their imagination to create a safe, regulated story that addresses the pros and cons of a given situation. And this type of safe, regulated story is exactly what Laura tells her own children at the poem's end. Laura hopes her children will benefit from her scary and life-threatening experience by understanding what constitutes proper behavior. In this scene, Laura is also speaking directly to child listeners of "Goblin Market," hoping they're now able to recognize and apply the lessons they've learned from the poem to their own individual lives.

When a story exists in a child's mind, she can replay it over and over, examining every possible outcome, punishment, or reward. Children learn quickly, however, that once they cast aside their imagination and perform their fantasies in the real world, there is often only one outcome and, whether good or bad, it cannot be changed. Using their imagination affords children total control, but in the real world they must relinquish such coveted control to adult figures. Children don't like to acknowledge their weaknesses and vulnerabilities; they don't want to admit they require adult supervision and aid. This is the reason why literature is so important to children. Novels and poems and picture books are training wheels that, along with parents and loved ones, provide children with the morals and values they'll need to develop into fully-functioning members of society.

The gothic atmosphere in "Goblin Market" forces children to experience intense feelings of vulnerability. Gothicism itself is characterized by gloom and darkness, distinguished by all the unknowns lurking in the shadows. "Goblin Market" implies that terror and horror can only affect children when they disregard the rules and wander off to explore that unknown darkness. Although adults realize that such emotions can happen anytime, and are often uncontrollable, the message is still an important one for children; it helps them progress through the anal stage, guiding them toward a daily routine in which they learn to be autonomous while still existing as part of a family unit that relies on support and trust. Through their familiarity with stories such as "Goblin Market," children realize that to misbehave is to cross imaginary boundaries and surrender what little personal control they already possess. The familiar may become dangerous, and the consequences may be deadly, but only when they make bad decisions that result in them unleashing their inner demons, gorging on sin, and indulging in reckless behavior.

The Myth of the Hero

The idea of crossing boundaries, whether physical or imaginary, is a trope that exists in many fairy tales. Consider how many fairy tale heroes and heroines must enter the woods to deal with a specific conflict, only to leave those same woods once they've matured. "Goblin Market" follows the traditional fairy-tale structure in that it details the journey of a young child who leaves home (a world of order and security) and travels to a foreign setting where she undergoes conflicts, becomes victorious, and learns such morals as honesty and truth. In "Goblin Market" Lizzie must leave her home and brave the goblin men to save Laura's life. She is then attacked by the goblin men who smear her face with their fruit and leave her soaked in syrupy juice. Although Rossetti describes Lizzie as experiencing an inward laughter while she runs away, in actuality she is exhausted and scared. Children, like adults, often mask fear with laughter because the act of laughing can relieve any tension and stress that builds up in the presence of fear. Consider how many people jump out of their seat during a scary moment in a horror film and then laugh immediately afterwards. Children, who have not yet learned how to understand and process their own emotions, can vacillate easily from laughter to tears to anger, often in the same breath. In fact, many children have been known to laugh, cry, and scream at the same time.

By mentioning the laughter, Rossetti actually enhances the horror that Lizzie endures. True, part of her laughter may be relief at not having succumbed to the goblins' taunts, as well as having helped her sister, but child listeners know Lizzie's laughter is not exactly genuine, and that it is manufactured as a means for her to cope with a scary and intense situation. Child listeners, then, will believe Lizzie to be simply veering from one extreme emotion to another. And, like Lizzie, they will experience fear and laughter at the same time, but view them as two separate emotional states, whereas an adult will recognize that the two emotions are equal halves of the same coin. For instance, children will be afraid of the goblin men because of how they pinch and claw and scratch at Lizzie; in the next moment they will smile at Raskin's depictions of the goblins' physical appearance and then laugh at the thought of Lizzie being smeared with the fruit. This humor also arises from a child's natural desire to play with food and create a mess, especially during the anal stage.

Because children can relate to Lizzie's conflicted movement between fear and laughter, they understand, at a basic level, that her fears stem from her recent interaction with the goblin men and her concern for Laura. This understanding, in turn, scares a child listener because she comprehends that another child, much like herself, is not only terrified and in danger, but alone and without parental supervision. Young children fear abandonment, which is why the poem generates anxiety. This is why babies and toddlers cry when their mother or father leaves the room. They don't understand that their loved ones are close by, and if the baby or toddler cannot see the mother or father, then their mother or father might as well be halfway across the world. Because young children share this fear of abandonment, they relate more closely with Lizzie and her plight. In essence, they are living vicariously through the characters. And this fear of abandonment that many children possess also enhances Rossetti's message about the dangers of misbehaving and surrendering to one's compulsions.

Once Lizzie returns home, she instructs Laura to "Hug me, kiss me, taste the juices / Squeezed from goblin fruits for you."[13] This sequence of action, beginning from when Lizzie leaves home to find the goblin men to when she returns home again smeared with the fruit, follows the standard path of the hero. The hero sets out on her own, encounters a series of difficulties and obstacles, must rely on her wisdom and strength to overcome those obstacles, and then returns home having matured and developed a more assured sense of her self-identity. This home-away-home scenario tantalizes every child because children fantasize about being heroes. They want the adventure, but they do not want to be hurt. They want the danger, but they do not want to show fear. Basically, they crave attention, and they crave compassion, but they don't want to show their dependence. In many cases, a child's urge to misbehave is simply a desire to make her presence known because she feels neglected or insignificant. Children relate to Lizzie by sharing in her euphoria of being victorious and escaping the goblin men. For children who don't experience victory often, whether during board games or team sports or personal accomplishments at school, living vicariously through a literary character can be a welcome surge of confidence and self-esteem.

In "Goblin Market," Rossetti also suggests that children should not confuse heroism with foolishness. Perhaps Laura thought she was being brave by meeting the goblin men instead of returning home with Lizzie, only to regret her decision when she fell ill and almost died. Laura makes a selfish decision to stay in the glen, whereas Lizzie acts unselfishly and places herself in danger for the sake of her dying sister. Lizzie learns the power of denial and the importance of resistance, while Laura, who has already left the security of home and made bad choices, learns not only the value of family and love, but also the consequences that can result when one does not listen to sense and reason. Or even sisters, since Lizzie had warned her.

Subconsciously, children are often attracted to the same emotions in others that they sense within themselves. These emotions arise from a child's need to find answers and understand her conflicted feelings, and it is this appeal for duality that lures a child listener further into "Goblin Market." The child listener is "holding on" to her own curiosity about the goblin men, as well as the fear produced by Laura's sickness. At the same time, the child listener is "letting go" of an urge to misbehave by observing Laura's actions and the strict consequences that follow. By acting vicariously through Laura, and thus experiencing her pain and trauma, the child listener can safely expunge her own compulsive desires without receiving punishment from parents, or without suffering through moments of shame and doubt in which she questions her own capabilities.

The Divided Self

Having a safe vantage point is important to a child's psychological development because it provides her with the courage and daringness to observe the unknown world around her. Yet it also affords her a needed sense of security and protection. To a child, the unknown is fascinating, whether it is the terror of being locked alone in an old, decrepit house, the startling discovery of a dead animal in the backyard, or being set upon in the woods by a horde of strange creatures. Children are drawn to countless dangers that surround them on a daily basis. They feel the urge to misbehave, but they also perceive their parents' desire that they maintain good conduct and adhere to societal norms. These warring impulses comprise the conflicting emotions that children experience, whether at school or at home.

Reading "Goblin Market," it becomes clear that a duality exists between Lizzie and Laura. Laura is impulsive and romantic, a "sweet-toothed girl" who ignores her sister's warnings and succumbs to the "sugar-baited words" of the goblin men, gorging on the fruits until she can eat no more. Lizzie, by contrast, is a sensible child who understands the power of resistance and denial. She warns her sister about the goblins, saying, "Their offers should not charm us / Their evil gifts would harm us."[14] Though both girls possess differing traits and characteristics, Ellen Raskin illustrates each girl as tall and austere, as independent and strong-willed. In the book's afterword, Raskin explains that her own daughter posed for both girls: "She is tall and straight and provided backbones to the usually languid Victorian maidens."[15] Raskin's illustrations not only provide strong imagery for children to gaze upon, but her depictions of Laura and Lizzie offer children a representation of characters who are not weak and scared, but aware of their surroundings and eager to explore them.

True, Laura falls into temptation and almost dies, but she does so precisely because she is strong-willed. She is not afraid of the goblin men and suffers because she is proud and overconfident. Together, these two young girls represent the conflicting impulses that children often encounter as they lose their innocence and stumble toward experience. These warring impulses relate to the anal stage, namely the child's apprehension between "holding on" and "letting go." Rossetti emphasizes this duality in the following lines: "Lizzie with an open heart, / Laura in an absent dream, / One content, one sick in part; / One warbling for the mere bright day's delight, / One longing for the night."[16] Clearly, Lizzie represents the rational part of the budding ego while Laura represents the compulsive will that continually tries to exert control over the child's ever expanding environment. Laura and Lizzie rely on each other to survive, the lesson being that children require warring impulses in their everyday lives. They need both pleasure *and* pain to mature and become adults. Thus, the poem suggests that a child cannot adequately develop her personality, or become a well-rounded individual, without tolerating both negative and positive experiences.

The girls' meeting with the goblin men proves beneficial to both of them. Laura learns that compulsive behavior can get her into trouble and cause physical and emotional pain. Initially, she suffers a loss of identity at the hands of the goblin men when they take a lock of her golden hair for payment, requiring her to surrender a part of her body that makes her unique. Later, she regains her identity because of her sister's love, upon which she gains a deeper appreciation for family. For children, Laura's parting with a lock of her hair is particularly effective; children tend to be selfish, especially during the anal stage, and many don't want to think about being told what to do or having to give up something precious they own, whether it's a material possession or a part of their own body.

Many children fear change, and a disturbance in their daily routine often upsets them. In "Goblin Market," Laura's lack of restraint disrupts her normal life, as well as her relationship with her sister. Children know how bad they feel when they're sick, and how frustrated they are when stuck in bed for days at a time. Having empathy for Laura helps children grasp the connection between Laura's misbehavior and the damage it affords her, both emotionally and psychically. They perceive the former as the cause and the latter as the effect, and for many children this realization is a crucial step in coming to terms with their own conflicted emotions during the anal stage.

Lizzie also matures as a result of her interaction with the goblin men, albeit in a different way. Her sister's sickness forces her to move beyond her familiar boundaries. Here, Lizzie displays the will and determination typical of stage two. Unlike her sister, she understands her limits and proceeds cautiously in her endeavor. Lizzie's journey into the glen helps her comprehend the larger world, as Rossetti suggests when she writes, "[Lizzie] halted by the brook: / And for the first time in her life / Began to listen and look."[17] For child listeners, this moment of clarity might enforce the notion that good deeds and proper behavior are healthy ways to develop personality and experience positive change. Although children often fear change, Lizzie's actions show that change, when necessary, can be positive when placed within the context of thought-out decisions and a high degree of confidence.

Another important point is that all the characters in "Goblin Market" are children, as is evidenced by the girls' actions several times throughout the story. At one point, as she tries to escape the goblins' cries, Lizzie "thrust a dimpled finger / In each ear, shut eyes and ran."[18] This innocent reaction to drown out the goblins' horrible cries is one that children can relate to, as they believe that doing so will erase all hints of danger. Nowhere in the poem is there mention of the girls' parents, or older friends who might assume the traditional role of guardian or protector. Although the radius of significant relations for stage two centers on parental persons, Lizzie, in addition to being a child figure, fills the parent role nicely because it's only through her constant courage and leadership and responsibility that she's able to save Laura. In many fairy tales, the hero or heroine must undertake the journey alone without parents' help and support. The lesson here is that in order to mature and progress to the next stage of psychosocial development, children have to rely on themselves and make their own choices, otherwise the experience will not be theirs to cherish, nor will it likely be a positive one.

The lack of any adult presence in "Goblin Market" also helps shift the poem's focus to an audience of children. To children, adults symbolize responsibility and sensibility. With no adult presence, except perhaps Lizzie, to preach morals and save the characters from temptation, an audience of children is left alone to accompany Laura and Lizzie on their dark journey as they strive to make sound decisions and learn from their mistakes. Rossetti wants children to understand that while temptation may look good in the beginning, the end result can often be painful and humiliating. Temptation can corrupt innocence, as it did Laura. Her survival is therefore contingent on Lizzie maintaining her own innocence and conquering those same compulsive feelings that led Laura to taste the goblins' fruit in the first place.

Rossetti's concentration on child characters can also extend to the feared goblins, for while Laura and Lizzie are two fair-haired maidens, one can view the goblins as mischievous "brothers" that engage in behavior associated with sibling rivalry. Ellen Moers suggests that "the brother-monsters tempt and harass the sisters with a twofold purpose: to intoxicate and to torture and destroy them with forbidden fruit."[19] The goblins' actions are typical of brothers who often taunt their sisters with a mixture of cruelty and coaxing. Like children on a playground, they goad Lizzie with their words and actions, turning misbehavior into a fun activity. Rossetti writes how they "trod and hustled her, / Elbowed and jostled her, / Clawed her with their nails..."[20] While the goblins' actions clearly symbolize aggressive male behavior, such actions also arise from the goblins' enjoyment at watching others behave badly and then suffer.

The idea that the goblins represent "brothers" who torment their younger sisters makes sense when one considers that in such sibling relationships the issue is mainly one of power. Raskin's illustrations of the mischievous goblins show them as cute and cuddly creatures, and this decision renders them less frightening to children because the goblins sometimes resemble stuffed animals rather than murderous rogues. These illustrations, coupled with the vivid descriptions, suggest that siblings, who can be cute and friendly and helpful one moment, can also be mean and hurtful and dominating the next. Raskin's illustrations emphasize an important idea that all children need to realize: danger and pain may lurk anywhere, and just because people or places might appear safe or nonthreatening does not mean children should surrender to their desires. Here, Rossetti and Raskin both highlight the lesson that children should not attempt autonomy before they have mastered their own compulsions.

The goblins are never punished for their actions, but children still realize that they never want to be one of the goblin men. They know that if they ever displayed those same actions, then their parents would punish them. And since most children don't enjoy feeling shame, or being punished and reprimanded by their parents, "Goblin Market" therefore succeeds as a deterrent. The lesson in the poem is that one should resist the temptation to partake in unsavory conduct and not indulge in any wrongdoing. And with no moralizing adult presence in the poem until the very end, the message would seem to be that children need to rely on their own judgment, which is an important concept for children who are striving to be autonomous.

"There is no friend like a sister"

Misbehaving is a necessary step in the maturation process because it educates children on precisely where their boundaries lie. Rossetti's warning in "Goblin Market" is that children should steer clear of such boundaries until they are physically and emotionally prepared, lest they find themselves afraid, alone, and separated from family. The poem teaches children that it is unwise to lose control and stray into an amoral landscape. And while there's a strong theme of disobedience, closer analysis suggests that perhaps Rossetti is stressing the power of peer pressure and the bad influences that children can exact on one another. Children can be as conniving and manipulative as adults, and in "Goblin Market" Rossetti emphasizes the loss of individuality that can occur when people succumb to peer pressure. This argument makes sense when one considers that the goblins actively try to make Laura and Lizzie interact with them. They shout into the night and literally attack Lizzie when she refuses to let them dominate her.

Upon further reflection, I realize the goblin men continually pester Laura and Lizzie, seeking them out day after day. They want Laura and Lizzie to give in to the fruit's allure; they want the girls to lose control of their own common sense so they can corrupt their fairy-tale lives. While this theme of temptation is important in the poem, it raises another important message, namely that children should not talk to strangers. This emphasis on stranger danger links "Goblin Market" with other classic fairy tales such as "Little Red Riding Hood" and "Snow White." Both of these themes—temptation and stranger danger—involve conflicted feelings of desire and apprehension, which all children experience during the anal stage. In this sense, the goblins not only provoke misbehavior, but symbolize the negative aspects of the anal stage. For children, they represent every ounce of pain, trouble, and unhappiness that results when adult authority is ignored and the mind wavers between "holding on" and "letting go."

Yet another question arises. If one misbehaves, then does one assume negative characteristics and become a malicious person? This is the warning many parents offer when they scare children into behaving properly, and in "Goblin Market" Christina Rossetti enforces this belief. If the goblins represent children who have misbehaved, and continue to misbehave by selling the dreaded fruit, then is it possible that child listeners will view them more as animals than as people, perhaps sensing that their evil actions are linked to their physical appearance? Rossetti herself suggests this when Laura chooses to linger and watch the goblins: "One had a cat's face, / One whisked a tail, / One tramped at a rat's pace, / One crawled like a snail, /

One like a wombat prowled obtuse and furry, / One like a ratel tumbled hurry skurry."[21] The goblins' physical descriptions match their wicked actions, and Rossetti's descriptions produce even more power when contrasted against the lush pastoral descriptions of babbling brooks and lofty crags. Just as there is a duality between Laura and Lizzie, there is also a duality between the landscapes in "Goblin Market." For example, the girls' cottage, which suggests innocence and peace, contrasts with the shadowy glen through which the goblins traipse. Even Raskin's illustrations emphasize duality in that her depictions of the goblins are rounded and present them as somewhat cuddly, but their strange features are also unsettling and grotesque.

After the goblins fail in forcing Lizzie to eat their fruit, they fling back her penny and storm off in anger. Rossetti writes that "some writhed on the ground, / Some dived into the brook / With ring and ripple, / Some scudded on the gale without a sound, / Some vanished in the distance."[22] The goblins are part of the natural world, and so, like animals, their instinct is to retreat and hide when they cannot get what they want. This mirrors a child who throws a tantrum when his parent won't let him have his way. Still, the child listener understands that the goblins, who misbehave, live subhuman lives in the woods, whereas Laura and Lizzie sleep in comfortable beds inside a cozy cottage. The message, then, is that good behavior is not only rewarded, but leads to happiness and security and fulfillment.

Ellen Raskin's illustrations during this pivotal moment when the goblins disappear into the earth are evocative of floods and drowning. While Lizzie runs back to Laura and the cottage, the goblin men sink into the landscape, which Raskin draws with lots of curving lines and swirls, suggesting an ocean brimming with sweeping waves. There is ambiguity between land and water, with obvious masses of green land rising up like pillars, one of which Lizzie stands on as she flees from the goblins. The hill on which she stands seems to hold her up like a hand that's helping her rise above the goblin's misbehavior. That the goblins appear to be flailing like wild animals on the left side of the page, while Lizzie is safe on the right side of the page, is a testament to children that those who behave can avoid danger and unhappiness, preserving the joys of their daily routine, while those who follow their compulsions can experience pain and sadness, as well as separation from loved ones. Again, the placement of the characters is key. The goblins on the left side of the page are mired in a perpetual state of juvenile behavior; Lizzie on the right side of the page is moving forward toward the next stage of development and a firmer awareness of her self-identity, from which Laura is sure to benefit.

To children, the thought of being transformed into an animal might seem exciting, but it tends to lose momentum when one ponders the lifestyle and treatment of rats, cats, and other creatures that aren't allowed to ride bikes, eat ice-cream, or attend sleepovers. Animals are also viewed as dirty and less intelligent than humans, lacking reason and judgment. To misbehave is to act like an animal, and the consequences are that one must then be treated like an animal, which, to a child, might suggest bullying or even abandonment.

Even Laura herself becomes animalistic when she first eats the goblin fruit. She loses herself in the moment, wallowing in her indulgence to gorge on soft, fleshy fruit until the juices smear across her face. Laura's sore lips symbolize the pain that indulgence may bring. She now has fallen prey to temptation and gratified the goblins with her misbehavior. The gothic atmosphere of the goblins' glen has saturated the pastoral, fairy-tale space of the sisters' own cottage dwelling. As Laura becomes sicker and sicker, more and more dark blues creep into the cottage scenes, strangling the bright greens that symbolize the girls' happy and carefree lives. This boundary that denotes a landscape consisting of mischievous children on one side and obedient children on the other is further symbolized by the gate that separates Laura and Lizzie's house from the glen.

Lizzie knows she must confront the goblins because Laura cannot hear their shouts of "Come buy, come buy," and thus she doesn't know where to find them. That Laura cannot hear the goblins' cries emphasizes her initiation into guilt and weakness. She cannot squelch her hunger unless she has the fruit. This hunger is a craving for naughtiness and misbehavior, an ache for delinquency that, quite literally, threatens to change Laura's manner of living. She became sick because she misbehaved, and children, who tend to be active and energetic, understand what it means to become sick and feverish. They fear the debilitating effects of any illness that restricts their playful world and saddles them with hurt and misery.

And yet one can argue that Lizzie receives just as much pain and torment as Laura. To save Laura, she attempts to buy fruit from the goblin men, but they refuse her money and insist she eat with them. When she refuses, they become upset and she must incur the goblins' wrath: "...The goblins cuffed and caught her, / Coaxed and fought her, / Bullied and besought her, / Scratched her, pinched her black as ink, / Kicked and knocked her, / Mauled and mocked her."[23] Lizzie defends her honor by not giving into temptation. She knows she has done nothing wrong and is being punished for her sister's behavior, but she sacrifices herself for Laura because they are family and depend upon each other.

Laura is surprised, as are most children, to find that her sister has braved the goblin men in an attempt to save her life. She shouts, "Lizzie, Lizzie, have you tasted / For my sake the fruit forbidden? / Must your light like mine be hidden, / Your young life like mine be wasted?"[24] For children who wish to be acknowledged and revered, Lizzie is the character with whom most will relate and emulate. When Laura sucks the juices off her sister's body, Rossetti writes that "her lips began to scorch, / That juice was wormwood to her tongue."[25] The bitter taste that Laura experiences is embarrassment at her own misbehavior, as well as shame for risking her sister's life. The kisses Lizzie gives Laura symbolize the healing power of family, and they may remind readers of other life-saving kisses in fairy tales such as "Snow White" and The Frog Prince." In addition to stressing the importance of family, the kisses illustrate to children that virtues are more important than material possessions.

Ellen Raskin emphasizes the importance of this scene even further by removing all background scenery and placing only Laura and Lizzie on the right side of the page. Laura lies in her sister's arms while Lizzie strokes her cheek and weeps. Without the greens and blues of the landscape, the girls stand out alone on the stark, white page. This artistic decision creates a more touching and intimate moment between the two sisters that underscores the intensity with which Lizzie wants to save Laura.

One has to respect the courage with which Lizzie stomps into the glen to demand the fruit. After witnessing firsthand Laura's experience with the goblin men and their wares, Lizzie still risks her own life to save her sister's. For children, this act illustrates the idea that selflessness and love will always defeat evil. Lizzie's intentions are pure and hopeful, transforming her into an angelic figure whose purity dispels the gothic atmosphere and drives away the goblins after they fail to corrupt her. Although Lizzie does not ask for attention, it is showered upon her at the end of the poem because of her heroic actions.

At the end of "Goblin Market" the girls are now mothers who warn their own children of the goblin men, and Peter Merchant believes that "the impression left by that tailpiece tableau of Laura gathering the little ones together and 'joining hands to little hands' is that the natural audience for Goblin Market is an audience of children."[26] The final stanza is an epilogue in which Rossetti presents a moral concerning the merits of denying one's passions. She also frames it as an important message regarding the value of sisterhood. As mentioned before, the two mothers speak as much to an audience of children as they do to the little ones who gather around them holding hands. For child listeners, the lesson not only concerns those who misbehave, but also those who save and redeem others through courageous acts of their own. Rossetti implies that in any frightening situation a child can find the means to triumph over her fears. Lizzie, after all, is terrified of the goblin men, but she remains strong and determined, refusing to succumb to the tempting fruit. She is able to succeed because she retains her innocence.

After reading "Goblin Market," it becomes clear that the gothic elements do not make the poem less appropriate for children, but actually more attractive to them. For Laura and all children, the terrible thought of being taken away from all they know and love forces them to question the decisions they make and how they behave. Maria Tatar sums it up best: "The goal is ecstasy, but the path to luminosity often winds through dark streets filled with gloom and terror."[27] The girls' intense experiences with the goblin men help to teach them how to acknowledge their faults, respect authority, and appreciate the boundaries in which they grow and mature. The gothic elements in the poem, namely the goblin men and their poisoned fruit, as well as the constantly shifting landscape, move the story forward and force the girls to make their own choices, for better or for worse. And for those children navigating through Erikson's second stage of psychosocial development, "Goblin Market" is an important text that can ease the conflicts and frustrations which often accompany the anal stage, namely the battle between retention and elimination, autonomy versus shame and doubt, and the growth of one's reason and determination when pitted against infantile tendencies and compulsions.

2

Fools' Trap:
Initiative and Guilt in
The Adventures of Pinocchio

Playland

When I was a young boy I had a puppet. I called him Pedro. He was dressed in black peasant clothes and wore a sombrero. In one hand he held a guitar. He had enormous, flat wooden feet that looked like shovels, and he hung from strings attached to the ceiling, a marionette sentry that guarded me from zombies and ghouls while I slept at night. Like most children with their toys, I pretended Pedro was alive, trusting him with useless secrets and labeling him as my sidekick. We carried on hours-long conversations, and my puppet's painted smile was a treasured constant in my constantly changing world. As I grasped at numerous identities, collecting and discarding other imaginary friends like cereal box prizes, I treasured my silly playtime banter with Pedro. I was entranced by a barrage of childish questions and answers that seemed perfectly normal in helping me understand the world around me.

Looking back, I realize that what attracted me most to Pedro was the idea of having an unlimited amount of power and control over another person, even if he was constructed out of cheap wood and tatty fabric. This is the reason why children tend to develop such an affinity to puppets and dolls and action figures. Being small and vulnerable, prone to moments of self-doubt and helplessness, they relish both the opportunity and the ability to manipulate and punish inanimate objects that they know cannot hurt, tease, or lecture them. Children enjoy controlling puppets because the act of pulling the strings and dictating someone else's actions also allows children to assume, at least temporarily, the coveted roles of mother or father.

Children don't like getting spanked or told to stand in the corner, but they have no problem spanking their dolls, or sentencing their action figure to a five-minute time-out. Usually, children will yell at and punish inanimate objects for an offense they themselves committed, such as not listening or hitting someone. And not only will children punish these objects, they will also tell said objects why they are being punished and state how disappointed they are in having to reprimand them. By acting out their aggressions on non-living things, children, much like Max in *Where the Wild Things Are*, can deal with their anger and frustration in a positive way that allows them the opportunity to calm down and learn from their mistakes before they misbehave again.

A child's fascination with dolls and action figures also relates to his inability to sometimes understand his parents' anger, or even his body's failure to move as he wishes it would, usually owing to still developing motor-sensory reflexes. As Freud explains, "In their early games children do not distinguish at all sharply between living things and inanimate objects, and they are especially fond of treating their dolls like live people."[1] As stated above, dolls become an outlet for a child's anger and frustration, as well as for a child's joy, sadness, or confusion. In essence, the puppet typically becomes an externalization, a physical symbol, of whatever emotional conflict might prompt the child to begin interacting with the puppet in the first place. Possessing a puppet allows a child to usurp the same power his parents wield over him on a daily basis. If the child becomes too violent or angry, however, he knows, at least on a subconscious level, that he will not inflict physical pain upon his toy, nor will it tattle and reveal any behavior of which the child's parents might disapprove.

Perhaps no puppet is more famous than Pinocchio, that naughty piece of carved wood who yearns to be a real boy but must first learn proper behavior by surviving a series of dangerous encounters and adventures. While the story of Pinocchio is fairly well known, most of us are more familiar with Walt Disney's animated film than with Carlo Collodi's original Italian version. Admittedly, Collodi's version of Pinocchio is extremely violent, even by contemporary standards. Throughout the course of the book, Pinocchio is burned, whipped, stabbed, hanged from a tree, swallowed by a shark, and almost cooked alive twice. The puppet's adventures provide a scary and thrilling narrative through the Italian countryside, and Collodi constantly emphasizes the idea that children are born naughty and mischievous, and it is only through a parent's positive influence, and also repeated punishment, that children can learn good manners and etiquette and hope to become decent and productive members of society.

Many parents might consider *Pinocchio* too frightening a novel for their children to read. They believe its gothic elements, such as the rabbits carrying Pinocchio's coffin or Pinocchio trapped in the belly of the shark, might be a detriment to a child's growth and development rather than a benefit. But Pinocchio is not a real boy. He is a wooden puppet. And many children are therefore able to accept the story's high level of violence because they view Pinocchio as an inanimate object, as just another one of their toys that assumes human characteristics but cannot share the same feelings and sensations that children themselves experience on a daily basis. Because Pinocchio is a wooden puppet, there exists an aesthetic distance between himself and child readers that softens the novel's frightening moments and allows children to focus their attention not so much on the physical pain that Pinocchio endures, but on the moral lessons that those nasty incidents provide for both Pinocchio and child readers.

Children find the story's gothic elements attractive and entertaining; they vicariously indulge in Pinocchio's misbehavior because they know he will be punished for it, whereas they will not. And if there's one thing that children particularly enjoy, it's watching another child get into trouble. As Claudia Card points out, the violence in *Pinocchio* "is not gratuitous but serves as a vehicle of the knowledge and sensitivity required for the transition from puppet to person."[2] Pinocchio, like all children, must come to understand the value of self-discipline, as well as how to trust and to be trusting. He must realize that laziness and egotism do not reap rewards, but instead cause difficulties and hardships that we can only overcome if we possess a firm sense of our own identities.

All children wish their life could be an eternal playland, but *Pinocchio* reveals that to live such a life is to isolate ourselves from family and friends, impeding our own identity formations and damaging the growth and development of not only our personalities, but also our future and all its possibilities. We must remember that it is because of his constant mistakes and dismissive attitude that Pinocchio lands himself in those dangerous situations from which he is often unable to escape. Reading the novel, it becomes clear that Pinocchio's encounters with the novel's gothic elements are crucial for his identity formation. Without them, he is unable to learn empathy. Therefore, it is only by suffering the consequences of misbehavior that Pinocchio is able to perceive the power of his conscience, shed his selfish desires, and realize the importance of relying on his family members for love and support.

Initiative versus Guilt

Pinocchio's gothic elements (such as when he is hanged by the assassins, caught in a steel trap, or has his feet burned off in a fire) all imply that the puppet cannot learn the consequences of his actions if he continues to misbehave. These dark and disturbing moments, when blended with the book's many ideas concerning etiquette and identity formation, make the novel an important text for preschool children, typically between three and six years of age. Erikson refers to this third stage of psychosocial development as the "play age," and he labels it "Initiative versus Guilt." The strengths in this stage are purpose and courage, the antipathy being inhibition. Having mastered the ability to walk and talk, the child is now able to move around more freely and explore his surroundings. His command of language also allows him to ask more questions, communicate more effectively, and inquire about the people and objects around him.

This enhanced command of language and mobility expands the child's imagination to the point where the child now dreams himself into many different roles. Erikson believes this surge in imaginative powers can sometimes scare a child and inhibit him from building a sense of courage that is needed to develop his own personality. He tells us that "being firmly convinced that he is a person on his own, the child must now find out what kind of a person he may become."[3] Certainly, Pinocchio undergoes a similar transition when he transforms from a block of wood into a puppet. As a block of wood, he represents a toddler, restricted in both language and mobility, and also dependent upon adults. His transformation into a lively puppet symbolizes the energy and excitement that a preschooler possesses upon discovering the newfound freedom of his imagination and his bodily movements.[4]

With these newfound freedoms, however, there arises a destructive need to test our boundaries. We often see this impulse in children who engage in playtime by building their own towers or houses with wooden blocks or Legos. They construct massive projects that they then delight in kicking or tearing down. Having built something with the power of their own imaginations, they next need to test their physical power by causing it to collapse. This active mastery parallels my previous ideas about children playing with puppets. In both cases, children engage in destructive activities because they are able to wield power and manipulate other objects. It's also important to note that the child must destroy his creation himself, for only then can he feel pride at having conquered something weaker than himself. If someone else destroys the child's creation, then the child will typically feel threatened and vulnerable, crying until he is able to reconstruct his creation and then tear it down himself as he had hoped to do originally.

A child who is denied this process of building up and tearing down all by himself might identify more with his ruined creation than with his budding ego. Identifying with such a negative and unfulfilling experience can then cause the child to recognize his own inadequacies and lose courage in any future attempts to test his strength or expand his boundaries. Pinocchio experiences a similar desire to test his boundaries, but by refusing to listen to Geppetto or the Blue Fairy he slips further away from maturity and remains mired in idleness and the pursuit of self-satisfaction. Pinocchio's self-destruction is particularly harmful because it occurs outside of a secure domestic environment in which a parent is able to monitor and guide his impulses to build and destroy. Also, Pinocchio's selfish actions create repercussions that directly affect his radius of significant relations. These negative consequences are more severe than those produced by a child who simply knocks down some wooden blocks and then returns to the safety of his own family.

Many of Pinocchio's conflicts stem from his constant inability to use good judgment and to learn from past experiences. The book's gothic elements tempt him with false promises of money and never-ending playtime, but the negative consequences that result from indulging in these vices do not deter him from misbehavior. From an adult standpoint, it's often frustrating to see Pinocchio suffer so many times and still not grasp the importance of proper behavior. But a young child will often view each individual episode on its own terms and not understand the cause-and-effect relationship that creates a pattern of misbehavior. By exaggerating the violence and misery that befall Pinocchio throughout the novel, Collodi strives to impress upon his readers the consequences that can happen when a child has a bad attitude and refuses to listen to reason. Children, who have short attention spans, cannot easily forget the powerful and startling images that drive the narrative forward.

The crises Pinocchio experiences throughout his many adventures seem to reflect an intense need to prove himself by testing his limits and capitalizing on a natural increase of locomotive and imaginative energy. In order to resolve the crises that often accompany stage three, Pinocchio must embrace his radius of significant relations, which during these preschool years consists of the basic family: a mother (The Blue Fairy), a father (Geppetto), and the voice of his own budding conscience as symbolized by the talking cricket. Collodi makes it quite clear that in order for children to mature they must listen to their parents and obey society's rules.

This idea corresponds to Erikson's belief that support from family members is crucial during stage three because a parent's influence can prevent intense feelings of guilt from developing within the child. Such feelings can often lead to anger and confusion, following the child through the rest of the developmental stages until the crises are resolved properly. Collodi shows us that Pinocchio's world is one "where children are endowed with the potential for full humanity that can be attained only if they learn to listen to and emulate wise counselors before they give in once too often to temptation and fall victim to predation or other logical consequences of their own actions."[5] During the course of the novel, Geppetto, the Blue Fairy, and the talking cricket will all guide Pinocchio as he strives to become a real boy. They offer him advice, lecture him on disobedience, and forgive him for his selfish behavior and poor decision-making. These three characters are moral anchors, for they protect Pinocchio from his inflated ego; at the same time, they allow him countless opportunities to experience danger and the threat of death, nurturing his imagination so that he may learn from his mistakes and find the courage to become caring, compassionate, and selfless.

We must remember, however, that an increased imagination, while supplying a child with initiative and a sense of purpose, can also fuel a sense of guilt. Erikson reminds us that "to initiate suggests a moving out into a new direction.... Initiative is brave and valiant, but when it misfires, a strong sense of deflation follows. It is lively and enthusiastic while it lasts, but the initiative instigator is often left with a sense of inadequacy and guilt."[6] Essentially, the child's imagination conjures up secret fantasies and dramatic roles that the child might then feel guilty for having invented in the first place. These pretend adventures often involve the child striving to attain the position of one of his parents, and the failure to do so results in the child feeling embarrassed and defective.

During the previous stage, "Autonomy versus Shame and Doubt," the child kept his rivals at bay as he struggled to establish his own independence while still remaining dependent on his parents. The child did not view himself as separate from his parents, and, in fact, viewed himself as merely an extension of their identities. During stage three, however, the child has now come to view himself as his own person, and this realization fuels the sense of initiative that is characteristic of stage three. Erikson believes that the guilt inherent in this stage tends to occur "over the goals contemplated and the acts initiated in one's exuberant enjoyment of new locomotor and mental power."[7] Basically, the dawning awareness of purpose and courage, coupled with surges of physical energy, instills intense feelings of rivalry toward those who occupy roles the child believes he can assume, namely the roles of mother or father. The child will battle these rivals in both his imagination and in reality, but he feels ashamed at having even entertained the thought of challenging two people who love and care for him. The ensuing guilt will often lead to anger, which only invigorates the child and encourages him to continue indulging in fantasies of control.

Like all children, Pinocchio wants to control his own life. Throughout the novel he tries to prove that he can survive in an adult world without parents or an education. He believes he can take care of Geppetto and that he does not need to work in order to live comfortably. His inflated pride and misplaced courage continually place him in harm's way, and it is only while suffering through these gothic episodes that he laments his poor choices and vows to be a dutiful son. We witness this sense of guilt after Pinocchio is freed from prison and sets out for the Blue Fairy's house: "How many dreadful things have happened to me! And I deserved them, for I am obstinate as a mule. I always wanted my own way, and never listened to those who loved me, and who had a thousand times more sense than I had. But from now I shall lead a different life, and become an obedient boy."[8] While these heartfelt epiphanies are short-lived, they still reveal Pinocchio's guilt at disappointing Geppetto and the Blue Fairy, as well as falling victim to gothic influences he does not understand. Even after suffering several near-death experiences, Pinocchio still refuses to learn, mainly because he lacks the necessary education.

More importantly, we sense that Pinocchio will never mature, and he will never establish his own identity, until he becomes an obedient child that listens to all the adults who care about him and try to help him learn from his mistakes. And not just a child that follows blind, "puppet-like" obedience and accepts without reason, but a child that questions and is able to think for himself. Part of achieving one's self-identity is the ability to develop a rational obedience and a value system based on experience. These are important steps in the growth and maturation process that Collodi continuously touts as prerequisites for being a real boy. To become a real boy, however, Pinocchio must first understand right from wrong, and this feat can only be accomplished by interacting with the novel's gothic elements. If he wishes to find his way successfully through this dark and dangerous landscape he must be wary of all the strange characters that cross his path, and he must also rely on a strong bond of love and acceptance with his basic family.

Fools' Trap

While the basic family is important during this third stage of psychosocial development, the child also seeks out the assistance of friends and peers with whom he can live out his fantasies. These associations often come into being outside of domestic spaces, and they allow the child to learn a variety of social or motor-sensory skills that fuel the child's sense of purpose and supply him with the courage needed to attain the goals he's created in his own mind. Erikson explains that "the tangible goals of the elementary practice of skills are shared by and with age mates in places of instruction (payer house, fishing hole, workshop, kitchen, schoolhouse) most of which, in turn, are geographically separated from the home, from the mother, and from infantile memories."[9] Indeed, Pinocchio spends almost no time inside his home. Throughout most of the novel he travels from place to place, trying to prove his self-worth to Geppetto and the Blue Fairy while also learning which characters he can trust and which he should not. Thus, in order to become a real boy and resolve the various crises that accompany this third stage of psychosocial development, Pinocchio must learn not only from his basic family, but also from his peers.

Pinocchio's repeated associations with characters his own age seem to play a vital role in the puppet's growth and development. Many of these peers reveal themselves as animal characters, and Collodi clearly delineates each one as good or bad. The bad characters (such as the fox and the cat, the shark, or the serpent) exist within the gothic landscapes that trap Pinocchio and punish him for his bad decisions. The good characters (such as the pigeon, the tunny fish, or the dog Alidoro) often invade the gothic landscapes to save Pinocchio from harm or even death. As the novel progresses, we begin to understand that the bad characters seem to symbolize children who, like Pinocchio, have yet to mature. These evil characters have not received the necessary skills to function in an adult society. As a result of their stunted growth and maturity, they remain embedded in gothic landscapes. They lack the parental guidance, as well as the initiative, to return to those domestic spheres that will nurture them emotionally and intellectually. Yet these evil characters are crucial to Pinocchio's development because he must interact with them in order to mature and to gain a sense of right and wrong.

Pinocchio's first meeting with his peers also coincides with one of the first gothic encounters outside of his home. Having ditched school to see a puppet show, he meets his fellow brothers, who are also puppets, and enjoys an affectionate reunion. This joyous occasion is short-lived, however, as the Showman decides to use Pinocchio as firewood so he can roast his mutton. When Pinocchio learns his fate he shouts, "O Daddy, O Daddy, save me! I don't want to die. I don't want to die."[10] That his first reaction is to shout for his father, who up until now he's abused and ignored, seems to suggest that, at least on a subconscious level, Pinocchio understands the importance of having parents and the protection that a basic family affords. His near-death experience has shocked him into this realization, and perhaps it's this need for help that prompts Pinocchio to save the life of Harlequin when the Showman decides to use *him* as firewood instead of Pinocchio. The reward for performing a good deed (which was initiated by a gothic moment) reveals itself to Pinocchio when the Showman gives him five gold coins to take back to Geppetto. For Pinocchio and child readers, the lesson seems to be that if we act selflessly and are willing to make sacrifices for other people, the benefits of demonstrating love and compassion might actually increase our own sense of happiness. And when we experience these surges of ecstasy and self-contentment, we also experience an intense feeling of purpose that invigorates us to work harder as we search out our identities.

Pinocchio's elation at receiving the five gold coins instills in him a desire to make even more money and also to show Geppetto that he can survive on his own and be an important contributor to his family. Pinocchio feels guilty because his father sold his own coat to buy his son a primer, which Pinocchio sold immediately so he could attend the puppet show. His intentions are clearly good as he heads home to greet Geppetto, but away from the family unit Pinocchio must learn who he can trust. His subsequent encounter with the fox and the cat distances him from Geppetto and propels him through each of the novel's gothic landscapes. Here we see how even children can be corrupted by greed and the lure of money. Part of Pinocchio's problem is that he's so concerned with earning more gold coins that he refuses to listen to good advice.

Pinocchio's behavior connects with Erikson's observations that children in stage three are so eager to explore their rapidly expanding environments that they frequently shun the counsel of their parents and pursue their own self-interests. Upon meeting the fox and the cat, the blackbird tells Pinocchio, "Don't listen to the advice of evil companions. If you do, you'll regret it."[11] That the cat quickly gobbles up the blackbird shows its attempt to hide its true nature from Pinocchio, as well as the cat's predilection for violence. Yet Pinocchio cannot be expected to show suspicion because he has never ventured out into the world before. His folly in trusting these two rogues is understandable. But we also realize that had Pinocchio gone straight to school like a well-behaved boy, he would not have put himself in danger at the puppet show, nor would he have met the fox and the cat. The message here is that young children should only move beyond their familiar spheres if accompanied by their parents. Doing so allows parents to teach their children why it's dangerous to talk to strangers, as well as the importance in knowing who to trust and what might happen if children place their confidence in the wrong people.

Pinocchio makes a bad decision in choosing to trust the fox and the cat, and he suffers for his ignorance. The two thieves abandon him at the inn and later, disguised as assassins, they attempt to rob him. As they chase the frightened puppet across the countryside, we cannot help but feel that Pinocchio is being chased not only by these two assassins, but also by his poor judgment and naughtiness. When they hang Pinocchio from the tree, his only words are, "O Daddy! If only you were here!"[12] Again, he reaches out for his father, and so it comes as no surprise that in the next chapter he is rescued by the Blue Fairy, who will function as his protector and mother throughout the rest of the novel. When rescued, Pinocchio is near death, but his rejuvenation by the Blue Fairy symbolizes another opportunity to learn proper behavior. If Pinocchio harbors any guilt at being tricked by the fox and the cat, the Blue Fairy will counter it by providing the puppet with the self-esteem and courage he needs to find Geppetto and become a real boy. And while Pinocchio has experienced several traumatic situations up to this point in the story, child readers are comforted by the fact that there are adult figures always looking out for him, even if Pinocchio himself is unaware of their presence.

Because Collodi tells us that the Blue Fairy is "good-hearted," we know she is a loving character who only wants to help Pinocchio. Yet he refuses her medicine because he doesn't like the taste, which is a decision most children can relate to on account of their hatred for medicine. In refusing her medicine, Pinocchio also seems to be refusing the help of adults. Like all children, Pinocchio must learn to trust the adults in his life; he must learn to differentiate between those who wish to help him and those who wish to harm him. His stubbornness disappears, however, when the black rabbits enter the room carrying a black coffin. This threat of death comes immediately after Pinocchio's hanging, which occurred because he lacked good judgment and put his faith in the wrong people.

When Pinocchio finally drinks the medicine and his health is restored, the Blue Fairy tells him, "Boys should know that the right medicine, taken in time, might save them from a serious illness, perhaps even from death."[13] In this statement she is also lecturing the puppet on the importance of accepting adult wisdom and ignoring the advice of those children (and sometimes adults) that seek self-gratification and are prone to abusing their power. This lesson is reinforced when Pinocchio lies to the Blue Fairy about the four gold pieces, whereupon his nose grows longer and longer with each lie. By making Pinocchio's nose become longer, Collodi shows that lying is naughty, and that it leaves a physical deformity. Children are often terrified of physical changes that occur inside and outside of their bodies, partly because they cannot explain such changes and fear they're sick or might be dying. Pinocchio's nose growing, and his hysterical reaction that follows, will certainly help younger readers contextualize and comprehend abstract ideas like shame and dishonesty and misbehavior.

Children also fear physical changes because they're afraid that said changes, which they often associate with sickness, will lock them in their bedrooms and prevent them from interacting with their peers. Collodi illustrates this idea of entrapment by telling us that because Pinocchio's nose grew so long, he "could not move in any direction. If he turned one way, his nose hit the bed or the window panes; if he turned the other, it struck the walls or the door."[14] This physical confinement emphasizes the types of punishments that can arise from lying and not trusting adults when they are only trying to help. Although this scene in the bedroom ends on a positive note, it is crucial for Pinocchio's development because he begins to learn and appreciate the consequences that result when we don't listen to our parents.

Collodi's message is that misbehaving children suffer greatly for their naughtiness, emotionally as well as physically. The black rabbits and the black coffin are strong gothic images that Pinocchio will never forget. He tells the Blue Fairy, "Another time I won't make so much fuss. I'll remember those black rabbits with the coffin on their shoulders, and take the glass at once, and down it will go!"[15] This scene illustrates how Pinocchio's inter-actions with gothic elements instruct him on how to behave and lead a bet-ter life. A less spooky approach might not have worked in this scene because child readers might have focused their attention on Pinocchio not taking his medicine, or on the introduction of the Blue Fairy as a new character in the novel. The gothic atmosphere presents strong and disturbing images that force child readers to respond to their own helplessness and vulnera-bility, as well as to the dependency they have on the adults in their lives.

When Pinocchio leaves the Blue Fairy's house, he again meets up with the fox and the cat, unaware that they were the assassins who hanged him from the tree. Although he is journeying to meet Geppetto, Pinocchio can-not help but be entranced by the possibility of turning four gold coins into a thousand. Admittedly, he expresses more hesitation this time, remem-bering the advice of the Blue Fairy, but he still agrees to travel to the Field of Miracles where he believes he can plant his money in the ground and it will blossom into a money tree. The Field of Miracles sounds like a place right out of a fairy tale, so named because it represents nothing more than idle fantasies in which only children would indulge.

Also, it's no coincidence that the Field of Miracles is located near the city of Fools' Trap. This connection implies that only fools engage in such wishful thinking, trapping themselves within their own dreams and thus inhibiting their own growth and maturity. And while children are expected to flirt with such imaginary ideas (even requiring them for the development of their personalities), Collodi also implies that to do so in an unfamiliar environment, and especially without one's parents, might be dangerous because it could inhibit our identity formation and prevent us from maturing properly. In *Pinocchio*, Collodi suggests that the optimal balance between parents' and peers' influence is one in which the parents step back and allow their children to interact freely with peer relations, yet the parents watch from a safe distance in case children should need their guidance, support, or protection.

And yet it's precisely because of this disappointing experience, after realizing he's been robbed, that Pinocchio finally understands the importance of associating with peers who are friendly and helpful, and not those who are mean-spirited and two-faced. When Pinocchio runs into town to tell the authorities about his money, he is thrown into jail. Although he is innocent of any crime, he is still guilty of listening to strangers and not following the Blue Fairy's advice. Again, as during the bedroom scene when his nose grew, we see Pinocchio confined for his behavior, trapped by his own actions and suffering the consequences. Being locked in a prison elicits strong feelings of horror from child readers, not because many children have ever been there, but because they identify a jail sentence with being given a time out or sent to their room.

Pinocchio's banishment for four months is a physical reminder that children must be careful in choosing their friends. Clearly, Pinocchio has allowed his fantasies to control his actions. His poor decision to enter Fools' Trap and test the Field of Miracles only leads to stronger feelings of guilt upon his release from prison. For example, he believes the Blue Fairy has died because of his own misbehavior and immaturity. This loss consumes Pinocchio with sadness, yet it forces him to redouble his efforts to find Geppetto and re-establish the family connections he now realizes are so important to his growth and development.

Although Pinocchio gradually learns right from wrong as the novel progresses, he still makes poor decisions and misbehaves. His actions support Erikson's theory that a child's development is not always strictly linear. Even after the Blue Fairy announces that Pinocchio will finally become a real boy, he decides to join his friend Lampwick and travel to Playland. She even cautions Pinocchio that "children who do not follow the advice of those who are wiser than they are, always come to grief."[16] Nevertheless, Pinocchio wants to indulge in foolish fantasies where he spends carefree days eating junk food and remaining idle, surrounded by other children without nagging adult supervision and having to go to school. But rather than provide him with bliss and entertainment, Pinocchio's time in Playland turns out to be quite the disaster. He transforms into a braying donkey, whereupon he laments the day he listened to Lampwick; he is then sold to a circus and injured during one of his performances.

Such a scary transformation finally forces Pinocchio to realize his mistakes. It's after this ordeal, having survived two more near-death experiences, that Pinocchio uses his energy and courage in positive ways. He frees Geppetto from the belly of the shark and then cares for him by earning money and studying his school lessons. In *Pinocchio*, as well as during the third stage of psychosocial development, it becomes clear that having achieved maturity denotes the ability to empathize with others, distinguish between right and wrong, and gain a sense of purpose that does not rely on excessive self-gratification.

It appears, then, as though these gothic encounters are necessary for Pinocchio's progression through this third stage of psychosocial development. Without them, he might not experience those feelings of guilt that spur his attempts to act like a proper young man. Likewise, these gothic encounters allow Pinocchio the opportunity to learn the valuable lesson that each one of us must choose our peers carefully. Surrounding ourselves with the wrong friends can separate us from our family and inhibit our maturation process. And although Pinocchio suffers greatly throughout his adventures, he still returns home in the end with a stronger sense of his own identity. No longer a wooden puppet, he is now able to move forward so he can enter the next stage of his psychosocial development.

The Blue Fairy

According to Erikson, the play age relies on the basic family, which instructs the child on where imagination ends and reality begins. And it's during this third stage of psychosocial development that "children now look for new identifications which seem to promise a field of initiative with less of the conflict and guilt which attach to the hopeless rivalry of the home."[17] The purpose and courage that children attain during this stage fill them with dreams of success in which they command attention. Pinocchio shares these same dreams, but he has not learned to curb his sense of initiative, and so he constantly finds himself in dangerous situations. It's natural that during this stage a child will want to experiment with a new radius of significant relations and assume different responsibilities. The child wishes to move beyond the home and seek out future roles, even if those roles exist solely in his own mind.

The narrative structure of *Pinocchio* is episodic. Each chapter is simply another adventure that lands Pinocchio in trouble and introduces one or more gothic elements that the puppet must overcome if he hopes to survive. Morals are reiterated, punishments are repeated, and Pinocchio escapes from one gothic encounter only to leap quickly into another. The structure of *Pinocchio* is similar to the moral stories of Horatio Alger, and Jack Zipes remarks that *Pinocchio* "is the consummate Horatio Alger story of the nineteenth-century, a pull-yourself-up-by-your-own-bootstraps fairy tale that demonstrates that even a log has the potential to be good, human, and socially useful."[18] On each of his adventures, Pinocchio must escape danger, refocus his goals, and strive toward maintaining some semblance of good behavior. Yet within the novel's repetition there also exists a gradual rise in character development. At the climax of each adventure, Pinocchio learns a bit more and becomes increasingly aware of the world around him, even if he continues to make bad choices. In all fairness to the wooden puppet, it seems that as the novel progresses, each of his poor decisions is accompanied by a stronger sense of guilt and doubt. At one point in the novel Pinocchio tells a dolphin that "[Geppetto] is the best father in the world; and I am very likely the worst son."[19] This increase in self-awareness and outward emotion also reveals Pinocchio's growing conscience, which fuels his intense desire to seek out those future roles that all children believe they are destined to pursue.

The Blue Fairy functions as a mother figure for Pinocchio, but she also symbolizes his hopes and dreams. She represents all those future possibilities the puppet continues to search out amidst his repeated requests and attempts to become a real boy. Fairies are known to grant wishes, and the Blue Fairy's presence in the novel suggests that if Pinocchio learns to behave himself and go to school, then perhaps he will achieve all that his heart desires. The Blue Fairy is also a complement to the novel's gothic elements. While the gothic elements tempt the puppet with false promises of wealth and eternal fun, the Blue Fairy reminds Pinocchio that "everybody must find work. Woe to those who lead idle lives! Idleness is a dreadful disease, of which one should be cured immediately in childhood; if not, one never gets over it."[20] Like the positive and negative thoughts that war inside Pinocchio's own mind, the Blue Fairy and the gothic elements both interact with the puppet to teach him the importance of pursuing one's dreams in a way that builds personality and contributes to a sense of identity.

For instance, Collodi tells us that inside the Blue Fairy's carriage "the cushions were padded with canary feather and lined with whipped cream and custard, with sweet biscuits."[21] This description differs from the gothic gloomy countryside in which Pinocchio once found himself running for his life from two assassins who stabbed him and then hanged him from a tree. Still, we need to remember that although the Blue Fairy seems to exist in competition with the gothic elements, both components work together during the novel, albeit in different ways, to teach Pinocchio the merits of gaining an education. Such an example occurs when the rabbits carry Pinocchio's coffin into the bedroom, thus enforcing the Blue Fairy's warning that Pinocchio's health will not improve if he does not drink his medicine. Together, the necessary presence of good and evil provides Pinocchio with an understanding of his own limitations as he continually strives to find an identity that will resolve his personal crises and propel him toward future stages of psychosocial development.

Collodi also makes it clear that the Blue Fairy symbolizes a joyful future that will reward the puppet for his good behavior, offering him far more pleasures than the gothic present from which he struggles to escape and find his way. She embodies a stable family life to which Pinocchio hopes to belong at some point in the future when he has turned into a real boy. This idea corresponds to Erikson's theories concerning the third stage of psychosocial development:

> [The initiative stage] frees the child's initiative and sense of purpose for adult tasks which promise (but cannot guarantee) a fulfillment of one's range of capacities. This is prepared in the firmly established, steadily growing conviction, undaunted by guilt, that "I am what I can imagine I will be." It is equally obvious, however, that a widespread disappointment of this conviction by a discrepancy between infantile ideals and adolescent reality can only lead to an unleashing of the guilt-and-violence cycle so characteristic of man and yet so dangerous to his very existence.[22]

Clearly, Pinocchio experiences a strong sense of purpose and yearning for adventure following his sudden delivery into Erikson's third stage of psychosocial development, and this is symbolized by his transformation from a block of wood into a walking and talking puppet. He wants to fulfill his adult capabilities so he can prove his self-worth, but his constant aversions to work and school prevent him from attaining the respect and control that adult tasks typically command and require.

Pinocchio wants to reap the benefits of being an adult, but he doesn't want to put forth any of the effort. He has not yet learned how to be responsible, and to do so he must first learn to rely on himself, which children gradually do as they mature and become less and less dependent on adults. And while Pinocchio possesses a high level of energy (which he should apply to labor and his studies rather than to trips to Playland and the circus), this energy becomes counterproductive because he uses it not for positive gain, but to indulge in mischief and idleness. In truth, most of his energy is spent fleeing from those very same gothic elements that he continually travels toward throughout the novel. He does not understand that such elements are limiting his growth and development, and so he rushes into them without a clear understanding of why, or even how, they affect his identity and personality.

When Pinocchio arrives at Busy Bee town he remarks, "I see that this place will never do for me. I was not born for work."[23] Because he is starving, though, he begs for money, and he is genuinely appalled when people offer to give him coins, but only in exchange for manual labor. He yells at the townspeople, telling them he is not a donkey, and this remark will prove ironic later in the story when he becomes so lazy that he actually does transform into a donkey and is then sold to the manager of a circus show. Pinocchio's anger at being asked to perform manual labor mirrors a child's frustration at being ordered about by an adult. Children know that adults have all the power and control, and the shame and helplessness they experience during these encounters can often create anger and frustration. Even when an adult says "please" and "thank you," the child is still upset because he knows the ultimate decision is not always his to make. The resentment that often builds up during these moments can inhibit a child from pursuing his own imaginary adventures, and from assuming those various roles and identities that, however unrealistic they might seem, are key in promoting his maturation process.

As grown-ups, we understand that Busy Bee town is a microcosm of the adult world; every person works for his share and earns his living. But because Pinocchio has not reached adulthood, he is unprepared for this manner and style of life. He is immature and impulsive, only agreeing to manual labor when he is seduced by the promise of tasty sweets. Although this indulgence does reveal Pinocchio's need for self-gratification, it still persuades him to carry the pail home for a kind little woman who turns out to be the Blue Fairy in disguise. If we admit that the Blue Fairy represents Pinocchio's hopes and dreams, and that she is a stepping stone to maturity, then it is no coincidence that she appears in Busy Bee town, for it is here that Pinocchio first performs manual labor and gives in (at least temporarily) to his penchant for laziness. This scene also represents the first moment in which Pinocchio says, "I'm sick of always being a puppet! It's about time I became a man, like other people."[24] Perhaps the appearance of the Blue Fairy, coupled with his journey through Busy Bee town, has prompted Pinocchio to see more clearly that a future does exist for him if only he will embrace it. And the Blue Fairy echoes these sentiments when she tells Pinocchio that the only way he can become a real man is if he deserves it. Her remark alludes to maturity as a process, a goal that one must work toward, and not as simply a gift. If Pinocchio wants to become a real man, he needs to earn that designation by showing adults that he is responsible and can take care of himself without supervision.

Despite the Blue Fairy's presence in his life, Pinocchio continues to make bad choices and eventually finds himself in Playland with his friend Lampwick. If Busy Bee is a microcosm of the adult world, Playland is a microcosm of a child's imaginary world. Collodi describes Playland as a place where "there's no school there, no masters, and no books. In that heavenly place, no one ever studies. There's no school on Saturday; and in every week there are six Saturdays and one Sunday.... The autumn holidays begin in January, and last till the thirty-first of December."[25] It is while celebrating at Playland that Pinocchio wakes up one morning to discover he has turned into a donkey. His transformation is a result of his idleness and misplaced energy, as well as his disregard for the adult world and all of its responsibilities.

Playland itself does not exude a gothic atmosphere, but the idea of transforming into an animal without our own consent can be frightening to a child. Children view this transformation as lowering themselves to a weaker position and thus becoming even more dependent on those who wield power over them. Claudia Card explains that "a donkey in Collodi's day was someone who was used by others and discarded when no longer useful."[26] The implication here is that children who choose to remain young and immature, and do not progress through the necessary stages of psychosocial development, will be considered worthless by society and treated as such. The squirrel reiterates this idea when she tells Pinocchio, "Lazy children who dislike books, schools, and masters, and who spend their time with toys, games, and amusements, must end up, sooner or later, by becoming little donkeys."[27] As a donkey, Pinocchio is whipped and ordered about, ridiculed and ignored. He has no control over his own life and he suffers, emotionally and physically, because of his idleness. Children can relate to these feelings of helplessness because they often feel slighted and restrained by the adults who control their lives. While Playland looks fun and exciting, it is only a fantasy because it disguises the horrible notion that to ignore one's mental faculties, and to shun a proper education, will diminish one's sense of purpose and ambition. The resulting laziness will then manifest itself into a physical transformation that a child cannot hide from others. And this public transformation results in the child then feeling ashamed and embarrassed, which stunts his growth even further because he now becomes afraid to test his boundaries in positive ways that will aid in his maturation and teach him to be responsible.

At the end of the novel, the Blue Fairy's love and patience finally results in Pinocchio shedding his egotism and learning from his previous mistakes. He works for a farmer so he can buy milk for Geppetto; he weaves baskets that he sells for money; and he begins to practice his reading and writing. The Blue Fairy tells him, "Children who love their parents, and help them when they are sick and poor, are worthy of praise and love, even if they are not models of obedience and good behavior. Be good in future, and you will be happy."[28] This realization that naughtiness can cripple identity formation and maturity is what enables Pinocchio to become a responsible boy who is now ready to begin Erikson's fourth stage of psychosocial development. His desire for parental figures, and his constant interactions with gothic elements, have both shown him that good deeds merit good rewards.

The Talking Cricket

As Pinocchio wanders through the novel, yearning to develop his own identity, he continuously makes poor choices and suffers from their consequences. Yet he also experiences moments of intense guilt in which, usually through fear and embarrassment, he admits his mistakes and vows to always behave and think logically. Over the course of the entire novel, these guilty feelings help form Pinocchio's conscience. Erikson believes that conscience governs initiative, and that the child "now not only feels afraid of being found out, but he also hears the 'inner voice' of self-observation, self-guidance, and self-punishment, which divides him radically within himself."[29] In *Pinocchio*, this "inner voice" manifests itself in the character of the talking cricket. Pinocchio has no conscience because he comes into the world during stage two of psychosocial development. Although he can walk and talk immediately after Geppetto carves him from the wood, Pinocchio has not spent any time learning to crawl and walk and become familiar with his surroundings. And because he is still learning how to control his new physical movements and motor-sensory reflexes, he cannot yet focus on the time that is necessary to develop his mental faculties. To do so requires the willpower and determination that children only gain from having successfully mastered motor coordination and assumed control over their bodies.

From the moment Geppetto carves him from the wood, Pinocchio acts cheeky and naughty, poking fun at Geppetto and landing him in prison. The talking cricket attempts to lecture Pinocchio on his misbehavior, telling him, "Woe to those boys who revolt against their parents, and run away from home. They will never do any good in this world, and sooner or later they will repent bitterly."[30] Pinocchio's anger at the cricket's preaching suggests that on a subconscious level he fears the cricket is correct in his observations. No child wants to believe that playtime will eventually end, and even Pinocchio admits that the only trade in life that attracts him is eating and sleeping and playing every day from the time he wakes up until the time he goes to bed. When the cricket disapproves of Pinocchio for having a wooden head (which also symbolizes those children who are lazy and selfish), the puppet seizes a mallet and throws it at the cricket, thereby smashing the insect against the wall. This murderous act implies that Pinocchio wishes to crush those ideas of having to earn his own way and be industrious; it also mirrors a child's desire to assert his own strength by conquering someone who is smaller and weaker than himself.

It is interesting that the only character Pinocchio kills during the entire novel is the one character that acts as his conscience and continually tries to correct his behavior. Perhaps the guilt associated with killing the cricket creates the "inner voice" within Pinocchio, for it is only after murdering the cricket that he begins to express verbally his frustration at making poor decisions, as well as his repeated failed attempts to live a dutiful and productive life. Immediately after Pinocchio kills the cricket, he says, "The talking cricket was right. I did wrong to revolt against my father and run away from home. If my father were here now, I shouldn't be dying of hunger."[31] Pinocchio is just now beginning to understand cause and effect, namely that without parental guidance a child cannot hope to survive and mature into a responsible adult. Here, we can see how the feelings of guilt and anger, which swell within Pinocchio following the murder of the cricket, become positive additions to his budding personality in that they initiate his self-reflection, as well as a gradual understanding of the differences between right and wrong.

Though the novel is episodic, each chapter a self-contained adventure that preaches the negative consequences of a child misbehaving, Pinocchio is the "thread that holds [the story] together, and he is depicted as an ungainly brat, naughty in a not particularly attractive way, who justifies his existence only toward the end of the story."[32] In another sense, however, the talking cricket, Geppetto, and the Blue Fairy also act as threads that hold Pinocchio (and his budding conscience) together. These three characters exist to remind Pinocchio and child readers that a parent's influence is crucial for successful growth and maturity. A parent's constant love and reassurances illustrate that while it is natural for a child to experience crises and setbacks as he progresses through various stages of psychosocial development, it is also natural that parents remain loyal to the child and guide him toward each successive stage, no matter how often the child might be indecisive or make bad decisions amid conflicting emotions.

For children navigating through this third stage, it is important to remember that while initiative can lead to an excess of energy and courage, as well as to a desire to conquer our rivals, it can also produce intense feelings of guilt that force us to question our sense of purpose. These moments of guilt often create doubt and hesitation that inhibit the child from pursuing any goals he might set, or any challenges he might wish to undertake. Having a conscience, as Pinocchio comes to learn, is important for one's personality development because it acts as a buffer to protect one from wild impulses and crippling self-doubt. The talking cricket's moralizing certainly comes off as preachy and didactic, but it also instills in Pinocchio a deeper understanding of pain and suffering. This understanding, which generates empathy and is so important in a person's growth and development, also invigorates him to perform positive actions and shows he is capable and worthy of becoming a real boy.

With the birth of his conscience, Pinocchio now begins to understand such concepts as love and compassion, as well as the idea of sacrifice. When Geppetto sells his coat to buy his son a primer, Pinocchio is overwhelmed with happiness and hugs and kisses his father. Although Pinocchio has never been to school, he still understands the importance of learning, even if he holds off attending for as long as he is able. Geppetto's actions teach Pinocchio that his father is willing to risk his own health to ensure that his son receives a proper education. In turn, this display of love and sacrifice expands Pinocchio's own imagination and, as is typical during the third stage of psychosocial development, he indulges in fantasies about the future. For example, on his way to school, Pinocchio dreams about learning to read and write, and how gaining those skills will allow him to earn lots of money; he imagines buying his father a new coat made of silver and gold with diamond buttons. He thinks, "That poor man really deserves it; for, that I should be a learned man."[33] While Geppetto's actions have sparked a sense of duty and responsibility within Pinocchio, the puppet is still unable to resolve the necessary crises that accompany his interactions with the novel's gothic elements, such as his encounter with the murderous assassins, as well as his fleeing from the police. These constant detours off the righteous path ultimately result in Pinocchio nearly being fried and eaten by a grotesque, green fisherman.

In many ways, Pinocchio's drive and ambition, fueled by a strong sense of courage and purpose, lead him toward these gothic elements. Without coming into contact with them he is unable to differentiate between decisions that further his own identity and those that stunt his growth and prevent him from moving forward, physically as well as emotionally. Reading the novel, it becomes clear that whenever Pinocchio misbehaves or makes a bad decision, he is immobilized. He is sent to prison for four months, caught in a steel trap, chained as a watchdog, tied up, hanged from a tree, and injured. Each of these detriments symbolize a stalling of mental growth and lead to an epiphany in which Pinocchio realizes he has exercised bad judgment. When the fox and the cat try to lure him to Dupeland, Pinocchio remains steadfast in his determination to return home. He reflects on the advice given to him by the talking cricket and realizes that misbehaving children endure many difficulties and hardships. His conscience tells him he should return home to his father, but his sense of initiative craves an opportunity to earn extra money and thus show Geppetto that he indeed possesses the power and intelligence to support his family.

Because he is consumed with greed and an overactive imagination, Pinocchio chooses to accompany the fox and the cat to the Field of Miracles. This trip adds another link in the chain of awful experiences that the puppet must suffer through on his way toward growth and maturity. It is no coincidence that the cricket's ghost appears at this point in the story, warning Pinocchio, yet again, about his poor judgment. The cricket tells him not to trust people who promise wealth and success, and that children who are selfish are never rewarded, but punished. The cricket's appearance is a physical manifestation of Pinocchio's own doubts about the sincerity of his two shady companions. And when Pinocchio ignores the cricket's advice and continues on his way, the path he now travels becomes darker and more ominous. The darkness represents the absence of Pinocchio's conscience, and the gloomy atmosphere is a foreshadowing of his brutal attack by the assassins, as well as the guilt he feels at disappointing his father.

Luckily, Pinocchio is rescued by the Blue Fairy, who brings him to her house and sends for the three most famous doctors in the neighborhood: a crow, an owl, and a talking cricket. Each of these characters represents a value that Pinocchio needs to embrace if he wishes to survive and become a real boy. The crow symbolizes self-preservation and cunning; the owl symbolizes wisdom and intelligence; and the talking cricket symbolizes Pinocchio's conscience and his desire to perform good deeds that will benefit his radius of significant relations. These three characters surround Pinocchio and offer their assessment as to whether or not he is dead. While their conversations center on the puppet's physical health, we can also interpret their words as being suggestive of Pinocchio's emotional state. In this sense, they seem to be discussing whether or not he has the ability to trust his conscience and learn right from wrong, as well as whether or not he has the ability to embrace his family and listen to Geppetto's advice and instruction.

This tense scene in the Blue Fairy's house supplies as much of an emotional awakening for Pinocchio as it does a physical one. After this pivotal scene, as Pinocchio progresses through the rest of the novel and attempts to resolve his numerous crises, he interacts more and more with the novel's gothic elements. The result is that his conscience becomes sharper and more defined, providing him with a valuable understanding of right and wrong, as well as reminding him of the vital role that basic family plays in one's growth and maturity.

Toward the end of the novel, having survived countless ordeals, Pinocchio grasps the importance of relying on family members when he realizes the Blue Fairy is his mother and that she is always there to help him in times of trouble, no matter how mean and disobedient he might act. This declaration occurs after the fiasco at Playland. Pinocchio has turned into a donkey, and the man who purchased him at the market ties a stone around his neck and pushes him into the ocean. The fish nibble at Pinocchio's ears and muzzle and neck and mane until they strip away his flesh to reveal once again the wooden puppet. This rebirth from the water is also a mental rebirth, for it leads to Pinocchio's encounter with an enormous shark that swallows him. Trapped inside the belly of the shark, Pinocchio risks his own life to save Geppetto, who has also been swallowed by the shark. These character-building events ultimately lead the puppet to finally work for money so he can help save the Blue Fairy, who is sick in the hospital.

In literature, water is often seen as symbolic of a new beginning; it suggests baptism and purification. Considering these ideas, it makes sense that "Pinocchio hits bottom metaphorically when he sinks in the pond and is eaten—that is *his* lowest point in the story—but *the* lowest point in the novel is the belly of *il pesce cane*, into which he goes voluntarily, having shed his egotism and need for immediate gratification."[34] Like many characters in children's literature, Pinocchio must enter and (eventually) leave the gothic environment if he hopes to develop successfully and progress to the next stage of psychosocial development. This home-away-from-home theme can be found in most children's stories. While I alluded to it during my discussion of "Goblin Market," we can see this theme play out in many classic fairy tales. Hansel and Gretel leave home, enter the woods to do battle with the witch, and then return home again to provide for their family. In *The Wonderful Wizard of Oz*, Dorothy becomes separated from her aunt and uncle, embarks on an adventure in Oz, and returns home having matured and gained a deeper appreciation for her home and family. Clearly, the implication in these stories is that to establish morals and self-identity, a child (or a wooden puppet) must be separated from loved ones and leave home where he will then be tested continuously and forced to rely on his own judgments.

That Pinocchio braves his way forward into the belly of the shark illustrates his newfound courage. The shark that has swallowed Pinocchio and Geppetto is the last gothic element in the novel with which Pinocchio must interact. Having developed a conscience, and learned from the consequences of his previous episodes, Pinocchio is now able to discard his selfish tendencies and focus his love and attention on family instead of on himself. Without the anger, laziness, and quest for control that has dictated his previous thoughts and actions, Pinocchio is free to embrace his radius of significant relations instead of viewing them as rivals for power. As a result, Pinocchio's escape with Geppetto from the shark's belly seems to suggest that he is ready to become a real boy and advance to the next stage of his growth and maturity. And, of course, at the end of the novel, Pinocchio finally admits that the talking cricket was correct all along in proclaiming that we should always treat one another with love and respect, and that how we treat another person often affects how those same people will treat us. This is a lesson that all children should learn, but it is only by interacting with gothic elements, and subsequently losing ourselves in the darkness, that we can rise up again with a better understanding of how our consciences can aid in our identity formation.

"How ridiculous I was when I was a puppet"

Pinocchio's countless adventures through gothic landscapes reassure children that they are not alone in feeling guilty about their power fantasies, nor are they alone in making mistakes and disappointing their parents. The patience and dedication that Geppetto and the Blue Fairy show throughout the novel in dealing with Pinocchio is a testament to the fact that all children have the potential to mend their ways and earn the respect and admiration of not only their parents, but also society. Pinocchio's closing lines of—"How ridiculous I was when I was a puppet. And how happy I am to have become a real boy"—comfort children with the knowledge that at some point in their lives they, too, will mature and reflect upon some of their past actions and misbehavior as nothing more than silly antics that might have produced negative consequences, but were still necessary moments in their maturation cycle.

Pinocchio reassures us that it is natural to feel extremely conflicted over our place in society, especially as we struggle to understand the differences between our own imaginations and the real world that we are constantly trying to navigate and understand. But if we focus our attention on our studies and skills, and pay attention to our parents' warnings and advice, we can learn from our personal experiences and exit those gothic landscapes with a deeper appreciation of ourselves and our surroundings. True, none of us enjoys being pulled by invisible strings, but it is a necessary and crucial part of everyone's childhood. Without our parents' love and support we cannot hope to move through these early stages of psychosocial development, nor can we hope to gain a more firm sense of our own identities. Eventually, having roamed a multitude of gothic landscapes, and having resolved our personal feelings of guilt and shame and doubt, we will feel confident enough to cut those hampering strings and cast them aside. We can then finally perform all by ourselves, moving freely across any stage of our choosing.

3

Games and Challenges:
Industry and Inferiority
in *Coraline*

Worlds to Explore

When I reflect back upon my childhood, it sometimes seems like it belongs to a completely different person. I often find myself laughing at all the thoughts and adventures that kept me occupied for hours or days at a time. I remember imaginary friends eating lunch with me, towering forts fashioned out of sofa cushions, and my asexual relationship with Daphne from the cartoon *Scooby Doo*. I remember hiking through quicksand (mud puddles), rescuing damsels in distress (my sister's Barbie dolls), and tending to my own special pets (dead ants I stuffed into Matchbox cars). Even now, I can still remember the excitement surrounding such special moments, the ease with which I moved between fantasy and reality, not always seeing that crucial line that divides the two.

During our early stages of development, namely our toddler and preschool years, we want nothing more than to eat, sleep, and play. We subsist on whims and wishes, and we possess no concept of words like *responsibility* or *accountability*. But as we learn to crawl and walk, as we learn to grasp random objects, we begin to familiarize ourselves with our environment. As we mature, we slowly abandon those make-believe worlds that once provided so much enjoyment and comfort. We sense that the world is much bigger than our own house, or even our own neighborhood. This dawning comprehension instills within us a desire to explore and discover our surroundings, not just geographically but emotionally, too. Possessing such an intense and natural desire to open up and investigate the world beyond our doorstep also helps to expand our imaginations, which in turn contributes to the long-term development of our personalities and the shaping of our self-identities.

At various times during my childhood I became Rambo, James Bond, and Indiana Jones, skulking through dark cellars and laundry rooms in my never-ending quest to find buried treasure that often revealed itself in the shape of plastic gold coins, cheap Mardi Gras beads, or action figures missing arms and legs. This insatiable longing to explore has followed me well into adulthood where it fosters my appetite for world travel and propels me to take chances, whether in the classroom or in my personal relationships. I appreciate a child's natural curiosity, her eagerness to make some semblance out of this immense, complicated world, and perhaps this is the reason why I relate so much to the character of Coraline Jones in Neil Gaiman's novel *Coraline*.

Although Gaiman never reveals Coraline's exact age, I would like to place her somewhere between eight and ten years old. Like most children who enter their school years, Coraline dreams of a world without parents and authority figures, in which she is loved all the time and allowed to engage in whatever activities she so desires. This natural craving to become independent, however, proves dangerous as it becomes the catalyst for the book's disturbing plot in which Coraline's parents are kidnapped by a second set of parents who live in a gothic world that darkly mirrors her own. In trying to escape from a fake mother who wishes to claim Coraline as her own daughter, Coraline eventually comes to appreciate the true and loving relationship between herself and her real parents.

In many ways, this story of a young girl who discovers another fantastic world is similar to Lewis Carroll's *Alice's Adventures in Wonderland*. In both novels, the main character must be brave and courageous as she encounters strange people and talking animals in her attempt to survive and return home to her family. Both novels contain the home-away-from-home theme and present young girls who must think for themselves and survive without help from loved ones. Throughout the course of their adventures, both Coraline and Alice gain a deeper sense of their own identities by navigating through a series of obstacles that create conflicts in their lives.

At the end of each novel, both characters must defeat these obstacles in order to resolve their individual crises and advance toward future stages of psychosocial development. As Hugh Haughton reveals in his introduction to *Alice's Adventures in Wonderland*, the novel "is not so much an adult's view of childhood as a child's view of adulthood."[1] Like many children,

Alice and Coraline do not always understand why adults are so busy and serious; they do not understand why adults' words and actions seem so confusing. Alice's and Coraline's transition into a fantasy world allows these two young girls the opportunity not only to grasp their own identity, and to better understand their own emotions, but also to feel more confident when interacting with the adult personalities in their lives once they return to the real world. That they survive their ordeals in the fantasy world, having achieved victory over creepy adult figures, instills in both of the girls a newfound self-confidence they can rely upon at home and in their respective communities.

Especially Coraline. The fantasy world in which she finds herself is certainly representative of many children's fears that adulthood is scary and restrictive, as well as unloving. This strange and surreal world is on the other side of a door hidden in the corner of her parents' drawing room. A long, dark, and narrow corridor connects these two worlds, and it is within this new fantasy world that Coraline will explore her own thoughts and feelings as she develops both courage and a sense of her own identity. The gothic atmosphere that permeates this other world is terrifying to child and adult readers alike. In it, there are rats and severed hands, a black cat, the trapped souls of children, and even a fake mother who enjoys munching on black beetles.

These disturbing images are emblematic of Nail Gaiman's work. Karen Coats explains how "certain gothic motifs in his work, including big old houses with secret spaces, doppelgängers, dream-visions, and dark tunnels, operate rather obviously as metaphors for unconscious depths." [2] These gothic motifs are externalizations of the psychological conflicts that often trouble many children as they move away from excessive play and attempt to become more productive in their lives. By achieving a sense of productivity and self-importance, children can establish a more intimate bond with their parents and peers, as well as experience a stronger affinity to their culture and society. In *Coraline*, Gaiman's descriptions, coupled with Dave McKean's illustrations, evoke a nightmarish landscape that mirrors the emotions and difficulties often experienced by school age children who are attempting to navigate through Erikson's fourth stage of psychosocial development.

Industry versus Inferiority

As children move through their school-age years, they begin to move outside their family unit and develop relationships with their teachers and peers. They gain a sense of self-importance and an awareness that their actions and behavior can be productive and influential in their home and community. This productivity, however, is dependent on the child's burgeoning personal skills and her knowledge of society's technology. "Technology," of course, can mean many things. Adults usually consider technology to encompass cars, computers, iPhones, or plasma TVs. Children, however, view technology in different terms. For them, technology is anything artificial they can manipulate to produce a given result. When Coraline uses the broom to knock the keys off the top of the kitchen doorframe she is demonstrating a mastery of technology, as well as when she uses the stone with a hole in it to find the three marbles that house the children's souls.

These traits involving technology correspond with Erikson's theories on the emotional changes that children undergo during the fourth stage of psychosocial development, which he labels "Industry versus Inferiority." This stage affects children between the ages of six and twelve; the strength of this stage is competence, the antipathy is inertia. Erikson explains that "while all children need their hours and days of make-believe in games, they all, sooner or later, become dissatisfied and disgruntled without a sense of being able to make things and make them well and even perfectly: it is this that I have called the *sense of industry*."[3] Put simply, the child starts to abandon playful tendencies and begins to re-identify herself with parents, seeing them not just as caregivers and supporters of love, but as workers who contribute to society. The child watches and imitates her parents, emulating their actions in an effort to reproduce within herself the same feelings of accomplishment that she now sees in them.

Perhaps this is why children become so excited when their parents arrive at school, stand at the front of the classroom, and speak for fifteen minutes about their jobs. Children are mesmerized by these lengthy and descriptive presentations. They often imagine themselves in such esteemed positions, earning large amounts of money and exuding an air of importance that every child envies and hopes one day to achieve. They understand that having a job equates to having money, and they understand that having money equates to having the power to buy items such as food and clothes and toys. These glimpses of adulthood and responsibility are tantalizing to children because they yearn to break free from the adults who wield control over them on a daily basis.

During these career presentations, children also experience a surge of pride in knowing that their parents are fulfilling an important role in society with the help of different technologies. That the child slowly grasps the many ideas and concepts behind the use of these different technologies is a testament to the child's growing impression of how every individual is vital to society and makes certain contributions depending on her occupation. And as the child considers these ideas, her radius of significant relations expands to realize concepts like "workplace" and "community" in addition to familiar ones such as "home" and "school."

These dawning moments in which a child comprehends the larger, intricate world outside of her home and neighborhood are vital contributors to her maturity and development. They comprise the initial steps she must take in order to produce a sense of accomplishment within herself. This fourth stage, which reflects a child's eagerness to learn about technology and problem solving, also illustrates her desire to establish a sense of discipline and use her budding intelligence to perform actions that signify she no longer relies on her imagination to solve problems.

During this fourth stage, children want adults to notice and praise their intellect; they want adults to acknowledge that they are moving toward independence, albeit slowly, and are beginning to understand more closely the link between technology and production that resonates so powerfully in the real world. For parents, stage four is crucial because it supplies children with the confidence and curiosity they will need in later years to solve those crises associated with adolescence.

Erikson tells us that during this stage the child "learns to win recognition by producing things. He develops perseverance and adjusts himself to the inorganic laws of the tool world and can become an eager and absorbed unit of a productive situation."[4] In essence, the child actualizes realistic roles, which she might have role-played previously, and she hopes that by assuming these new roles and grasping the concepts of certain technologies, she will eventually earn the same recognition that adults command. It makes sense, then, that the main strength emerging from this stage is competence, a growing sense of ability that fuels self-assurance within the child and allows her to begin those necessary steps toward maturity and sexual awakening.

We must remember, however, that, without the proper care and guidance from parents and peers, some children might not be able to resolve successfully all the crises that arise within this fourth stage of psychosocial development. Erikson admits that one of the dangers inherent in this stage is a tendency for the child to develop a sense of inferiority. Basically, the danger at this stage "lies in a sense of inadequacy and inferiority. If he despairs of his tools and skills or of his status among his tool partners, his ego boundaries suffer, and he abandons hope for the ability to identify early with others who apply themselves to the same general section of the tool world."[5] Confidence, then, is crucial during this stage in a child's development. The child needs to feel secure in her ability to contribute to society. She must feel that she is progressing toward a moment when she will be regarded as equal to her parents and she will master technology and become a mature adult.

One of the dangers inherent in this fourth stage is a tendency for the child to revert back to primal urges and fantasies. If the child believes she has been unsuccessful in her attempts to be productive and master technology, then she is liable to view herself as a failure. Erikson believes that a feeling of inferiority "can drive the child to excessive competition or induce it to regress—which can only mean a renewal of infantile-genital and oedipal conflict, and thus a preoccupation in fantasy with conflictual personages rather than an actual encounter with the helpful ones right at hand."[6] Consequently, the child might become afraid to take chances and so retreats into the safety of her own imagination. Instead of relying on parents and family for support, the child might feel ashamed at her lack of productivity and create imaginary relationships with people who shower her with the attention and praise she feels she cannot earn in the real world.

Conversely, the child might become angry at having not achieved the same success as other children. This frustration might result in an extreme rivalry with anyone else the child views as competing with her for success. A growing sense of competition will then isolate the child even further from family and peers by causing her to distrust or disregard those adult influences that are so beneficial to her growth and development. In her quest to prove herself capable of success, the child might also tackle larger problems and crises that she's unprepared to approach, whether emotionally or physically.

These futile attempts at self-justification will only cause more moments of failure, thus intensifying the anger and resentment that continue to cripple the child's self-esteem. In an effort to extinguish this shame and frustration, the child might now direct her negative emotions toward those parents and friends whom she blames for her feelings of inability and powerlessness. A child who feels inadequate and useless, unable to develop those necessary skills and ideas with which we all learn to master technology, will often enter adolescence unprepared to deal with sexual issues and identity crises. Creating a sense of industry, then, is integral to the formation of a child's personality.

Because the child needs to establish a strong sense of industry, the radius of significant relations is especially important during this fourth stage of psychosocial development. During this stage, the child's radius extends beyond the family unit to encompass school friends and neighborhood friends. The child begins to understand the importance of community and starts to emulate those around her. She looks to these people for guidance and reassurance, especially teachers and school friends with whom she will likely spend most of her days.

Although Coraline does not go to school during the course of the novel (she is on summer vacation), we can assume that the other neighbors living in the large house, such as Miss Spink and Miss Forcible, represent not only neighbors, but also school age friends that contribute to her sense of industry. This idea is especially true when one considers that many of the adult characters in the novel act like children by engaging in weird activities and speaking words that Coraline interprets as confusing and crazy. Likewise, there are animal characters in *Coraline*, such as the black cat and the circus mice, and these animal characters certainly seem to represent childhood friends that assist Coraline in her physical and emotional journey to free her parents. By surrounding herself with this radius of significant relations, Coraline is able to gain the confidence she needs to triumph over the Other Mother and develop further her own identity.

Charcoal Scribbles and Misty Whiteness

In *Coraline*, Neil Gaiman uses the gothic landscape to symbolize the conflicts and emotions that Coraline undergoes as she moves away from a reliance on her imagination and toward a sense of industry and productivity that will aid her in adolescence. From the very first page Gaiman evokes a creepy atmosphere as he describes the house in which Coraline lives with her family. It is so big that it's divided up into several apartments. There are passageways and attics and cellars, and the grounds are expansive as well, allowing Coraline the opportunity to explore. Reading about such places, which are often associated with Gothicism, we anticipate Coraline encountering danger at some point in the story, especially given the old well she is warned to stay away from, and the elusive black cat that slinks through the tall grass.

Looking down into a well is scary because there is complete darkness. One cannot see the bottom, and so the imagination begins to produce feelings of claustrophobia at the thought of being trapped way, way down underground with whatever creatures might be lurking. Black cats, historically, have been associated with witches and bad luck. By bringing in the black cat as a character, Gaiman instills into the story a sense of anxiety, as well as a forewarning that Coraline might soon find herself in trouble. By introducing all of these elements into the first chapter, Gaiman begins to build a gothic mood that creates apprehension and a growing sense of unease.

Being a child, Coraline ignores the adults and investigates the well along with the rest of her new surroundings. That she wants to explore this landscape symbolizes her desire to move outside of her boring home environment and to create her own personal experiences. Donna Heiland reminds us, "Gothic fiction is about transgressions of all sorts: across national boundaries, social boundaries, sexual boundaries, the boundaries of one's own identity."[7] Coraline's identity is rooted to her family and her possessions, but she is bored with all her toys and her parents who, occupied with their adult responsibilities, are too busy to play with her. Clearly, Coraline's family is not supplying her with the love and attention she needs to mature. Likewise, her toys have lost their appeal. These feelings of loneliness and inadequacy are what compel her to begin exploring new spaces.

Coraline needs to move beyond childhood and make-believe, crossing her imaginary boundary into a landscape that can offer her a sense of productivity and self-importance. We often see this pattern in children progressing through stage four. As they begin to understand the importance and value of technology, as well as their growing desire to perform positive actions of consequence, they lose their childhood sense of wonder and crave experiences outside of the home that can stimulate them intellectually. In order for Coraline to progress through stage four and resolve any necessary crises, she must mature emotionally and gain self-confidence. Gaiman illustrates this important process by having Coraline first move beyond her home environment, which is comfortable and secure, and into a new and unfamiliar landscape, which subsequently leads Coraline to the door in the drawing room and then into another world where her Other Mother attempts to hold her captive.

Essentially, her physical journey through that strange, misty world is an externalization of the mental process that she, as well as all children, must eventually undergo as they move away from childhood and begin to integrate themselves more regularly into an adult culture and society. This means that the external environments symbolize Coraline's internal feelings. Botting further illustrates this idea when he explains that "the loss of human identity and the alienation of self ... are presented in the threatening shapes of increasingly dehumanized environments, machinic doubles, and violent, psychotic fragmentation."[8] Coraline's conflicts over her budding identity manifest themselves in the Other Mother who tries to trap Coraline in an adult-controlled world. The oppressive atmosphere and limited boundaries of the Other Mother's house also symbolize the dependence children feel toward adults, as well as the fear children often possess when faced with moving past childhood boundaries and stretching themselves beyond the limits of their own imaginations.

When Coraline finally enters the old, dusty passageway that separates the two worlds, it feels very much like a transitory location, and the reader senses that her exploration has now taken a serious turn. This new adventure will not be safe or fun, and there will be no one to protect her or offer her guidance. She is alone and must depend only on herself to survive. As with all stages of psychosocial development, making this necessary journey is a part of growing up. By experiencing multiple crises, grappling with fears, and resolving our conflicts, we are able to gain self-confidence and learn unique abilities in ways that foster our independence and develop our personalities.

Throughout the novel, the gothic landscape becomes more dangerous as Coraline becomes more frightened. But it also becomes less defined and pronounced as she begins to conquer the rats and the Other Mother. As Coraline collects the three marbles housing the children's souls, the gothic landscape becomes more childlike and imaginary, assuming the characteristics of a painting or a sketch. Gaiman tells us that "the house had flattened out even more. It no longer looked like a photograph—more like a drawing, a crude, charcoal scribble of a house drawn on gray paper."[9] The altering landscape signifies a growing maturation within Coraline. As she gains confidence and becomes industrious (such as using the stone with a hole in it to find the marbles), she no longer needs to rely on childlike play and make-believe. The environment, which once seemed ominous and threatening, now transforms into an innocent figment of Coraline's imagination, one that she has tamed and controlled with her emerging productivity.

Gaiman emphasizes this newfound confidence that has rejuvenated Coraline when he writes, "Normally, on the night before the first day of term, Coraline was apprehensive and nervous. But, she realized, there was nothing left about school that could scare her anymore."[10] Because she has undertaken a dangerous journey alone, during which she rescues her parents and asserts her independence, she now understands the intense feelings of pride and self-respect that often accompany productivity and industriousness. She understands that imagination alone will no longer aid her in promoting growth and development; she must become more active in forming her own identity and making her own choices. For children progressing through stage four, Coraline's mastery of the gothic landscape illustrates that they, too, can brave their way through the darkness if they believe in themselves, remain composed, and do not seek constant protection within the safety and comfort of their own minds—or within their own mental projections of their parents.

The parallel world that Coraline visits is also symbolic of her own consciousness. The brick wall that separates the two worlds is a barrier between the fantasy world and the adult world, namely the link between the child's imagination and reality. Gaiman's use of a brick wall is especially powerful as it stresses that moving from childhood into adulthood is not easy. On the contrary, it requires a great deal of thought and effort to break through all the emotional and imaginary walls that children have built around themselves, and that they must now tear down as they slowly gain a deeper and more defined understanding of reality. The people and objects Coraline encounters are representative of those very same fears and anxieties that nest within her own mind, namely her own inferiority and the doubts she possesses about finding a sense of achievement in an adult world.

The Other Mother signifies an alternative version of Coraline's own mother. True, the Other Mother allows Coraline to do anything she wants, as well as to receive anything she wants, but she also smothers Coraline with love and attention as though the young girl is nothing more than a pet or a piece of property. For children who often wish their parents would ignore their misbehavior and lavish them with constant praise and attention, *Coraline* forces them to consider the idea that changing one's parents into mere puppets can also have its disadvantages. In witnessing the overload of love and attention she receives from her Other Mother and her Other Father, Coraline understands that she is now viewed as an object instead of a person, and that in order to be loved unconditionally she must sacrifice a part of her identity and act in accordance with the Other Mother's wishes. Likewise, she comes to appreciate the fact that even though her real parents have strange quirks and idiosyncrasies that bother her, she must still accept those traits as being an important part of their own identities.

At first, Coraline delights in this new gothic world that offers an exciting contrast to the drab and boring life she lives with her parents, as well as to all the neighbors that constantly forget her name. In her other bedroom there are "books with pictures that writhed and crawled and shimmered; little dinosaur skulls that chattered their teeth as she passed."[11] This fantasy world excites Coraline because, while it's new enough to generate wonder and excitement, it's also an extension of her own imagination and thus feels familiar and comfortable. But when the Other Mother tells her she can play with rats, Coraline feels uncertain about remaining in this fantasy world. She begins to understand the old adage that if something is too good to be true, then it probably is.

Because children are fascinated, to a certain extent, with the dark side of human nature, Coraline's adventures in this other world seem interesting and fascinating so long as they aren't threatening or dangerous. Part of this attraction stems from Schadenfreude, the sense of comfort and pleasure we feel at the expense of someone else's pain and emotional duress. Children know that if they feel afraid they can shut the book and return to the story at a later time. They are the ones in control, unlike Coraline who is at the mercy of her Other Mother and Other Father. Child readers do not envy Coraline her journey through the gothic world, especially once she becomes trapped, but they do enjoy accompanying her on it because they are able to learn from her mistakes and also to relate her predicaments to those same dilemmas they often experience in their own lives.

The claustrophobic environment of this gothic world mirrors Coraline's growing sense of entrapment at the way her friends and family tend to ignore her and treat her like a child. Sandra Gilbert and Susan Gubar explain that "heroines who characteristically inhabit mysteriously stifling intricate or uncomfortably stifling houses are often seen as captured, fettered, trapped, even buried alive."[12] Although Gilbert and Gubar place their ideas within a feminist context, I don't think that Coraline's gender is relevant here. Both girls and boys experience moments in which they feel dominated by the adults who control their lives. Like Coraline, most children believe that adults limit their freedom and trap them in roles from which they desperately want to escape. The gothic house in which the Other Mother and Other Father live echoes the stifling environment that children often experience when they live in a household that is commanded by adults and directed by adult rules. As grown-ups, we must remember that a child's desire for autonomy and self-justification is not an attack on the parents' decisions regarding how to raise and nurture her, but a natural yearning to assimilate her parents' role in society, thus earning respect from the community and establishing a sense of industry that will contribute to identity formation during adolescence and early adulthood.

Another extension of the gothic landscape that proves beneficial to Coraline's emotional development is the mirror at the end of the hall inside the Other Mother's house. When Coraline refuses to accept the Other Mother as her real mother, the Other Mother locks Coraline behind the mirror and tells her she cannot come out until she has learned how to behave according to The Other Mother's instructions. The Other Mother hopes that by confining Coraline to this small, cramped space she will scare the poor girl into submitting to her demands. This process mimics a familiar parenting technique in which parents sometimes use fear and darkness to terrify their children into obeying their instructions and behaving properly. But identity formation cannot occur suddenly under moments of extreme stress. Nor can it develop naturally and positively if a child lacks the necessary time to process her own feelings and then reflect on the consequences of her actions. Children that constantly live in an atmosphere of fear and submission cannot grow and mature because they are unable to thrive in a healthy environment. Trapped behind the mirror, Coraline does have the freedom to explore her own conflicted emotions, and Gaiman illustrates this idea by having Coraline put out her hands in the darkness that imprisons her. She does not know where to go or what to do, and rather than being an active learner she is now reduced to being a passive observer.

At some point in their lives all children progressing through stage four will spend a fair amount of time behind the mirror, but hopefully it will happen on their own accord. The crucial moments that children spend ensconced in this gothic gloom are often their first attempts at productivity, sparking within them a sense of industry that will allow them to move beyond the mirror and begin making decisions that will help them to survive in an adult world rather than an imaginary one. For example, it is while locked within this dark space behind the mirror that Coraline finally comprehends the danger that surrounds her, as well as the consequences she will suffer if she remains with the Other Mother. The entire sequence feels like a nightmare, and in dreams a mirror often symbolizes the power of the unconscious. If we interpret the Other Mother's world as a nightmare world, then it becomes clear that the mirror at the end of the hall functions as a reflection of Coraline's internal conflicts and identity crises, namely her fear of not gaining a sense of competency. These intense feelings of helplessness and incompetence are emblematic of all children during the fourth stage of psychosocial development, no matter how much they might try to mask them with false confidence and bravado.

Coraline's imprisonment behind the mirror symbolizes an externalized repression. This means that the cramped physical space behind the mirror, weighed down with darkness and the unknown, represents all the confusion and anger that she experiences at being constantly pinned down by adult expectations. Like most children trying to assimilate themselves into society, Coraline faces daily pressures to assume an identity that grownups expect of her. Back in the real world, living with her real mother and father, Coraline feels repressed as she struggles to establish an identity separate from that of her parents. The souls of the other children that Coraline encounters behind the mirror illustrate what she will become if she does not gain the courage and confidence to break away from her Other Mother and establish her own identity. One of the child voices tells Coraline that the Other Mother "stole our hearts, and she stole our souls, and she took our lives away, and she left us here, and she forgot about us in the dark." [13] What these lost souls have experienced is precisely what every child fears most: abandonment and isolation. Coraline's learning experience during her encounter with these lost souls is comparable to a child reader's learning experience during his or her interactions with Coraline as she progresses through Gaiman's gothic story.

In *Coraline* the gothic landscape reminds our heroine that to remain trapped in the dark is to never mature and become independent. By immersing herself in the gothic, Coraline eventually comes to realize, as do all children, that it is only by losing herself in darkness and gloom that she is able to explore her own feelings so she can develop into a fully functioning individual. Given these two seemingly contradictory ideas, we might wonder if there is a thin line that separates a child's need to explore gothic worlds from the dangers of being trapped there and regressing to a more infantile state. A child should probe the darkness, and interact with her own identity crises, until she understands her emotions and feels confident that she's established some command over them. Only then is the child ready to embark upon a new challenge and progress to the next stage of psychosocial development. And only then can those gothic elements be left behind until they are needed during future stages of growth and maturity. Even though we leave behind certain gothic elements at the end of each stage in order to grow up, we still find ourselves traveling into the darkness during every stage of our development, even as experienced and responsible adults. We must remember that children and adults possess the same fears, such as abandonment, inferiority, or role confusion, but those fears take on different forms depending on one's age and maturity.

To remain in the Other Mother's gothic world means that Coraline will be objectified and lose her identity, as illustrated by the big black buttons that the Other Mother wants to sew onto the girl's eyes. If everyone in the fantasy world has black button eyes, then everyone looks the same and behaves the same, which will stunt Coraline's identity formation and personality development. And if eyes are said to be the windows of the soul, functioning in many ways like a mirror, then we understand how covering them with black pieces of plastic can erase one's identity. Functioning as eyes, the black buttons are emotionless. The act of stitching them onto someone's eyes suggests that that person is nothing more than a puppet that can be molded to fit a certain category or role. This use of adult control is scary to child readers because a child often sees herself as a malleable object that is constantly told how to think and how to act. But the more a child is ordered around and forced to adhere to certain expectations, the more the child "seeks to test and perhaps throw off the stifling ego-ideals that he or she has internalized as a child under the rule of parents, and find ones that will reflect his or her individual desires and sense of self."[14] As Coraline grows tired of being threatened and manipulated by the Other Mother, she is able to look beyond the mirror and move past those feelings of helplessness and inadequacy that have plagued her in the past. Emboldened by a strong determination to save her family, she spends the rest of the novel searching for the three marbles so she can emerge victorious and establish a sense of competence.

The Other Mother

In *Coraline*, the Other Mother is also a doppelgänger. The doppelgänger is the double of a living person, and it typically functions as a ghostly omen or a portent of danger. In some countries, the doppelgänger casts no reflection in a mirror, so it's not surprising that Coraline doesn't see the Other Mother's reflection when she stares into the mirror at the end of the hallway. This idea of an evil double often appears in children's literature because children tend to separate their parents into good and evil personalities. The good personality assumes the shape of a kind, benevolent parent that loves and nurtures the child. This parent hugs and kisses the child, buys toys, and sits with the child to watch cartoons. The bad personality assumes the shape of an evil stepmother or father that berates the child and prevents her from maturing and achieving autonomy. This parent reprimands the child for not cleaning her room, or for fighting with her brothers and sisters.

Because children don't want to view their parents as having bad qualities, it's often easier for them to consider their parents as two entirely different people. This is one of the reasons why there are so many stepmothers in fairy tales. The process of separating the parent into two distinct characters helps children process their emotions because they can then focus all of their hurt and anger on those individual aspects of their parents' personalities that they dislike. For children learning how to express their feelings, and how to comprehend abstract terms like jealousy and anger, it's much easier to view the world in black and white rather than in shades of gray.

At the same time, children feel comfortable and secure in knowing there are caring and lovable aspects of their parents' personalities. They find solace in the kind and nurturing parent who adores them and makes them feel special, not the evil double who shames them, enforces rules and bedtimes, and punishes them for their bad choices and misbehavior. As children grow and mature, however, they begin to understand the complexities that exist within the human mind. They realize that people possess both good and bad attributes, and that these traits define who we are and how we function in society.

These are important lessons that Coraline must learn the hard way. Since she is an only child, and since there are no other children for her to play with, the time she spends with her parents is doubly important. And since her real parents are too busy typing and doing housework to pay her much attention, Coraline must learn these lessons by interacting with her Other Mother and Other Father. Every character that Coraline meets in the fantasy world is another opportunity for her to gain self-confidence and to realize her identity as separate from that of her real parents.

The subject of Coraline's identity is even broached by the black cat, which seems to be an extension of her curiosity. He says to her, "Now, *you* people have names. That's because you don't know who you are."[15] Though she has seen the cat many times during her explorations of the grounds, it only speaks to her once she enters the fantasy world and meets her Other Mother. The cat is composed and intelligent, offering sound advice, and in this way it functions as an aspect of Coraline's conscience, much like the ghost of the cricket in *Pinocchio*.

We can assume that Coraline's confusion about her identity is what prompts the gothic world to appear suddenly on the other side of the doorway. Her new friendship with the cat, as well as her confrontations with the Other Mother, represents those subconscious desires to meet and conquer her own fears and inadequacies. These uncertainties have arisen from Coraline's fear of being an inferior and incompetent young adult who is too dependent on her parents. Again, we see a young person's search for identity and the growing need to no longer rely on childish whims or the power of the imagination. It is only through her exploration of the Other Mother's gothic world that Coraline can learn to have faith in herself and to trust her own emotions.

As children progress through Erikson's later stages of psychosocial development they no longer need a doppelgänger to absorb all of their negative feelings and confusion. Terry Castle explains that "what makes the doppelgänger now seem uncanny is precisely the fact that we have grown out of that 'very early mental stage' when the double functioned as a figure of existential reassurance.... Thanks to the estranging force of repression, says Freud ... the double 'has become a thing of terror.'"[16] Coraline needs to resolve her crises during this fourth stage if she hopes to mature to the point where she no longer requires the doppelgänger to explain her parents' actions and behaviors. In fact, the repression she experiences as a young child (which manifests itself in the gothic landscape) becomes a hindrance, instead of a comfort, because she has matured enough to recognize it as such. While she once enjoyed being dependent on her parents and having them make decisions for her, she now wishes to separate herself from them and assert her independence. To accomplish this task, Coraline must master her emotions and gain a sense of industry that will aid her in future identity formation as she strives to become even more autonomous.

We witness Coraline's desire to become autonomous when she asks her mother if she can choose her own school clothes. As a young girl progressing through stage four, Coraline is aware of cliques and social groups; she understands the link between fashion and popularity, and she is embarrassed by what she perceives to be her mother's clinginess and interference. Coraline's desire to select her own clothes implies a longing to be unique and to make her own decisions. When Coraline's parents disappear after her first trip to the Other Mother's world, she revels in being alone. She eats canned spaghetti for breakfast, and snacks on apples and blocks of chocolate. She walks down to the grocery store all by herself and buys food with her own money. During these scenes, Coraline is trying on an adult identity, slipping into various roles as she depends on herself for those basic needs that children rarely consider because their parents are taking care of them on a daily basis.

These moments of independence fuel an innate desire for productivity and self-fulfillment that all children possess, and they attempt to foster these desires through their interactions with gothic elements. But if Coraline hopes to continue being an active learner, and not to suffer from the inertia that can affect children who are unable to resolve their crises during stage four, then she must battle the Other Mother and defeat the oppressive authority that this evil parent represents. Only by doing so can Coraline finally move past those early stages of childhood in which the doppelgänger provided her with comfort and reassurance by offering her a temporary outlet for her anger and fear.

The Other Mother is truly a gothic character. Gaiman describes her as having skin "white as paper" and long fingers that "never stopped moving, and her dark red fingernails were curved and sharp."[17] The Other Mother also sports large, black buttons for eyes and is known to chomp on beetles whenever she is hungry. That this doppelgänger is a natural part of every child's development becomes clear when Coraline says, "I didn't know I had another mother," to which the Other Mother replies, "Of course you do. Everyone does."[18] The meaning here is that we all experience negative thoughts during our childhood, most often caused by confusion, frustration, and a sense of inadequacy. The Other Mother symbolizes those dark thoughts that form when children try to make sense of the world; she is a physical target at which children can aim their aggressions. By having an Other Mother, children can release their anger in healthy ways that allow them to nurture and maintain positive relationships with their real parents.

Coraline herself is aware that she's going through an identity crisis. The morning after her first encounter with the Other Mother, Gaiman writes that she "was not entirely sure *who* she was."[19] This confusion is natural because it reveals an awakening in the young girl. Coraline is now able to comprehend life without her parents and, in doing so, she can begin to question her role and obligations in navigating such an independent life. Coraline's meeting with the Other Mother has sparked a moment of self-reflection and forced her to consider her responsibility not only within her household, but also within the community. And it is this process of self-reflection that will force Coraline to become industrious, in both a physical and an emotional sense, throughout the rest of the novel.

The problem that most of us experience, however, as does Coraline, is that it is much easier to surrender to the Other Mother's seeming displays of love and compassion than to explore our own feelings and emotions. In the fantasy world, there is a crazy old man upstairs who tells Coraline, "We will listen to you and play with you and laugh with you. Your other mother will build whole worlds for you to explore, and tear them down every night when you are done. Every day will be better and brighter than the one that went before."[20] The crazy old man appeals to a desire for control that most children crave because they witness their own parents wielding it morning, noon, and night. What *Coraline* teaches us is that although such control is a coveted part of human existence, it must also be earned through intelligent decisions and positive actions. Children cannot earn this control and respect without venturing into gothic landscapes. Wandering through such dark and gloomy spaces, and exiting them with a sense of pride and victory, reassures children that while they will certainly experience difficult times, they possess the abilities to overcome any conflicts and crises, no matter how dangerous or overwhelming they might seem.

In *Coraline* the gothic landscape appears enticing and non-threatening, but it masks the absence of genuine affection. Like most children, Coraline initially bases her perception of the other world on a sensory level, amazed at the delicious food and strange new toys, ecstatic at the thought of living with parents who will allow her to do whatever she wants, whenever she wants. But as Coraline becomes accustomed to this other world she begins to contemplate the core emotions that comprise such a world, and she realizes that the Other Mother's genuine affection is as false and empty as Coraline's own dream of attaining perfect parents who award her unlimited freedoms.

When Coraline asks the black cat why the Other Mother wants to keep her forever, the cat replies, "She wants something to love, I think.... Something that isn't her."[21] The term "something" alludes to the Other Mother's treatment of Coraline as an object, but the cat's answer also suggests that the Other Mother has a desire that needs to be fulfilled, much like Coraline's desire to rescue her real parents and return to her normal world. This conversation between Coraline and the cat prompts Coraline to challenge the Other Mother to a game, the stakes being her parents' lives versus Coraline's permanent place in the Other Mother's world. Coraline understands that the Other Mother is using love as an excuse to kidnap her parents and hold her captive. If Coraline hopes to win the challenge, she will need to be proactive and act like an adult, especially since indulging in childish fantasies is what caused her parents to disappear in the first place. Here, Gaiman implies that devotion and family bonds tend to wither in the presence of misplaced productivity, and this is a lesson that Coraline, as well as all children, need to learn before they reach adolescence.

In their minds, children create the perfect picture of how their parents and family should treat them, so it comes as no surprise that Coraline is entranced by the Other Mother's tender words when she says, "We're ready to love you and play with you and feed you and make your life interesting."[22] As adult readers, we understand that the gothic landscape represents an underlying level of false emotions that are based more on the Other Mother's obsession with parental control rather than on her ability to supply Coraline with respect and guidance.

Subconsciously, Coraline knows this, too. She is aware that her expectations to have perfect parents and unlimited freedoms are a dream, but it is only by exploring the gothic landscape that she can accept those imperfections and appreciate them. These thought processes and physical movements mirror key components of Gothicism, which Linda Bayer-Berenbaum defines as "an intensification of consciousness, an expansion of reality, and a confrontation with evil."[23] Coraline's adventures in the Other Mother's world contain all three of these characteristics, and they give tangible shape to a growth process that most children undertake within the confines of their own minds. As the novel progresses, we see how the uncomfortable atmosphere in the Other Mother's world prompts Coraline to embark on a journey of self-discovery in which she eventually gains a deeper sense of her own identity.

Within this gothic world, parts of Coraline's own personality transform into physical characteristics. If the black cat, which speaks to Coraline and offers her advice, seems to be the bodily manifestation of her childish curiosity, then it makes sense that the rats represent the bodily manifestation of the Other Mother's cunningness and treachery. Both animals are also associated with gothic literature, black cats being evil omens and witches' familiars, and rats often symbolizing filth, decay, and sneakiness. Gaiman emphasizes this connection between the characters and their animals by telling us that the Other Mother despises the black cat, while Coraline is fond of the animal and treats it like a trusted friend.

It makes sense that the Other Mother, who is associated with lies and deceit, would fear the possibility of Coraline thinking on her own. The more a child is able to think for herself, the less control a parent has in influencing the child's decisions. If Coraline assumes a personal identity, the Other Mother cannot have power over her. While Coraline and the Other Mother wage an emotional battle based on power and control, the cat and the rat engage in a physical battle. Naturally, when the cat kills the rat at the end of the novel, thus assuring that Coraline possesses all three of the coveted marbles, we comprehend that on a deeper level this action symbolizes Coraline's triumph over the Other Mother. Because we view the rat as a physical extension of the Other Mother's personality, we know that its death signifies a victory for Coraline. She will find her parents and return to her own world.

Coraline escapes from the Other Mother by throwing the cat into her face whereupon it claws and scratches her. This scene illustrates through physical action the same process that is occurring emotionally within Coraline, namely curiosity and productivity defeating those controlling forces from which children must escape to mature. In illustrating this idea, Gaiman also validates a child's natural desire to move away from a secure family unit as she seeks out her own identity and tries to bring semblance to all the conflicts and emotions that dot her mental landscape.

In *Coraline*, Gaiman teaches us the merits of being active rather than passive, productive rather than destructive. And he reminds us that being evil and dishonest will often bring about its own retribution in the form of intense isolation, inertia, and the further deepening of an already visible identity crisis. But in order to learn these important lessons, we must first venture beyond the comfort and safety of our own domestic spheres, and in doing so we must hike across the gothic landscape to confront our fears and doubts.

Coraline's struggles, and her subsequent triumph over the gothic landscape, assure us that if we can remain brave and motivated in our quest to mature, then we will persevere and become assets not only to our families and friends, but also to society. The struggles Coraline must endure as she searches for the three marbles, such as battling with the Other Father or escaping from the creatures in the sac, represent the efforts that all children must tackle if they hope to defeat the doubts and anxiety that prevent them from taking chances in life and developing emotionally and physically.

Games and Challenges

The plot structure of *Coraline* revolves not only around the gothic landscape and its influences on the story's characters, but also around the idea of games and challenges. In fact, there exists an interesting similarity between Gothicism and game-playing. Gothic literature is often about power, specifically the struggles between those who have it and those who do not. Likewise, playing a game also involves power, namely the desire to win and achieve victory over another person or a group of people. These two ideas resonate throughout *Coraline* because children often see maturity and identity formation as a means to achieving the same command that adults possess. They tend to equate age with wisdom, believing that time will blossom into authority, which will then lead to power. The only time that most children are able to reign over adults, however, is when they play a game. Children enjoy the process of game-playing because it involves a series of steps that are fun and exciting, yet it also allows children to show their skill and intelligence. It is while playing a game that a child is in control of her own thoughts and actions, and during that time she will not be reprimanded if there is a negative outcome, which is often harmless in the context of game-playing. In this sense, games help give children power over adults while still socializing them into adult habits of industry such as decision-making and assuming personal responsibility. We all know that children love games and competition, and so most readers can identify easily with Coraline's journey as she attempts to outwit the Other Mother and win not only her parents, but also a return to her own normal life.

When the black cat first suggests that Coraline challenge the Other Mother to a game, it tells her, "There's no guarantee she'll play fair, but her kind of thing loves games and challenges."[24] In stating "her kind of thing," the cat seems to reference not only the Other Mother, but also children who share a love of problems and puzzles and board games. This is especially true during Erikson's fourth stage of psychosocial development, when the child is trying to prove her understanding of technology and show that she can compete in an adult world. Children want to play games because they enjoy feeling superior when they win. Being victorious gives them power and control, which they associate with being an adult. So when the black cat says, "Her kind of thing loves games and challenges," it might as well be referencing Coraline, too.

Games prove beneficial to children because they force children to be active while also improving their mental power and reasoning. Elena Gianini Belotti believes that "the more a child moves the more chance he will have to have sensory experiences of his surroundings and the more his brain cells and his intelligence will develop. To reduce his opportunities for movement means reducing his curiosity, his experiences, and hence his intelligence."[25] A child whose parents limit the time she spends playing games might fear that her parents are attempting to stifle her identity formation because they do not want her to become an adult. The child might also consider that her parents are not accepting of the person she is or the person she wishes to become. A child who does not feel validated and supported by her parents is liable to retreat inside her imagination, become a passive observer, and isolate herself even further from those wishing to aid in her development. Coraline does not suffer these setbacks because she is able to be productive throughout the entire novel, able to satiate her curiosity and investigate her surroundings.

On one of these exploratory trips Coraline encounters a theater where the Other Misses Spink and Forcible perform nonstop antics onstage, every day and night. In many ways, the idea of a performance echoes the various roles that children assume as they adopt different personalities in an attempt to discover their own identities. In their quest for the self, they don many costumes, test many different voices, and perform a wide range of behaviors. The reactions that these performances elicit from adults, much like the applause from an audience, often influence a child's perception of herself and her environment. Also, watching a theatrical show is a classic form of entertainment, much like a game. Indeed, Coraline enjoys participating as a volunteer in this theater performance. She stands on the stage and allows Miss Forcible to throw a knife at a balloon that sits atop her head. In addition to enhancing the creepy atmosphere in this gothic landscape, and perpetuating the entire fantasy world as nothing more than a game, this scene illustrates further the great danger that exists within those spaces controlled by the Other Mother.

There is a constant threat of death that simmers beneath all the excitement and wonder in the novel. Coraline, like all children, thrives on the originality of this gothic landscape, and even convinces herself that it is safe: "*In danger?* thought Coraline to herself. It sounded exciting. It didn't sound like a bad thing. Not really."[26] As is typical of most children, Coraline sees only what she wants to see. She believes she can handle the danger, that she is unbeatable and unable to be hurt. Most children will experience this intense feeling of invincibility, and it is only by exploring gothic landscapes, which symbolize their own conflicted feelings, that they are able to understand their own limits. Realizing their capabilities will then allow children to discover unique opportunities to hone their intellect and thus put into action those cravings for productivity that were previously pushed down by their own imaginations. It seems, then, that Gaiman does not draw a line between productive games and dangerous ones, and by doing so he suggests that growing up consists of many perilous moments that are threatening and risky, but are necessary nonetheless for our own maturity and personal development.

When Coraline asks one of the dogs in the audience how long the show lasts, the dog tells her that it doesn't ever end. This answer reflects the reality that identity conflict never really ends. We will always question who we are. We will always struggle throughout certain periods of our lives. And we will always need to rediscover ourselves under the cover of darkness, armed with past experiences and an arsenal of recognized emotions. It's important to remember that even the most passive person needs to hike across these gothic landscapes every once in a while. Yet it's equally important to remember that we do not always undertake this journey alone. Guiding and encouraging us is a radius of significant relations. And even though Coraline seems to be alone in the Other Mother's world, she still clings to that radius, and it still aids her in winning the game. The stone with a hole in it is a constant reminder of Misses Forcible and Spink, and Coraline's concern over winning the game forces her to remember her own parents whose lives now depend on her actions. Likewise, the black cat proves to be an invaluable part of Coraline's support group, and although the cat is symbolic of Coraline's childish curiosity and daringness, it is also the only living thing besides herself that travels between the two worlds, thus providing her with a sense of comfort and familiarity.

The thought of seeing her parents again plays an important role in helping to maintain Coraline's confidence as she roams the gothic landscape in search of the three marbles that will ensure their escape from the Other Mother. But parents are typically associated with the radius of significant relations connected to the second and third stages of psychosocial development. As Erikson explains, the radius of significant relations during the fourth stage revolves around neighborhood and school friends. In this sense, both Miss Forcible and Miss Spink prove crucial in helping Coraline defeat the Other Mother. The tea leaves that they read predict danger for the young girl. Even the mice belonging to the crazy old man upstairs have a message for her when they warn her not to go through the door. Coraline's neighbors try to warn her of impending danger, but she doesn't listen to them. As a child, it's natural that she wants to ignore adult advice and make her own decisions, even those that prove to be negative and cause her trouble. And while some might assume that the radius of significant relations does not help Coraline (because she doesn't heed her neighbors' warnings), we must also remember that Miss Spink and Miss Forcible do give her the stone with a hole in it, and it is this stone that allows her to find the marbles and eventually win the game.

Like most children in novels dealing with growth and development, Coraline herself must decide how to use the tools she is given. Her neighbors prove beneficial in her identity formation because they provide her with warnings and advice upon which she will later reflect when she returns to the real world and contemplates the value of family and community. As well, the stone with a hole in it is just one of the objects that Coraline uses in the novel to win the game against the Other Mother, and it is this desire to win the game and reclaim her real parents that forces Caroline to master technology and, in the process, become a productive adolescent.

The Stone with a Hole in It

The definition of the word "technology" changes when applied to children. For them, technology is anything artificial that they can manipulate to produce a given result. For instance, we know the black key unlocks the door in the drawing room that leads to the Other Mother's world; but the key rests at the top of the kitchen doorframe and Coraline cannot reach it. In order to obtain the key, Coraline uses her intellect to push a chair next to the door, climb onto the chair with a broom in her hand, and then knock the set of keys onto the floor whereupon she removes the single black key she needs. Each of these objects becomes a form of technology that Coraline uses to produce a given result, the last one being the black key she uses to discover what lies behind the door in the drawing room. Gaiman tells us that after picking up the keys, Coraline "smiled triumphantly."[27] Obviously, she feels a surge of pride at having used these objects in a way that transcends their practical use and becomes not only creative, but also industrious.

And while the black key unlocks the door in the drawing room, it also symbolizes the unlocking of Coraline's mind. It suggests a dawning awareness in regarding the way she can manipulate technology for personal gain. That this comprehension reaches its peak within a gothic environment corresponds to William Patrick Day's assertion that the heroine "approaches the Gothic world ... with a heightened apprehension and a restless curiosity.... The vision of the Gothic world evokes in the protagonist both fear and desire. The stimulation of desire comes from the apparent possibilities of self-creation and gratification."[28] This sense of self-creation and gratification occurs during the fourth stage of psychosocial development precisely because the apprehension and curiosity both pressure the child to explore her own feelings. Without this pressure the child cannot gain a sense of her own identity, and without this identity the child cannot find the courage to progress through future stages of development. The black key, which is an extension of the gothic landscape, frees Coraline to enter a deadly game in which she emerges victorious and can then re-enter her familiar community with a new identity and a new sense of self-worth.

The other vital piece of technology that aids Coraline in the novel is the stone with a hole in it. Without it, she cannot hope to obtain the marbles and win the game. In order to see the glowing marbles, she must hold the stone up to her eye and look through the hole. This act reminds us that we need to carefully examine the world around us. People and objects that might pass by unnoticed sometimes tend to take on a deeper significance when viewed from a different angle or with a bit more intensity. For children navigating through stage four, who are attempting to prove they are capable of being productive and also forming ties with their community, it's especially important that they take the time to study and observe not only the actions and behaviors of all those around them, but also the physical and emotional conflicts that rage inside their prepubescent bodies and minds.

The stone with a hole in it also suggests that we must not become too confident in our own surroundings. Clearly, the gothic landscape entices Coraline because it seems fun and interesting, but she does not sense its underlying horror until it is too late and the Other Mother has already kidnapped her parents. The stone reveals the truths about Coraline's new surroundings, namely that just as a positive environment can possess negative attributes, so, too, can a negative environment possess positive attributes. This is an important lesson because children need to learn to think before they make a decision. They cannot remain naïve in thinking that good and evil exist separately in the world. That Coraline is able to use a special stone to collect the marbles and save her parents is testament to the tremendous impact that gothic elements can have on a child's growth and development. Had she not interacted with these gothic elements, it seems possible that Coraline might not have become an active learner. In turn, she might not have learned to appreciate her parents or even trust herself. If Coraline did not resolve the main crisis that accompanies stage four, she almost surely would have become passive and withdrawn, envious of productivity, ashamed of herself, and unwilling to seek help amongst those within her radius of significant relations for fear of being mocked and ridiculed.

Once Coraline is safe at home in her own world, she believes her ordeal is finally over, but the Other Mother's hand has followed the young girl, and it desperately wants the black key that Coraline now wears around her neck. This continuation of danger from the fantasy world to the real world is yet another reminder that the process of identity formation never quite ends. And it makes sense that the Other Mother, who represents Coraline's subconscious and imagination, would want to possess the black key, which symbolizes the unlocking of Coraline's mind and the initial steps needed for her to secure a stronger identity, gain a sense of industry, and become more independent. The Other Mother does not wish for Coraline to break away from her power and influence. She believes that if she possesses the black key, she controls the door in the drawing room, which also represents, at least in Coraline's mind, the gateway between imagination and reality.

For Coraline to successfully resolve this crisis and begin the next stage of development she must find a way to destroy the Other Mother's hand. It is fitting that she finally chooses the well near her house as the prison where she'll trap the hand. In many ways, this "brick-lined hole in the ground" mirrors the brick wall that hides the dark passageway on the other side of the door in the drawing room.[29] Both the well and the passageway represent darkness and depth, and the Other Mother's hand falling into the well suggests that Coraline has now banished her childhood fears and doubts. She will no longer rely on the power of her imagination to influence her decisions. And having unlocked her mind, she no longer requires the black key, which is now reunited with the Other Mother at the bottom of the well. This last triumph over the Other Mother is also accomplished with technology, as Coraline uses cups of water to weigh down the sheet so it appears to be a harmless and innocent surface. Again, we see how a newly realized sense of industry, attained by roaming the gothic landscape, has enhanced Coraline's intellect and given her the ability to create logical ideas that she can then put into productive action.

In the final pages, Gaiman tells us that Coraline is getting ready to begin a new school year. This is a fitting end to the novel, as the beginning of a new school year mirrors the new changes that have occurred within Coraline. Being at school will allow Coraline to expand her radius of significant relations and also find more new and exciting ways to expand upon the grasp of technology that the gothic elements have afforded her. We believe that Coraline has the strength and confidence to face any conflicts or challenges that might place themselves in her path. Having steered her way through Erikson's fourth stage of psychosocial development, Coraline has now become a competent child. For children and adults alike, *Coraline* is especially important not just because it informs us that the Other Mother is a crippling yet necessary influence on our constantly evolving emotional states, but because it reassures us that the Other Mother can be conquered and defeated if only we have the courage to explore those gothic landscapes that lie hidden away within the darkest recesses of our minds.

4

Genital Dystopia: Identity and Role Confusion in *Little Red Riding Hood*

Genital Dystopia

Lately, I've been reading about Little Red Riding Hood Syndrome, a popular phrase that has wormed its way into pop culture vernacular. While it sounds fairly innocent, its implied meaning is as loaded and dangerous as the vicious wolf that ushered the very phrase into existence. Initially, I thought Little Red Riding Hood Syndrome might be a second cousin to Stockholm syndrome, a psychological event in which young children fall desperately in love with their stuffed animals, or cry incessantly when their grandmothers leave the room. Later, I imagined it as some rare disease that targets young children while they sleep, a deadly virus comparable to AIDS or Ebola, but made tolerable because of cartoon Band-aids and fairy-tale stickers.

Little Red Riding Hood Syndrome is classified as the public's fear and misperception of wolves. Not wolves and sex. Not wolves and sex and little girls. Just wolves. At its most basic level, Little Red Riding Hood Syndrome concentrates on the mistaken belief that wolves will attack humans with no provocation, and that, should you ever just happen to stumble upon one, it will sink its teeth into your throat and tear you apart. And when that happens, there's not much you can do except thrash around and scream.

While Little Red Riding Hood Syndrome is predominantly an adult fear, it arises from the same feelings of weakness and inferiority that are shared by children who are afraid of the dark or of being abandoned. So it's no surprise that this adult fear references one of the most famous fairy tales. True, Little Red Riding Hood is a story about stranger danger, but it's also a story about a young woman on the verge of adulthood. The word "syndrome," which is often synonymous with disease, echoes the sexual undertones found in numerous versions of Little Red Riding Hood, as well as the social taboos that accompany blossoming sexuality.

Listening to parents trying to discuss puberty and sexual activity with their child is usually awkward and uncomfortable for everyone involved. When confronted with the reality that many adolescents engage in sexual intercourse, adults sometimes choose to wear blinders and promptly change the subject, hoping to convince themselves that their children are channeling Puritan virtues and will wait until adulthood before diving under the covers. In truth, many of the themes and issues connected with sex (such as love and communication, contraception, and ownership of one's body) have been topics of debate for hundreds of years. Such issues are not evil or taboo, but natural and important contributors to identity formation, especially when it comes to resolving adolescent crises and progressing into those early stages of adulthood.

While there are many different versions of Little Red Riding Hood, the two most widely read are "Little Red Riding Hood" by Charles Perrault and "Little Red Cap" by the Brothers Grimm. I also want to focus my attention on "The Story of Grandmother," the earliest known version that originated as a folk tale. Each of these tales presents a young girl set upon by a wolf on her way to her grandmother's house, and each tale demonstrates that women must possess important knowledge about their own sexuality to survive. While Perrault's version is highly erotic and warns women against the dangers of sexual frivolity, the Grimms' version stresses the importance of proper etiquette and behavior. "The Story of Grandmother" combines the two approaches, however, and succeeds in illustrating the importance of self-reliance and obedience, as well as the adolescent challenge to control and understand one's body. All of these lessons are important when dealing with the wolf, for he represents not only those primitive urges that lurk within every human being, but also the male seducer and charged sexuality.

The main character in all three tales is a young peasant girl who faces the immediate threat of being devoured by a male predator. In "Little Red Riding Hood" and "Little Red Cap," however, she is dominated by the wolf and forced to relinquish control over her own body. These moments of surrender damage the tales' lessons about sexuality by denying her the ability to think for herself and preventing her from exploring those feelings of intimacy that she, along with adolescent readers, should respond to and learn from. In each story, the peasant girl is not prepared for sexual discovery or for the many challenges involved in being an adolescent. After reading the three individual tales, we realize that the mother figure has not provided this girl with the necessary knowledge for such an important journey. She sends her daughter into the dark forest without alerting her to the dangers that lurk therein, which proves costly. "The Story of Grandmother" does end with some sense of hope, though, as the child survives her gothic encounter and finds her way back home. There, she will hopefully reflect on her traumatic experience, and the lessons she learns will then prove beneficial in contributing to her psychosocial development.

Some might ask why there is a need to study the tales of Little Red Riding Hood within the context of adolescent growth and maturity. After all, our culture is so insistent that fairy tales are for small children, and it seems that many adults believe fairy tales provide them with no educational merit. But most fairy tales were originally written for adults. And most fairy tales explore themes of change and identity formation, so it makes sense that we should examine the different ways in which these tales stimulate and foster one's growth and development, not only during adolescence, but during all stages of identity formation. After all, it was Albert Einstein who once remarked, "If you want your children to be intelligent, read them fairy tales. If you want them to be more intelligent, read them more fairy tales."

Reading any version of Little Red Riding Hood will also raise the question of how we can blame the wolf for acting in accordance with his natural instincts, as well as for acting within his own established territory. Prowling through the woods, how can he be expected to do otherwise? A wolf hunts for food in his familiar surroundings, and when he comes across a weaker animal he pounces on it because he needs to eat. Here, the wolf is doing nothing more than trying to survive, and the point, though bloody, becomes quite clear: the will to endure is powerful, and it transcends trivial facts like species or class or gender.

Shouldn't the same be said of Little Red Riding Hood? She is an adolescent on the verge of puberty, brimming with curiosity about her own body and the strange world around her. She teeters between childhood and adulthood, confused about relationships and peer groups. In each of the three tales, this young girl stops along the path on the way to her grandmother's house and indulges in childish whimsies, such as picking up needles, gathering nuts, and collecting flowers. Her fascination with nature, represented by the gothic forest that harbors a cunning wolf, illustrates that she acknowledges the importance of the gothic as an educational tool.

She wishes to immerse herself in it and discover its secrets. Perhaps she is aware that a loss of innocence requires bad experiences as well as good experiences, and that maturity, especially sexual maturity, must be gained through sensible choices and honesty, neither of which is demonstrated by any of the adults in these three classic tales.

What most casual readers do not understand is that it is necessary to Little Red Riding Hood's physical and emotional growth that she enters the gothic forest and meets the wolf. She is going through many of the same changes that Erikson emphasizes as crucial to an adolescent's maturity, namely the idea that "a state of acute identity confusion usually becomes manifest at a time when the young individual finds himself exposed to a combination of experiences which demand his simultaneous commitment to physical intimacy, to decisive occupational choice, to energetic competition, and to psychosocial self-definition."[1] Little Red Riding Hood experiences all these emotions as she journeys to her grandmother's house. She must contend with not only the wolf, but also with her mother's strict instructions to stay on the path, as well as her responsibility to bring food to an ailing elder whose role she will someday assume.

In these three tales of Little Red Riding Hood, the gothic elements, namely the wilderness and the wolf, as well as cannibalistic elements in "The Story of Grandmother," represent the undiscovered and dark side of human nature. It is only through interacting with these outer elements that Little Red Riding Hood can begin to understand her inner self. Because the gothic is often portrayed as an externalization of the psychological, it makes sense that Little Red Riding Hood's blossoming sexuality leads her into a gothic atmosphere that exudes those very same emotions that are raging constantly inside her own pubescent body.

Identity versus Role Confusion

On one level, the message implied in the various tales of Little Red Riding Hood is that children should not talk to strangers lest they fall into dangerous hands and become separated from their family. On another level, the tales relate closely with many of the same themes and ideas that Erikson explores in his fifth stage of psychosocial development. He defines this stage as "Identity versus Role Confusion," and it comprises the adolescent period between the ages of twelve and twenty. The strengths in this stage are fidelity and loyalty, the antipathy being repudiation. Erikson sums up this fifth stage quite well when he writes, "The greatest problem we encounter is who we think we are versus who others may think we are or are trying to be."[2] During this tumultuous period of growth, the child searches for fidelity in social ideas and theories, as well as in cliques, fashion styles or places that will allow her to establish a sense of trust with others. She must deal with intimate relationships, develop a personal ideology that's her own and not merely an extension of her parents, and undergo significant physical changes. Oftentimes, she enters the workforce through a part-time job and must learn how to organize and manage her finances. In experiencing all of these changes, the adolescent strives to prove herself capable of being viewed as a trustworthy person who is ready to be initiated into adulthood.

At the same time, however, those childhood fears that still resonate can often result in confusion and foolish behavior. This behavior, in turn, will foster moments of deep mistrust for adult authority. Little Red Riding Hood displays such behavior when she ignores her mother's warning and engages in a conversation with the wolf. She wants to make her own decisions, yet knows she must listen to her mother. The resulting anger at this lack of personal control is what fuels her desire to disregard her mother's words and not only become friendly with a male predator, but also to reveal the way to grandmother's house. As is typical of stage five, the adolescent is concerned with how she appears to others, yet she also wants to make her own choices and remain individualistic.

Adolescence is the last stage of childhood, although, for some of us, the resolution of its crises may extend well past twenty years of age and perhaps even into our thirties or forties. We can move successfully past adolescence and enter adulthood only when we shed childhood labels and identifications in favor of new ones that society accepts as representative of an adult personality that's ready to consider more serious goals like securing a job or maintaining a committed relationship. This is one of those *fin de siècle* moments in which the child looks forward to becoming an independent adult, but looks back on childhood with more longing and nostalgia, especially as she begins to comprehend her own mortality.

When confronted with the passing of childhood, and the inevitable onset of adulthood, many adolescents become scared, angry, and confused. They want their parents and friends to help guide them toward maturity, but they also desire the freedom to explore their identity on their own and to make mistakes that will aid them in learning how to better understand the world around them. That Little Red Riding Hood disobeys her mother and interacts with the wolf is evidence of an adolescent desire to break free from her childhood identity and become a woman in her own right. Julian

Fleenor emphasizes the connection between Gothicism and this fifth stage of development by explaining that "the Gothic world is one of nightmare, and that nightmare is created by the individual in conflict with the values of her society and her prescribed role."[3] Like most adolescents, Little Red Riding Hood experiences stress and anxiety as she struggles with becoming the woman she wants to be while also becoming the woman she believes everyone expects her to be. The fears and mood swings inherent during this stage of development often mirror the emotions experienced during a nightmare. Little Red Riding Hood's behavior thus corresponds with a teenager's need to break free from parents and family, and to discover an entirely new radius of significant relations.

During this fifth stage of psychosocial development, the adolescent's radius of significant relations centers on peer groups, outgroups, and models of leadership. These relations might extend to adolescent siblings, as well as to high school peers, many of whom are almost certainly experiencing similar identity crises in their lives. These crises can encompass appearance and class structure, as well as intelligence or a reconsideration of familial and societal values. Because conflict and confusion is such an important part of an adolescent's growth and maturity, adults must accept the fact that bad decisions and immature actions will be natural sidekicks in the adolescent's quest for crisis resolution and identity formation. This is especially true when we consider that those same peers an adolescent often approaches for help and advice are themselves feeling conflicted and confused.

Adolescents often attach themselves to outgroups because many experience feelings of displacement during this time in their lives. They feel stuck between two crucial stages, and they are distrustful of parents who they firmly believe do not understand adolescent problems and, therefore, cannot offer sound advice. Also, an adolescent may find comfort in the roles and behaviors of certain societal figures such as movie stars, politicians, and athletes. The images of these famous people in films and magazines often provide the adolescent with goals (though not always realistic ones) that she hopes to achieve in her future.

In attempting to complete their own identity, many adolescents will often mirror the actions and behaviors of others. This might occur in the way they dress, the language or slang they use when they speak, and in the beliefs and opinions they share with others. Such a trial and error process is important in stage five because, as Erikson reiterates, "we play roles and try out for parts we wish we could play for real, especially as we explore in adolescence."[4] Just as the wolf assumes the role of a nonviolent friend, and later the role of the grandmother, so does Little Red Riding Hood assume the role of an independent woman and also, in some versions of the tale, the role of a family patriarch.

Many adolescents feel the urge to seek out new and challenging experiences, surrounding themselves with peers who will respond more constructively to their hardships and moods. To feel validated in their emotions, teenagers want their friends to express sympathy and reassurance rather than the pity and criticism that teenagers often expect and misinterpret from their own parents and family members. This fifth stage is tumultuous for adolescents because not only do they need to transition into adulthood by casting off their childhood identities, but they must do so while experiencing a variety of moods caused by all those hormones raging inside their maturing bodies.

In considering the connections among Little Red Riding Hood, sexuality, and Erikson's fifth stage of development, it's important to remember that in most fairy tales the gothic elements symbolize bad decisions, negative thoughts, or amoral behavior. For child readers it's important they understand the significance of Gothicism as it relates not only to cause and effect within a given story, but also how these gothic elements contribute to identity formation. Added to this is the reality, as Peter and Iona Opie state, that "most events in fairy tales are remarkable for their unpleasantness."[5] The horrible experiences that befall most heroes and heroines help children to learn and understand that life is not always fair, that danger constantly lurks in the background, and that people, no matter their age, will often find themselves in scary situations that test their judgment. Violence and gruesomeness are an integral part of life, both physically and emotionally, and it's important for parents to send their children into the woods—metaphorically speaking, of course.

From a psychological standpoint, the woods represent future challenges and the unknown, as well as the dark side of human nature, especially during adolescence. The forest is an important setting in most fairy tales, from "Hansel and Gretel" and "Rapunzel" to "Snow White" and "The Brave Little Tailor." Children cannot remain innocent forever, and only by journeying into the woods and confronting those gothic elements can they initiate and foster a search for their self-identities that will allow them to mature. For Little Red Riding Hood, her experience in the forest is connected to her sexual awakening. Seth Lerer suggests, "It is as if the girl's body is itself a kind of forest for the fairy-tale imagination: something dark and inexplicable, something in need of management, of clearing, of cleansing."[6] This idea highlights an important message in the tales of Little Red

Riding Hood, namely that sexual discovery is a natural and important part of all our lives. And while these discoveries can be fraught with uncomfortable moments of sadness and confusion, and sometimes difficult to endure, they can strengthen our characters if we remain confident and composed.

Parents who understand the process of maturation should not be afraid to let their children travel into the woods alone. To enter the darkness at any age, to engage in a physical or emotional battle and then return home again, is to participate in a select rite of passage that prepares one for future stages of development. Because Little Red Riding Hood enters the woods to mature, she should also exit those same woods at the end of the tale, thus stressing the themes of rebirth and enlightenment that are integral to most fairy tales.

By placing Erikson's theories within the context of three very different versions of Little Red Riding Hood, I hope to highlight ways in which the gothic elements in each tale illuminate various methods for dealing with adolescent challenges like sexual discovery, confronting the dark side of human nature, and formulating positive choices. Each of these tales touches upon key ideas relating to the fifth stage of psychosocial development, and they show that teenagers can indeed benefit from reading and analyzing fairy tales. In this regard, "The Story of Grandmother" is arguably the most successful at promoting a necessary cycle of pubescent growth and maturity.

The Story of Grandmother

"The Story of Grandmother" is a French folk tale that's not nearly as well known as the two other versions by Charles Perrault and the Brothers Grimm. While not generally considered a children's tale on account of the cannibalism motif, it is precisely this motif that helps contribute to the tale's importance as a comment on sexual maturity. "The Story of Grandmother" presents an unnamed peasant girl who already displays some intelligence about the world around her. She meets the *bzou* (wolf) at a crossroads, which clearly symbolizes the different paths we all might take in life. When questioned by the *bzou*, the peasant girl tells him that she wishes to take the Needles Road rather than the Pins Road. Jack Zipes tells us that "the references to the pins and needles were related to the needlework apprenticeship undergone by young peasant girls, and designated the arrival of puberty and initiation into society in specific regions of France where the oral tale was common."[7] The peasant girl chooses the Needles Road because she is a hard worker and understands the importance of labor; it is easy to fasten items together with pins, but needlework requires time, commitment, and concentration. That the peasant girl already grasps the connection between work and survival is testament to the realization that she is maturing as a young woman and accepting her designated role in society.

Because the little girl likes picking up the needles, the reader understands that she possesses a strong work ethic, one that will conflict with the *bzou's* idleness. The girl's decision to take the Needles Road also reveals why her mother did not perform a safety lecture when the girl said goodbye and left for Grandma's house. Clearly, this peasant girl has spent time in the woods, and she is not afraid of wild animals or the darkness. She understands that one path illustrates maturity while the other illustrates laziness. That the *bzou* exploits this positive attribute reveals the male gender's relentless pursuit to lure young women off the virtuous path and engage them in naughty behavior.

Unlike the other versions of the story by Perrault and the Brothers Grimm, the young girl in "The Story of Grandmother" is not terrified of the *bzou*, nor does she tell him where her grandmother lives. She answers his question without revealing crucial details concerning the exact location of her grandmother's house or even the appearance of the house itself. Her unwillingness to aid the *bzou* does not stem from naiveté, as it does in the other versions, but from a mature personality who realizes that her maturation into an adult, as well as her usurpation of Grandmother's role, is an inevitable occurrence. On a subconscious level, she understands that she doesn't need to rush this important growth process, as it will simply develop at its own natural pace. Perhaps this is why she isn't afraid to experiment with her adolescent feelings and explore a newfound interest and curiosity in the male gender.

Of course, the *bzou* arrives at Grandmother's house first and promptly devours her. After slicing the grandmother into bite-size snacks and draining some of her blood into a bottle, the *bzou* crawls into bed. When the girl arrives, the *bzou*, who seems to be a gracious host, suggests she eat some meat and drink some wine. Because the peasant girl is diligent and hardworking, she is also well-mannered. She eats the flesh and drinks the blood. The act of gorging on the remains of her grandmother shows that "the grandmother's death signifies the continuity of custom through her granddaughter, who symbolically replaces her by eating her flesh and drinking her blood."[8] The flesh may symbolize the grandmother's strength and knowledge, while the blood may symbolize the onset of menstruation that all women must experience before achieving sexual maturity. That the young girl crawls into bed with the *bzou* immediately after drinking grandmother's blood helps to strengthen the sexual connotations implicit in such a cannibalistic act. She now feels more confidant and assured, and is curious to play the role of the mature adult.

As is most often the case in adolescence, a person will not always know an important event has transpired, or even created a lasting impact, until well after it happens. There needs to be a period of reflection in which the person can consider what a specific event or experience has meant to her and how that experience will affect future decisions and behaviors. Sexual maturation is a process that yields many of these experiences, and we do not always comprehend their effects until we have undergone numerous physical and emotional changes.

The peasant girl understands that a change is taking place within her body, and this realization excites her, even if her fluctuating adolescent emotions cause her to react against what she knows to be proper behavior. Instead of leaving the house and removing herself from this tense situation, she feels emboldened by the *bzou's* attention and indulges in its plan to tempt and seduce her. Doing so definitely adheres to the theme of repudiation and rebellion that many adolescents display throughout their teenage years. Like many young men and women, the peasant girl is simply searching out new experiences and roles that will contribute to her psychosocial and psychosexual development, and will also aid her in assuming an adult identity.

As she consumes her grandmother's remains, a cat says, "A slut is she who eats the flesh and drinks the blood of her grandmother."[9] Clearly, the word "slut" is a derogatory remark, but this remark seems out of place in the tale, as the girl has no idea she is eating her grandmother. Also, it is important that we interpret the cannibalism not in a literal sense, but in a symbolic one. The cat's remark seems to exclude the fact that such actions symbolize a vital and necessary stage in a person's life. The girl's ingestion of her grandmother's body represents her own growing maturity and the eventual role she will assume as mother and protector. Another idea, however, is that the cat's remark could represent the more negative views of sex as taboo, especially centuries ago when the tale was first shared. While sexual awakening is undoubtedly an integral part of the maturation process, many people still consider it sordid and unmentionable. It is interesting, though, that the peasant girl does not respond to the cat's remark, or even seem to notice it. This point certainly parallels my earlier statement that the entire sequence of events in grandmother's house is a growth process that the girl does not yet understand. She might also simply be acting like any normal teenager who does not want to listen to what adults have to say, especially if the cat in this scene represents adults' perspectives on sex.

While the other versions of Little Red Riding Hood focus on the gothic landscape and the danger of the woods, "The Story of Grandmother" reveals its gothic imagery in the flesh and blood that the peasant girl consumes, as well as in the threatening figure of the *bzou*. Not only is the *bzou* a vicious beast with sharp claws and teeth, but he is also representative of the male gender, often seen as seductive, oversexed, and dangerous. These characteristics parallel the representation of most male characters in gothic novels, especially when applied to the gothic motif of the "pursued maiden." This gothic idea of a woman fleeing for her life from an oppressive male also relates to themes of isolation and abandonment, both of which surface in the various tales of Little Red Riding Hood. The peasant girl's absorption of the gothic, through her consumption of grandmother and through her intimacy with the *bzou*, represents her passage into womanhood and stresses that while the gothic is an integral part of maturity, it should also be treated with respect as a rite of passage, and not indulged as a sexual whim that simply satiates one's curiosities.

In consuming her grandmother's flesh and blood, the peasant girl assumes the role of her grandmother and attempts to act out an adult love affair with the *bzou*. These theatrics echo Erikson's theories concerning stage five of psychosocial development that "to a considerable extent adolescent love is an attempt to arrive at a definition of one's identity by projecting one's diffused self-image on another and by seeing it thus reflected and gradually clarified."[10] In seeing how the *bzou* acts, immediately after she assumes the role of her grandmother, the peasant girl then gains a deeper understanding of how a mature adult woman might act when confronted with intimacy. Surely, she might be afraid of the encounter, and even confused by all the emotions she experiences, but it is still a vital learning experience that serves as a jumping-off point for any future liaisons she might develop, or any sexual decisions she might need to make.

"The Story of Grandmother" also suggests that although the gothic is a necessary contributor to our growth and development, there are mature and immature ways to accept the more negative aspects of life, much like the choosing of the Needles Road versus the Pins Road. Had the peasant girl been lazier, or perhaps more eager to sacrifice her grandmother to the *bzou*, she might have been completely seduced by the *bzou* and lost her life at the end of the tale. Such an ending would then undercut the pedagogical value of the gothic by denying her an important learning experience that she needs in order to resolve those crises associated with identity and role confusion. As in the two other versions of Little Red Riding Hood, the gothic elements in "The Story of Grandmother" provide the young girl with the firm understanding that maturation, especially of a sexual nature, involves both good and bad moments. These moments combine over time, during various stages of psychosocial and psychosexual development, to provide lifelong lessons that will help to form our individual personalities.

In French slang, when a girl loses her virginity it is said that she has seen the wolf: *elle avait vu le loup.* This historical connection helps illuminate the sexual undertones inherent in the tale. The phrase alludes to the fear and danger that can accompany physical maturation and it also alludes to the idea of men as being sexual predators. In "The Story of Grandmother," the peasant girl encounters both of these scenarios. To mature, she must first validate her grandmother's death and assume her natural role in the cycle of life. Second, she must climb into bed with the *bzou*, experience the onset of sexuality, and make her own choices about whether or not she is ready to begin engaging in erotic activity. She also expresses herself in new and exciting ways, such as when she undresses in front of the *bzou*, a seductive act she probably does not perform in front of her grandmother. During this scene, she performs a deft striptease and tosses her clothes into the fire. This act reveals a newfound interest in her body, and in this instance her identity is determined by the positive attention the *bzou* showers upon her. Because she feels special and wanted, she is willing to move past familiar boundaries and to venture into adult-oriented territories.

The scene in which the girl takes off her clothes is sexually charged for many reasons. First, the wolf symbolizes our primal, ferocious urges; his actions represent those moments when we allow our emotions to overpower reason. Second, the fire blazing represents the heightened feelings of lust and passion that often accompany adolescence. The burning of the girl's clothes symbolizes her vanishing childhood. The *bzou's* refrain of "you don't need it any more," in reference to each article of clothing, emphasizes the notion that she is embarking on a new path, namely womanhood. Traveling this new path also means she can never return to that state of childhood she has known up to this point. The tale describes the girl's disrobing as a slow process, much like the stages of life, or even the different events that culminate over years to lead us to a better understanding of how the world functions.

After the peasant girl and the *bzou* engage in what can only be called foreplay, she climbs into bed and realizes that the *bzou* plans to consummate their relationship. While he wishes to devour her, there is still an intimacy involved, especially when we consider that the acts of devouring and fornication both involve levels of control and submission. The *bzou* is excited about this rendezvous, exhibiting the same sort of giddiness and frustration expected of a teenage boy. That the peasant girl feels excitement *and* apprehension during this pivotal moment in her adolescence is an experience to which most teenagers can relate. They want to prove themselves as being capable of handling such a mature moment, but their inexperience causes them angst and anxiety that can generate shame and self-doubt.

Once she's in bed with the *bzou*, the peasant girl becomes agitated and begs to go outside so she can use the bathroom. The *bzou*, preoccupied with sex, and obviously not worried about health issues, suggests that she relieve herself in bed. The act of relieving oneself in bed is itself immature and filthy, but when coupled with the addition of the *bzou*, it heightens the tale's sexual undertones. This scene suggests that the gothic components function not only to provide essential steps she must undergo to become a mature woman, but also to create uncomfortable moments that force her to feel awkward about the situation and perhaps realize that she isn't quite ready to experience the level of intimacy that the *bzou* desires. That the *bzou* instructs the girl to relieve herself in bed emphasizes even further society's attitude that indulging in sexual curiosity as an adolescent is dirty and vulgar.

Knowing she is unable to satisfy the *bzou*, the girl refuses to relieve herself in the bed. This decision illustrates that she is making conscious choices about her own body. With her grandmother dead, and with her mother many miles away, there is no one else around to make this important choice for the young girl. Her firmness and resolve to step outside and relieve herself is representative of how a mature and intelligent woman responds to a situation involving the male gender and intimacy. The girl's decision also reminds adolescents that they alone possess the ability to make sound, sensible choices concerning their sexuality; they have the freedom to express their physical and emotional desires in ways that will allow them to feel comfortable, safe, and able to share trust with a partner. Likewise, such intimate moments may come at any time during one's adolescence. Such moments should not be rushed lest they disrupt the maturation process, fueling negative emotions and increasing the risk of repudiation that most teenagers display during stage five when they are confused and conflicted.

On some level, the peasant girl is definitely aware that the figure in the bed is not her grandmother, which is why, in addition to becoming flirtatious, she exhibits self-defense and preservation when she asks the *bzou* if she can leave the bed to relieve herself. We must also consider the fact that the girl doesn't really need to go to the bathroom, but is simply making an excuse so she can escape this uncomfortable situation. Either way, the girl does not remain in bed with the *bzou*, but chooses instead to leave her grandmother's house and return home. The *bzou* follows her, but she arrives home safely before he can snatch her up.

The peasant girl's entrance into the house at the end of the tale completes the cycle. She entered the woods as a child, chose the mature path, and confronted Gothicism in the form of the *bzou*, as well as in the form of her grandmother's flesh and blood. Although there appear to be no peer groups in the tale with whom the peasant girl can converse, we can assume that the family unit, consisting of the mother and the grandmother, acts as the radius of significant relations. Her loyalty to them, as displayed through her diligence and independent thinking, allows her to learn from the tale's gothic elements without being corrupted by them. As with other versions of Little Red Riding Hood, the point is that the peasant girl must encounter the *bzou* and become intimate with him, whether she crawls into bed naked with him, or he eats her (an act which clearly implies sexual connotations of its own). The choices she makes throughout the tale are what create conflict and contribute to her identity formation. Had she remained passive the entire time, either by remaining silent or having those choices made for her by other adults, this young girl would have arrived home just as naïve as when she entered the woods at the beginning of the tale.

"The Story of Grandmother" illustrates Erikson's theories about identity and role confusion in that it presents a young girl who discovers her blossoming sexuality and experiments with the *bzou* (up to a certain point, though, as any normal adolescent is prone to do). Her encounter with the *bzou* functions as a practice round in which she can learn about intimate relationships, and also how to mediate and resolve sexual crises. That she decides she isn't quite ready for such an adult experience doesn't mean she is immature. On the contrary, her realization is another important step in navigating the fifth stage of development and becoming an adult. In making the decision to leave her grandmother's house and return home, the young girl has successfully handled the male gender and shown she is well on her way to becoming a woman. To complete this significant cycle, however, and to illustrate that she is beginning a gradual development toward womanhood, the young girl must now exit the woods. At the end of the tale she returns to the place where she originally started, albeit more experienced and cautious. In Charles Perrault's version, however, he does not allow this rebirth. His Little Red Riding Hood does not make choices, nor does she exit the woods.

Little Red Riding Hood

In his story "Little Red Riding Hood," Perrault dispenses with the scenes of cannibalism and creates a high amount of sexual tension and eroticism that saturates the tale and changes the original folktale's meaning.[11] Whereas "The Story of Grandmother" was a tale that advocated maturity and sexuality, Perrault's tale is a dire warning to any girls who might stray past the borders of their own chastity to indulge in sexual intercourse. His tale presents an image of woman as helpless and naïve, necessitating punishment for surrendering to her natural sexual desires. Perrault's tale is also the first version of the story in which the young girl wears the red hood. Zipes remarks, "For a village girl, in Perrault's story, to wear a red chaperon signified that she was individualistic and perhaps non-conformist."[12] While teenagers should be praised for striving to be individualistic, Perrault suggests that Little Red Riding Hood should not think for herself. She should be an extension of her family, embracing its values and customs. Her red hood, then, highlights what Perrault interprets as teenage misbehavior rather than adolescent discovery.

Zipes' comment resonates even more when we consider that peasant girls during this particular time in history were unable to make choices concerning their own future. The girl's suitor, as well as the entire wedding, was orchestrated by the girl's parents for social or financial gain. Often, love did not play a part. It makes sense that since emotional love was controlled by parents and family, so, too, was physical love. Parents and family suppressed physical love at the onset of puberty. They chided their adolescents for questioning the sexual maturation process, rendering the topic of sex taboo and effectively removing those adolescents from a stage that is crucial in the formation of one's self-identity. Throughout "Little Red Riding Hood," Perrault, as a member of the aristocracy, illustrates the dangers inherent in letting innocent, young women choose their own path in life.

Women of Perrault's day were warned constantly about the repercussions of choosing devious and deceitful suitors. Perrault emphasizes Little Red Riding Hood's innocence and careless thinking by linking her with the color red. Clearly, the color red symbolizes lust, passion, and even the menstrual blood that arrives at the onset of puberty. Whereas "The Story of Grandmother" celebrates this color by showing the consumption of blood as a symbolic ritual that passes on knowledge and strength to successive generations, Perrault implies that its presence can be destructive, and he exaggerates this idea by shrouding the girl's head in a red hood.

The red hood becomes her identity, labeling her as different from those pious and dutiful children who obey their parents. In providing Little Red Riding Hood with this physical marker, Perrault sets her apart from a society comprised of mature adults who don't wish to school their children on the importance of adolescent themes. He implies that the red hood prevents the girl from behaving like a proper, virtuous woman, and it becomes a symbol of misbehavior and negligence. In the context of Perrault's version, the hood's purpose is to heighten the claim that not only is Little Red Riding Hood experiencing the onset of untamed sexuality, but it is precisely her willingness and consent to engage in immoral behavior that eventually leads to her death at the jaws of the wolf.

Perrault presents Little Red Riding Hood as an immature girl, both physically and emotionally. Her lack of worldly knowledge, and her inability to understand the dangers inherent in talking to strangers, is what allows her to offer the wolf exact directions to her grandmother's house. Her directions are so detailed and explicit that she might as well draw him a map or lend him the house key. Her eagerness suggests that, at least on a subconscious level, she is interested in the attention she receives from the wolf and wants to prolong his advances. Nevertheless, her mistake in telling the wolf where her grandmother lives relates to many of Erikson's theories concerning stage five, namely an adolescent's predilection to learn about her sexuality and emotions by suffering the consequences of bad decisions. Bruno Bettelheim emphasizes the tale's focus on adolescent growth:

> [Little Red Riding Hood's] danger is her budding sexuality, for which she is not yet emotionally mature enough. A premature sexuality is a regressive experience, arousing all that is primitive within us and that threatens to swallow us up. The immature person who is not yet ready for sex but is exposed to an experience which arouses strong sexual feelings falls back on oedipal ways for dealing with it.[13]

As is typical during stage five, there exists some jealousy between a sexually naïve adolescent and her older, more experienced family members. This envy fosters conflicted emotions in that, subconsciously, Little Red Riding Hood wishes to act the part of those older family members, and this is a role she plays when she crawls into bed with the wolf.

Yet she also becomes fearful of her own burgeoning sexuality. This fear generates a desire that those same family members now assist her in resolving any personal crises. For example, she is certainly entranced by the wolf, but also a bit frightened of what he might do. By sending the wolf to her grandmother's house, Little Red Riding Hood might also be assuming that because her grandmother is an older mature woman, and most likely knowledgeable about the male gender, her grandmother can handle the wolf and any bad intentions he might possess. The girl might also believe that by placing the wolf inside the cottage, a setting typically associated with femininity, the wolf will be emasculated and easier to manage. Although Little Red Riding Hood might believe she's being faithful to her grandmother by trusting that Granny is experienced enough to handle the wolf, she also displays repudiation by assuming the role of an opportunist who tests her grandmother's womanliness.

As it does in "The Story of Grandmother," the wolf in Perrault's tale functions as a gothic element that represents the male predator. In his version, however, Little Red Riding Hood is actually eaten by the wolf at the end of the story. This violent act stresses Perrault's warning that proper women should not succumb to their erotic desires. The wolf's consumption of Little Red Riding Hood echoes the childhood fear of being devoured, thus linking sexual activity with death and abandonment. It is also clear that the wolf's "eating" of Little Red Riding Hood is a punishment for her sexual curiosity. Or perhaps sex as punishment, since being eaten would still seem to emphasize sexual overtones by suggesting the act of oral sex.

Again, the forest is a gothic element that symbolizes the unknown, as well as the conflict and angst that adolescents experience as they mature. Here, however, the gothic elements are not viewed as learning tools, but as hindrances that can contribute to immoral behavior and a degenerative society. In order to soften the tale's sexual undertones, and also to reduce the level of violence for his aristocratic audience, Perrault dispenses with the elements of cannibalism found in "The Story of Grandmother." By editing out the vital scene in which the girl drinks her grandmother's blood and consumes her flesh, Perrault ignores the previous tale's perspective on heredity and custom, rendering Little Red Riding Hood's encounter with the wolf not as a rite of passage that brings about growth and enlightenment, but as a detrimental meeting that eventually kills her.

The cannibalism scene is important in "The Story of Grandmother" because it symbolizes lust and passion, suggesting how an adolescent's charge onto the sexual battlefield might be the result of her natural need to feel wanted and loved. Adolescents constantly feel the urge to talk and act like adults, even when they are not quite sure how to do so. They want to assert their independence and show they are ready to become involved in adult relationships. The cannibalism scene in "The Story of Grandmother" illustrates this hunger for attention and closeness, and Perrault's removal of it fuels the message that sexual feelings can be controlled and halted by strict codes of moral behavior. The cannibalism scene also appears to emphasize physical love and eroticism, as well as the joys and troubles that often arise when we release our inhibitions and surrender to carnal desires, and so it's no wonder that Perrault removed the scene for an audience that prided itself on civilized behavior. Removing those gothic and sexual elements from the domestic setting within grandmother's house is damaging to the tale because it reduces the wolf to an evil villain whose sole intent is to seduce Little Red Riding Hood and then kill her.

In Perrault's tale, as well as in "The Story of Grandmother," the peasant girl is not warned beforehand by her mother. But whereas the peasant girl in "The Story of Grandmother" displays a positive work ethic and a sense of maturity, Little Red Riding Hood is clearly unprepared to think on her own in a world where sexual desires must be regulated by adults. Perrault's emphasis on discipline exists only to save young women from experiencing those very same inner forces that constitute psychosocial and psychosexual development during Erikson's stage five. Indeed, the bedroom scene in "The Story of Grandmother," during which the peasant girl tosses her clothes into the fire, is omitted in Perrault's version, replaced by the traditional banter in which the wolf and Little Red Riding Hood discuss the various sizes of grandmother's extremities. "What big eyes you have!" "What big ears you have!" And so on. The message here seems to be that sexual curiosity should be curbed if we value our health, family connections, and overall manner of living.

Had Little Red Riding Hood been lectured on the negative consequences that can result from interacting with the wolf, perhaps she might have ignored him or run away when she first encountered him in the forest. Either way, she would have made a conscious choice based on pre-existing knowledge, and not one based on ignorance. Eventually, Little Red Riding Hood must encounter the wolf and all that he represents, but only later when she has matured emotionally and physically enough to understand his intentions and how she should respond to his advances. When Perrault thrusts her into the woods with no prior warning, he essentially sets her up for failure, as many parents do when they choose to ignore the onset of adolescence and refuse to speak with their children about intimacy and sexual activity.

By having the wolf devour Little Red Riding Hood at the end of the story, Perrault alters the original tale's intent, transforming the main character into a little girl who misbehaves by indulging in her deviant thoughts and fraternizing with a stranger. Perrault's moral, then, is that virtuous girls should avoid strange men, and that any sexual desires are sinful, inappropriate, and extremely harmful to one's growth and development. Clearly, this ending contradicts Erikson's belief that sexual discovery is crucial in stage five, and that without it we cannot properly progress to stage six. Bettelheim elaborates on the new meaning that emerges from Perrault's changed ending:

> Since in response to such direct and obvious seduction Little Red Riding Hood makes no move to escape or fight back, either she is stupid or she wants to be seduced.... With these details, Little Red Riding Hood is changed from a naïve, and attractive young girl, who is induced to neglect Mother's warnings and enjoy herself in what she consciously believes to be innocent ways, into nothing but a fallen woman.[14]

Being a fallen woman was a label that no woman wanted, as she often found herself shunned from society, without friends, and unable to make a living unless she became a prostitute. Most fallen women either ended up poor and miserable, locked away in a mental institution, or dead. Like Little Red Riding Hood at the end of Perrault's version, a fallen woman is essentially dead to the world.

Like "The Story of Grandmother," Perrault's tale seems to imply that parents who don't wish to speak with their children regarding the topic of sex are setting them up for situations laden with frustration and anxiety. Such situations are obviously not the ideal ones in which children should mature, and often they result in psychological traumas that can last for many years and impact future relationships and decisions. And just in case his readers might not understand the tale's message, Perrault smacks them over the head with a moral stating, "Young lasses / Pretty, courteous and well-bred, / Do very wrong to listen to strangers."[15] In Perrault's tale it seems that Little Red Riding Hood must fail to learn so that Perrault's readers can learn from him instead.[16] Rather than being the learner, as she is in "The Story of Grandmother" and "Little Red Cap," this character of Little Red Riding Hood is simply the object in a cautionary tale. Perrault seems to favor violence as a way of instilling obedience, but the tale might succeed better if the mother had delivered the moral to her daughter at the beginning of her journey rather than at the end when Little Red Riding Hood has become nothing more than a sexual appetizer.

My problem with Perrault's version is that he doesn't allow Little Red Riding Hood the opportunity to make a choice. He makes her an object, and not a subject. In "The Story of Grandmother" the peasant girl *is* allowed to make a choice. She chooses to go outside, whereupon she runs home to escape the *bzou*. Having survived the *bzou's* advances, she learns her lesson and will certainly be more cautious the next time she cavorts in the forest. Much like the Grimms' version of the tale, however, Perrault depicts women (both Little Red Riding Hood and his implied audience) as needing to obey older, wiser men in order to stay safe. His Little Red Riding Hood has that right taken away from her. She doesn't assume the grandmother's role, nor does she remove her clothes like the young peasant girl in "The Story of Grandmother." Perhaps Perrault believes that sex should be devoid of flesh, blood, and good old fashioned skin against skin. His presentation of the coupling between Little Red Riding Hood and the wolf lacks passion and sexual discovery because there's no intimacy. They exchange words and then he gobbles her up. What Perrault doesn't realize, however, is that the chance to make independent choices is exactly what allows children to mature in the first place, for without these choices they cannot resolve the crises associated with stage five and continue on toward future stages of development.

What we have, then, at the end of Perrault's version is a tale in which Gothicism appears as dangerous and threatening; it acts as an inhibitor and brings nothing but harm to the main character. Rather than serving as an educational bridge between childhood and adulthood, the gothic elements in "Little Red Riding Hood" seem to suggest that women should not mature; instead, they should remain children forever so as to depend upon men for their guidance and survival.

Little Red Cap

Jacob and Wilhelm Grimm's version of Little Red Riding Hood, "Little Red Cap," also fosters an image in which women are inferior to men. Echoing the misogynistic undertones of Perrault's version, the Grimms' take on this classic fairy tale also promotes the idea that women will survive only if they rely on a man's cunning intellect and strength.[17] However, like Perrault's version of the tale, it moves away from the erotic elements found in "The Story of Grandmother" to celebrate more openly the concept of obedience and the consequences of misbehavior.

This theme of compliance is evident from the opening paragraph, as Little Red Cap's mother tells her daughter, "Walk properly like a good girl and don't leave the path or you'll fall down."[18] Here, the path symbolizes virtue and traditional values while the forest represents sin and wickedness. Even the wine she carries into the woods suggests conformity. Maria Tatar agrees with Erich Fromm's belief "that the bottle carried by Red Riding Hood on the way to her grandmother's house stands as a symbol of virginity, hence the warning not to break it."[19] This analysis highlights the tale's sexual undertones and, like Perrault's version, suggests the evils inherent in allowing an adolescent to explore her own feelings, especially when they relate to physical and emotional changes inside her body.

Little Red Cap's mother instructs her daughter to greet Granny when she arrives at the house, but not to look in all the corners. This command illustrates a prevalent belief that curiosity should not be satisfied, especially when it concerns adolescent emotions. To look into the corners and to investigate all those dark nooks and crannies would suggest a daringness, not to mention a heightened level of independent thinking, that unnerves adults because it illustrates they have less control over the child and are no longer the main influence. However, adolescents are naturally curious during stage five, mostly because of their newfound interests in relationships and peer groups. This process of self-discovery is crucial because it contributes to the formation of an adolescent's adult identity. To deny them such an experience is to impede their psychosocial and psychosexual development.

"Little Red Cap" is different from "The Story of Grandmother" and "Little Red Riding Hood" in that the mother warns the young girl before she leaves home and enters the forest. But the warning in this version is more of an obligatory throwaway than compassionate advice. Her mother orders Little Red Cap to stay on the path, but she never explains why the young girl should stay on the path, what she might discover if she veers off the path, or even what she should do if she does veer off the path and encounters something horrible and threatening. What her mother doesn't realize is that it's completely natural (and to be expected) for a pubescent girl to want to veer away from such a straight line of moral rigidity.

Bruno Bettelheim praises this version of the tale because he believes that Little Red Cap is indeed a young girl who not only struggles with puberty, but, because of her walk into the gothic forest, also experiences a conflict between the reality principle (her parents' teachings) and the pleasure principle (her budding sexuality). Bettelheim suggests that "Little Red Cap" succeeds in helping adolescents understand the ideas of temptation, mainly through the wolf, a character that "also represents all the asocial, animalistic tendencies within ourselves."[20] The idea of temptation arises at the very beginning of the tale when Little Red Cap promises to obey her mother, but as soon as she steps into the forest she strikes up a conversation with the seductive wolf. Having entered a new and unfamiliar landscape where she is now free from her mother's influence, this young girl begins to test her boundaries.

In the versions by Charles Perrault and the Brothers Grimm, the young girl tells the wolf where her grandmother lives, whereas in "The Story of Grandmother," the *bzou* knows exactly where to locate Grandmother's cottage. In the original tale the girl is polite and courteous, but she cannot be held responsible for the *bzou* killing the grandmother. Clearly, each girl's encounter with the wolf stems from her naivety in dealing with the male gender, but in "Little Red Riding Hood" and "Little Red Cap" her tendency to reveal too much information arises from a flirtatious and overconfident disposition that places her in danger and creates a traumatic situation from which she does not learn, but suffers instead.

Still, Little Red Cap's disobedience cannot be attributed fully to her own poor judgment. As the Grimms reveal, she "didn't know what a wicked beast he was, so she wasn't afraid of him."[21] As in "The Story of Grandmother" and "Little Red Riding Hood," there are two paths that the young girl can choose from. One path represents goodness while the other represents evil. Little Red Cap's mother desires her to follow the path of obedience and proper etiquette. That the girl does not recognize the wolf for what he is—basically a male predator that preys on naïve young women— is simply a testament to the negative effects that can result when parents refuse to communicate with their children.

Little Red Cap's mother has sent her daughter into the gothic forest with only a few words of caution. She seems to be more concerned with societal appearances and expectations than the personal safety of her own child. The mother's actions imply a thought process that seems to link complete honesty with strong temptation, namely that the more open and truthful a parent acts, the more tempted a child will become, eventually falling victim to those very same dangers from which the parent initially attempted to shield her child. Perhaps her mother thinks that by not saying anything about the wolf, she will eliminate the possibility of Little Red Cap meeting the wolf and falling under his influence.

Because the Grimms' version of the tale excludes the eroticism, Little Red Cap does not undress when she encounters the wolf at Grandma's house. In fact, she does not even climb into bed with the wolf. The physical distance that Little Red Cap places between herself and the wolf symbolizes a societal belief that young ladies should suppress their sexual feelings until they are adults and also display proper etiquette in the presence of men.

As in Perrault's tale, the wolf eats her up and then decides to follow the tasty meal with a quick nap. Again, the wolf's "eating" of Little Red Cap hints at oral sex, although in this case the experience is negative for the child. In fact, when Little Red Cap first enters her grandmother's house she says, "My goodness, I'm usually so glad to see grandmother. Why am I frightened today?"[22] Her body is giving her signs that hint at adolescent conflict and turmoil. And because her mother did not instruct her properly, Little Red Cap is not prepared for either the wolf's seduction of her in the forest (when he appeals to her girlish nature by convincing her to pick fresh flowers), or the instinct that now halts her at the doorway to grandmother's cottage and cautions her about entering.

As in Perrault's version of the tale, the Grimms present the forest as a gothic element, and the wolf is an extension of this environment. Through the wolf's charming demeanor and manipulation of Little Red Cap, the Grimms go beyond Perrault in illustrating how the forest (albeit the unknown) can seem quaint and charming, yet also harbor sinister people that wish to harm innocent young ladies who might allow themselves to be corrupted. Because she is in the midst of stage five, however, Little Red Cap falls prey to her thriving sexual desires. Subconsciously, she wants the wolf to seduce her. In her adolescent mind, his attention and interest validates her beauty and worth as a young woman. Little Red Cap knows she shouldn't listen to the wolf or allow his kind words to entrance her, but she desires to play a role she knows is forbidden because she wants to try on an adult persona.

This same dilemma occurs when she arrives at her grandmother's house and senses that something is amiss, but proceeds inside anyway to engage the wolf in conversation. Erikson explains that an adolescent "is afraid of being forced into activities in which he would feel exposed to ridicule or self-doubt.... He would rather act out shamelessly in the eyes of his elders, out of free choice, rather than be forced into activities which would be shameful in his own eyes or in those of his peers."[23] This conflict between good and bad behavior defines stage five, illustrating the various roles children test out when their bodies begin to develop, as well as the anxiety they often feel when adults expect them to assume certain responsibilities such as securing a part-time job. The gothic woods, which contain both beauty and ugliness, represent those same conflicting impulses that adolescents battle as they attempt to establish some sense of camaraderie and loyalty with their friends, often through cliques or peer groups, yet still maintain a sense of individuality and self-control.

Again, as in Perrault's "Little Red Riding Hood," the wolf's consumption of Little Red Cap symbolizes the childhood fear of being devoured. Unlike Perrault, however, the Grimms allow their main character to re-emerge from the belly of the wolf. Her disappearance into the wolf and subsequent redemption symbolize the birthing process, an act clearly associated with sexual intercourse, and one that will surely traumatize Little Red Cap given her near-death experience. The implication here seems to be that misbehaving and defying one's elders will lead to dire consequences, but so will sexual curiosity and indulgence. Little Red Cap survives her ordeal, and is able to leave the woods, but she does so at the expense of crippled identity formation and a traumatic experience that might cause her to fear intimacy and mistrust men.

At the end of the tale, we get the impression that Little Red Cap has actually regressed in her psychosocial and psychosexual development, restrained by a society that considers sexual maturity a forbidden subject rather than a natural progression in a person's life cycle. When adolescents associate sex with punishment or inferiority, the possibility arises that they'll dislike themselves for having sexual thoughts or for engaging in sexual behavior. Adolescents will then judge themselves too harshly, believing that perhaps they are abnormal, and that such self-inflicted anger can damage their self-identity and personality growth.

Whereas Perrault kills Little Red Riding Hood at the end of his story (a tactic directed toward his aristocratic audience), the Brothers Grimm choose to remind their child audience that we can learn from misbehavior by remembering to adhere to society's rules and norms. This message is conveyed by Little Red Cap at the end of the tale when she says to herself, "Never again will I leave the path and run off into the wood when my mother tells me not to."[24] The problem with this statement is that her epiphany comes after she has already suffered irreversible trauma by being devoured. Her subsequent interactions with any male predator, whether he is a wolf or a suitor, will render her scared and vulnerable, unable to form the kind of mature decisions that tend to accompany women who have been allowed to discover the joys of their own body and to resolve their individual crises during stage five.

The Brothers Grimm also introduce a hunter into the tale. While logging away in the forest, he hears the wolf snoring, which he believes to be the grandmother. The hunter, thinking Granny might suffer from sleep apnea, breaks down the door, discovers the wolf, slits open the beast's belly, and frees Little Red Cap and her grandmother. As in Perrault's version, the young girl is not allowed to make a choice. She remains helpless until the male hunter arrives to rescue her and her grandmother. By having a man charge into the cottage with his gun, the Brothers Grimm celebrate the father as the head of the family, as well as his accepted role as both a peacekeeper and a law-abiding citizen. This final scene implies that while men can be no-good seducers (the wolf), they can also be protectors (the hunter). Either way, it is in their nature to behave a certain way, and it is up to a woman to know what kind of a man she associates with and how she should behave in his presence.

It is no coincidence that the wolf seduces Little Red Cap in the woods while the hunter saves her inside a domestic setting. The message here suggests that women should never linger in the woods, and that they are most safe in a domestic setting where a man can watch over them. Through their ending, the Grimms make it clear that if women wish to survive in a male-dominated world, then they must adapt to their environment, and this can only be accomplished by having them suppress their adolescent desires and follow a model of behavior and etiquette that has been dictated by their parents and society.

The Grimms also present another ending in which the grandmother and Little Red Cap encounter a second wolf. Having learned her lesson the first time, Little Red Cap ignores the wolf on her way to grandmother's house. Upon arriving, she tells her grandmother about the wolf and they bolt the doors. The message here implies that men are relentless. Shrug them off and they will continue to follow, salivating with anticipation and bursting with sexual energy. But what is the value of being told to stay away from a wolf if he continues to maintain his pursuit and becomes more aggressive with each encounter? For Little Red Cap, it might be more beneficial to know how to manage the male predator once he invades her personal space. If she lives in constant fear of all men, then how can she be expected to one day establish and nurture an adult relationship?

In this second ending to the tale, Little Red Cap and her grandmother finally kill the other wolf by luring him off the roof with the scent of cooked sausages, whereupon he drowns in a trough. In essence, he is seduced by two women, much like he tried initially to seduce Little Red Cap. The use of smells in this scene also echoes the importance of pheromones to attract members of the opposite sex. While this addition to the tale hints further at the theme of sexual discovery, the Grimms still refuse to present this tense moment as an opportunity for Little Red Cap to engage in an honest and constructive dialogue with her grandmother. Such an opportunity represents a positive step in an adolescent's growth and development, and it is one that all children should be having not only with their parents, but also with themselves.

The problem with this alternate ending is that Little Red Cap is still not allowed to make a choice. Although she is not devoured by the wolf, her grandmother makes all the decisions and saves them both from the wolf. As in "The Story of Grandmother," Little Red Cap should now begin to assume the role of an adult so she can aid and protect her grandmother from the wolf, rather than vice-versa. Cristina Bacchilega emphasizes this point by suggesting that "just as the protagonist must enter and exit the older woman's house successfully, she must also negotiate the older woman's changing nature and death."[25] By having the grandmother survive, and then continue to make important choices, the Grimms suggest that women should mature through obedience and respect for their elders, not through sexual discovery and independent thinking. Little Red Cap basically stands on the sidelines as her grandmother outwits the wolf. Instead of being an active participant who helps to find a solution to this problem, she is just a passive observer. She is still a naïve child rather than an emerging adult.

The gothic elements in "Little Red Cap," as well as in Perrault's version, are portrayed as dangerous and threatening. The Grimms do not employ the gothic as a learning tool. They believe obedience and maturity should be learned by listening to one's parents rather than through chance occurrences and self-discovery. Indeed, the gothic elements in "Little Red Cap" are not viewed as vital components that help to form an integral part of everyone's life experiences. From this perspective, the tale fails as an odyssey of sexual discovery precisely because it preaches that children learn best by direct moral teachings when they actually learn best by personal, hands-on experience. Children should be put into situations where they can learn safely by trial and error. And it is this manner of trial and error that recurs continuously throughout adolescence, creating various roles and conflicts that allow us the necessary time to reflect on our emotions in a healthy way. Positive growth promotes fidelity to our bodies, and it celebrates all the physical and emotional processes associated with identity versus role confusion.

Journey Into the Woods

After reading the three different versions of Little Red Riding Hood, we understand how the theme of sexual discovery forms the crux of each story's conflict, whether it's between the peasant girl and the wolf, or even between the peasant girl and her grandmother. The tales' preoccupation with sex should not be ignored, for it's an important tool from which children and their parents can benefit. Even younger children, who understand that the tales warn them against talking to strangers, are aware on a subconscious level that there exist sexual undercurrents between the young girl and the wolf. Bettelheim stresses this idea:

> Most children view the sexual act primarily as an act of violence which one partner commits on the other.... Because this strange coincidence of opposite emotions characterizing the child's sexual knowledge is given body in "Little Red Riding Hood," the story holds a great unconscious attraction to children, and to adults who are vaguely reminded by it of their own childish fascination with sex.[26]

At the beginning of these three tales, the young women are not aware of the strong dynamic that exists between their inner emotions and the external world. And because the gothic elements in each tale do symbolize certain aspects of their inner emotions, these three young women, through their various interactions with these gothic elements, should be able to start the gradual process of questioning their own conflicted feelings and gaining a more secure comprehension about their own bodies. The girl in "The Story of Grandmother" does begin this process, as does Little Red Cape to a certain extent, but the same cannot be said of Little Red Riding Hood. Through her demise at the tale's end, Perrault makes it clear that it was considered taboo for a young woman to consider her budding sexuality, as well as the decisions that might accompany such an important process.

The peasant girl in "The Story of Grandmother," however, succeeds in tricking the wolf and then returning safely home. She played the role of a young, inexperienced lover, albeit awkwardly and with a fair amount of trepidation, and is now aware of her body's changes. In contrast, Little Red Cap (although she survives to exit the woods) is never given the opportunity to make conscious choices concerning her own pubescent body. While she might learn important lessons about misbehaving or not listening to her mother's advice, she is still unprepared to deal with the sexual identity that has already begun to impress itself upon her. Like Perrault's version, the Grimms' version chooses to stress ideas of conformity and domesticity rather than to view adolescence as a tumultuous period of growth in which parents should help their children mature by acting as facilitators instead of judges.

It is also interesting to note that the Little Red Riding Hood tale that best corresponds to modern theories about adolescent and psychological development, namely "The Story of Grandmother," is also the least well known, while the tales that stress conformity and obedience, namely "Little Red Riding Hood" and "Little Red Cap," are extremely popular. This observation is certainly ironic, and the irony itself seems to reveal the ignorance and naivety with which American/Western popular culture still views young women and their sexuality. It is a subject that few parents wish to explore with their children because many of them believe that by addressing sexual issues with their children they are actually promoting an interest in sexual activity. But by not being open and honest about sexuality, many parents actually put their children at risk to rebel against adult authority. These rebellious acts, whether physical or verbal, can often stall the growth process in adolescents by fueling a deep sense of identity confusion. These victims of identity confusion can often be found in their twenties, thirties, and sometimes even their forties, trying to escape the crises of stage five while wandering aimlessly in search of the love and intimacy that define stage six.

At some point during our lives, every one of us must travel into the woods. It is necessary and inevitable, and while it might not always be positive and rewarding, it is always a learning experience. We must travel outside of ourselves in order to gain a deeper wisdom and appreciation of how we function on the inside. Certainly, a journey into the woods will provide this insight, but prior knowledge, usually offered by our parents, can ease the often rocky transition between childhood and adulthood. In adolescence, we must assume different roles and weigh different options; we must suffer innumerable defeats and even feel at odds with our own bodies. For those adolescents who are beginning puberty, the story of a young girl who travels to her grandmother's house is a great asset in understanding Erikson's fifth stage of psychosocial development.

Given the public's apprehension toward sexual activity (including abstinence programs, teen pregnancies, contraception, and sexually transmitted diseases) the tales of Little Red Riding Hood are just as relevant today as they were hundreds of years ago. If more parents embraced their child's maturity and endorsed her journey into the woods, warning her of specific dangers and allowing her to make personal choices, then perhaps more children might enter the woods with determination and understanding. To do so would allow them to shed their innocence more freely while crafting intelligent decisions that can aid them throughout the rest of their lives.

5

An Awfully Big Commitment: Intimacy and Isolation in *Peter and Wendy*

"All children, except one, grow up"

Like many adults, I miss those idle days when nap time was mandatory and any stress during my day was caused by nothing more than bad dreams or misplaced toys. To grow up is to endure a constant tug-of-war between innocence and experience. Just ask any hero in children's literature. For some, maturity is a concept that pushes them closer to death; for others, it's a rite of passage that replaces simplicity with responsibility. Unfortunately, maturity is unavoidable. Yes, it brings about joy, fulfillment, and happiness, but it is also causes misery, pain, and frustration. Seen from one angle, it's a dazzling rainbow that stretches across a vast blue sky; from another it's an oily puddle choked with drab, muted colors. It seems the older we are, the less interested we are in maturity and the more we crave nostalgia and the comfort of our own memories.

Why is it that adults often wish to be children and children often wish to be adults? Why is it that children want days and weeks to rush forward while adults grip their faded memories like a tired swimmer clinging to a buoy in the middle of the ocean? Perhaps because children don't seem to understand the concept of time, and thus have no reason to fear it. Children want to live in an adult world, but they want to continue playing by childhood rules, and the reality that this cannot happen is usually hurtful. Adults, however, are sadly aware that time is constant and indifferent, and so we feel powerless in its presence. For children, time is an imaginary friend promising countless adventures; for adults, it is a familiar acquaintance that we know is there, but would rather not acknowledge.

As adults, we wear responsibility like a cloak, wanting to shake it off periodically, but unable to loosen the clasp. For us, always striving to create some semblance of meaning in our temporary lives, the future is rife with flashes of clarity that help to propel us toward future stages of psychosocial and psychosexual development. As we gain new ideas and theories, so, too, does the past become a shimmering haze, slipping out of our grasp like a shadow that refuses to be caught. For despite those needed moments of peace and tranquility that punctuate the intensity of our daily lives, we still understand that time is a second cousin to death, as securely hidden, but ever-present, as a clock ticking away inside some ferocious alligator.

Left alone to fester, the concept of time will breed anxiety and apprehension, and its effects on people can sometimes be disastrous, not just physically but also emotionally. At some point in life, typically during early adulthood, many people will suffer, to some varying degree, from the Peter Pan Syndrome: they will refuse to commit; they will refuse to settle down; and they will refuse to grow up. While this apathy toward maturity can center on one's job, finances, or family issues, it most often surfaces in our adult relationships. Clearly, being in a relationship mandates a certain level of maturity in order to ensure its success, and some people are either unwilling or not ready to cross that rugged terrain between adolescence and early adulthood. They fear opening up to their partner; they fear revealing their own quirks and insecurities; and they fear the danger in allowing someone else to infiltrate their own private stock of personal memories. For some, these looming concerns can also raise inevitable questions about sex and marriage, as well as the possibility of having and caring for children.

To be sure, many of these adult themes and ideas might seem out of place in a work of children's literature, but J.M. Barrie's 1911 novel *Peter and Wendy* is an engaging story about adult relationships and the conflicts associated with them. While children can enjoy the novel for its portrayal of Neverland (which functions as a transitional/liminal space) and the countless adventures to be had there, adults can recognize, in the characters of Peter, Wendy and Captain Hook, the struggles inherent in wanting to be in an adult relationship, yet also wanting to remain single and assert one's exclusivity. The character of Peter Pan represents the tension that exists between carefree childhood and responsible adulthood. While adults relate to Peter Pan in their envious desire to experience the same freedom of youth that he enjoys on a daily basis, they also pity his inability to establish intimacy with other people.

If Peter is an adult trapped in a child's body, Wendy is certainly a child trapped in an adult's body, a consequence of both her gender and her Victorian upbringing. During the nineteenth century, girls were expected to act prim and proper, helping their mother with household chores and preparing themselves for a life of domestic servitude. Often, girls were not provided with the same quality of education as boys, and any "playtime" was usually a form of "training" for their future roles as wife, mother, and caregiver. Wendy certainly acts the role of proper Victorian woman, acting out motherly duties with the Lost Boys, telling bedtime stories, and cleaning their underground home. Yet she knows these roles are an extension of playtime and make-believe that allow her to indulge in Neverland's countless games and adventures. And while Wendy does enjoy being a child, she also seems to appreciate the inevitability of growing up and the ways in which it will lead to more complex relationships. Captain Hook, however, seems to represent those adults that have lost the ability to laugh and smile, and the novel suggests that this is because Hook lacks not only female companionship, but intimacy on any level.

Reading *Peter and Wendy*, one understands how the three main characters—Peter, Wendy, and Captain Hook—symbolize the pitfalls and obstacles of entering into an adult relationship. The love triangle among them sets out three different ways of reacting to the demands of an adult relationship. Neverland, like many relationships, is a place of banishment as well as escape. Alison Lurie explains that "Never-Never land is the world of childhood imagination; it is also a refuge from the adult universe of rules and duties."[1] Neverland is a place where people are liable to lose their identities if they don't choose to move past the present moment. Such movement affords them the opportunity to reflect on the past and contemplate the future. Thus, the island is meant to be a temporary retreat, and not a final destination. In terms of psychosocial and psychosexual development, Neverland seems to be a transitory place that prepares one for the trials of early adulthood.

In *Peter and Wendy*, the gothic elements contained in Neverland (such as pirates, alligators, poisonings, and decapitations) heighten the novel's conflicts and help to illustrate the themes of intimacy, isolation, and sexual repression that affect the novel's main characters and also help to shape the story's action. These gothic elements, while seemingly innocent and childlike in the context of Neverland, echo much of the anger and frustration that are integral in maintaining a healthy, personal relationship. Barrie's use of Gothicism, fused together with Neverland's exclusive vacation package of lagoons, fairies, and Lost Boys, reveals the tug and pull that adults feel when they prepare to share part of their lives and identity with another person. While obviously focusing its attention on the joys of childhood, *Peter and Wendy* also employs these gothic elements to remind us how difficult and stressful adult relationships can become when we allow ourselves to love another person. By generating fear and horror, these gothic elements reflect the dangers inherent in establishing intimacy, as well as the anxieties that often result when we attempt to maintain healthy levels of commitment. In essence, the gothic elements in *Peter and Wendy* lead us toward a mature understanding of the different ways in which identity and personality development are vital factors in the formation and longevity of our adult relationships.

Intimacy versus Isolation

At some point in our lives we usually feel the need to move beyond the comfort zone of family and friends, not simply to engage in adolescent love and frivolity, but to saddle up commitment and take it out for a long run, holding onto the reins as we speed along some winding path toward a dark future. Such is the nature of adult relationships. They are exhilarating, yet scary; they are frustrating, yet promising. While some relationships may blossom into lifelong bonds of devotion, others collapse under the weight of so many hopes and expectations. When the latter happens, the emotional danger that results from a debilitating relationship is a gradual withdrawal from intimacy followed by a subsequent exile into isolation. These two extremes are the strengths and antipathies in Erikson's stage six of psychosocial development, which he terms "Intimacy versus Isolation."

This stage typically affects those of us in early adulthood, usually between twenty and forty years of age. This is the period in life when we gain a sense of our own mortality and begin to seek out relationships that might prove to be more fulfilling and durable than those we chased down as rambunctious teenagers. As we open our minds to the possibility of marriage and commitment, so, too, do we expand our radius of significant relations to include lovers and sexual partners. When I use the term "intimacy," I don't mean to imply that its definition in this context only relates to a sexual nature. In many of his texts, Erikson emphasizes that an intimate relationship also presents shared trust between partners, proper care for offspring during all stages of development, and joint management in regulating the constant cycles of work, fun, and, of course, sexual intercourse.

In this sense, intimacy involves physical and emotional desires, both of which contribute to a healthy personality. Having intimacy in our lives also contributes to further identity formation. Erikson reminds us that "only a firm sense of inner identity marks the end of the adolescent process and is a condition for further and truly individual maturation."[2] If we enter an adult relationship without understanding our own personal feelings and behaviors, then we run the risk of corrupting the current relationship, as well as all future ones. And not just personal relationships either. Because as we move into early adulthood, and continue moving into our forties and fifties, we must also learn to share parts of our lives with not only our lovers, but also with our friends, family, and coworkers. Gaining a sense of community is necessary for helping us cope with the crises we undergo as we progress through early adulthood. As we enter into adult relationships, caring for past generations while ensuring the survival of future ones, we depend more and more on those around us with whom we have already established intimacy and trust.

Sometimes, though, intimacy is an albatross hanging around our necks. We all want to feel loved and appreciated; we all want romance, intimacy, and the fulfillment of physical desires. We want to roam the landscape until we find our special prince and princess, and then live happily ever after in a towering castle, basking in domestic bliss. But this sugarcoated wish is just another ideal that shrivels up in the presence of reality. In the real world, relationships require patience and dedication. They survive on a large amount of sweat, blood, and tears, not to mention useful clichés. Ideally, we begin a relationship because we hope to forge and share crucial life experiences with someone who not only understands our wild assortment of trials and tribulations, but accepts them, as well. Maybe even appreciates them, too. But it's clear that a healthy relationship cannot survive without both participants having achieved a firm sense of their own identity as well as a healthy personality. In his explanation of stage-six characteristics, Erikson supports Marie Jahoda's definition of what constitutes a healthy personality in an adult, namely that it "*actively masters* his environment, shows a certain *unity of personality*, and is able to *perceive* the world and himself *correctly*—it is clear that all of these criteria are relative to the child's cognitive and social development."[3] Yet again, we see how the successful completion of previous stages of development can lead to the successful completion of future stages, thus ensuring we possess the ability to develop loving and intimate relationships with a wide radius of significant relations.

It is important to remember that loving someone can sometimes be a selfish and impetuous act. Often, we will love another person so we can feel needed and wanted in return. To love someone is to demand that they validate us with their own personal stamp of approval. For some of us, to enter into an adult relationship is a narcissistic process in which we strive to define and understand our own identity by interpreting the various ways in which our lover reacts and responds to our own behaviors and idiosyncrasies. In a way, this process is an adult version of what psychologists refer to as a "startling spectacle," that pivotal moment when a child first looks into a mirror and realizes that the reflection is not just another person, but is the child himself. Basically, the child sees himself as an individual, and somewhere in his spongy skull he begins to associate "I" with his reflected image. Many adults continue to experience this "startling spectacle" as they move through later stages of psychosocial development. Instead of a mirror, however, they use another person who can now verbalize all those varying degrees of denial and acceptance that tend to accompany commitment and intimacy.

In *Peter and Wendy*, Peter Pan demonstrates this narcissistic tendency through his constant desire to hear stories about himself and his many adventures. He wants to hear Wendy and the Lost Boys preach about his strength and greatness, touting him as the most fearless and courageous person in all of Neverland. Because Peter Pan lives in the present, oblivious to the past and indifferent about the future, he cannot establish a firm sense of identity. Although Peter is incapable of love, his seeming projection of intimacy and friendship toward Wendy and her brothers, as well as toward the Lost Boys, is merely flashy showmanship that reveals his shallow self-interests and glaring lack of human complexity.

Nevertheless, Peter Pan does exhibit moments of weakness and curiosity that suggest an underlying struggle between wanting always to remain a boy and wanting to share intimacy in an adult relationship. Throughout *Peter and Wendy*, Barrie creates a love triangle involving Peter, Wendy, and Captain Hook. Their interactions with each other, ranging from tragic and comical to romantic and frustrating, echo the same pitfalls that affect every adult relationship. Even the healthiest ones.

Still, many of us continue to believe that we will find the perfect relationship, that our blessed union will be the exception to the rule. This ideal is a leftover wish from childhood, corrupted by hormones and adolescence, and it does not necessarily disappear as we move into early adulthood. In fact, this transparent ideal can damage our own idea of what constitutes an adult relationship, often instilling us with false hopes and expectations that project failure before the relationship even has a chance to begin. This failure then leads to isolation, which is a result of, "the incapacity to take chances with one's identity by sharing true intimacy."[4] Like Peter Pan, we want so much to fly away from our struggles and responsibilities, refusing to plant our feet on solid ground lest we fall down and bruise our egos. We sometimes avoid experiences that will allow us to master our own environments, and this refusal to embrace intimacy, on any level, will often lead to self-absorption and character flaws such as anger, indifference or timidity. These powerful emotions can then hinder our impending identity formation and personality development.

To maintain an adult relationship is to walk a thin line, one that shifts its position from day to day. While some of us cannot find this line, others refuse to see it, and so walk their life in a constant never-ending circle. Some of us even expect that another person will take us in their arms and carry us forward, absolving us of the effort and accountability that we know are necessary to sustain a healthy adult relationship. Still others try to erase this line so they can simply draw another in the hope that it might prove more manageable and accommodating. In *Peter and Wendy*, Peter Pan draws his own imaginary line so he can separate childhood from adulthood, so he can separate rewarding experiences from impulsive moments. Peter's imaginary line encircles the island of Neverland, and so it is there we begin our fantastic journey.

"To be wrecked on an island"

J.M. Barrie was a lover of islands, so it's no surprise that Neverland itself, symbolic of a child's imagination, is an island, set apart from the mainland of adult responsibilities. In his critical introduction to *Peter Pan and Other Plays*, Peter Hollindale remarks that Barrie, in his own preface to R.M. Ballantyne's *The Coral Island*, wrote that "to be born is to be wrecked on an island."[5] We must remember that children, and even adolescents to some degree, are isolated from the adult world. They have not yet formed their own identities, and so they mimic and repeat the words and actions of all those around them. Children use the power of their imaginations to sort out and understand the real world and all of its crises and obstacles. To be a child is to be stranded on Neverland, enjoying the adventures of childhood and adolescence until, eventually, we become conscious of a faraway land somewhere on the other side of the ocean. It tempts us with commitment, money, and a newfound sense of accountability, convincing us to leave our island home, to wade across channels, and to swim across unknown depths on our way to another important identity that helps to define and to shape our personalities.

Barrie's use of the word "wrecked" suggests the trauma and intensity associated with birth. If one can liken the suspension of an infant in amniotic fluid to floating on a tranquil ocean, then the violence of the birth process is the same as being washed ashore on a desert island. In this sense, the island is a home away from home (the second "home" being a fulfilled state of adulthood). Certainly, especially as it pertains to Wendy and her brothers, the island is nothing more than a temporary refuge. Barrie seems to be reminding us that as much as we cling to childhood, it inevitably slips through our fingers and disappears, relegated to a hazy cloud of memories. And though we certainly cherish all our years stranded on those tropical shores, we must always remember that those of us who wish to engage in adult relationships and share intimacy must eventually learn to swim away from our own Neverland.

In literature, water tends to symbolize an awakening or a rebirth, so it makes sense that Neverland is an island, and that to gain one's identity and progress through early adulthood the characters must cross an immense body of water. Of the three main characters in *Peter and Wendy*, however, Wendy Darling is the only one who succeeds in completing this necessary transition. She understands that Neverland is a point of refuge between childhood and adulthood, and unlike Peter Pan and Captain Hook she does not become entranced by and dependent upon repetitive days or the island's endless adventures. While Peter Pan and Captain Hook delight in their daily battles and taunts, the novel's constant stream of dangerous escapades only further illustrates Neverland's absence of stable and rewarding relationships, and Barrie demonstrates this point by replacing genuine emotion with an overabundance of physical exploits. Eventually, though, having interacted with and learned from the island's gothic elements, Wendy is able to move away from Neverland and begin her own journey through early adulthood.

To remain always on such an island is to spend our lives groping randomly for any identity that fits us. We become jaded in the process and experience intense moments of sexual repression, much like Peter Pan and Captain Hook. Both characters share more in common than they would care to admit, such as an inability to reveal personal feelings as well as an unwavering reluctance to progress toward future stages of psychosocial development. Peter Pan and Captain Hook have not yet learned that while Neverland is an escape from reality into a dream world, it can only be a temporary escape.

Peter himself echoes this idea when he relates the story of how his mother barred the windows and forgot about him, replacing him at home with another little boy. His story resonates with readers because these themes of abandonment and unrequited love reflect major fears that often constitute being in an adult relationship. An underlying point of Peter's cautionary tale seems to be that a visit to Neverland is attractive and pleasing so long as it is short-lived. This should be a strong reminder that while we all engage in immature behavior from time to time, refusing to act like responsible adults, to do so over a considerable length of time risks sabotaging our own personal relationships. If we accumulate enough of these damaged emotions, we're liable to wreck ourselves on our own private Neverland. There, we will likely miss out on important opportunities to learn from our mistakes and to enrich ourselves with rewarding relations.

Although there are three main characters in *Peter and Wendy*, the island of Neverland is a fourth major character of importance. For Wendy, Neverland is a transitory location where she can test out the waters of early adulthood. Here, on the island, she can practice being a mother and a wife before she must return home to Victorian England and fulfill her social expectations as an "angel in the house."[6] For Peter Pan, the island is akin to a Fountain of Youth, enabling him to escape the real world and live in a fantasy land where he can assume the role of the hero and act out adventures of his own choosing. If Peter Pan is an asexual boy afraid of intimacy, then Captain Hook is surely a sexual figure who longs for companionship. Like Peter Pan, though, he remains fixated on childhood adventures. Captain Hook represents various adolescent fears concerning adulthood, namely the tirades of anger, the profound moments of loneliness, and the seeming absence of fun and excitement that Hook lacks in his own life, and for which he envies Peter Pan.

In *Peter and Wendy*, Neverland becomes a training ground for early adulthood. Those of us still trapped in previous stages run the risk of making childish decisions to solve adult problems, a serious detriment when trying to negotiate a mature relationship. To spend time on Neverland is to learn how to survive all the dangers and obstacles inherent in establishing intimacy. Even though Neverland represents a child's world, its lessons still carry over to adult relationships. We sometimes need to perform childish actions, and even remember childhood emotions, in order to identify our faults and imperfections. Regressing to a former stage often reminds us why we needed to leave that stage in the first place. The emotional distance that separates how we *do* behave from how we *should* behave will often reinvigorate our attempts to resolve individual crises, which, in turn, will prompt us to look ahead toward future stages of development rather than seeking solace in past ones.

By exploring the terrain of Neverland, Wendy is able to sort through her own personal conflicts such as relinquishing playtime and having to assume female responsibilities. As a result of these self-reflections, she is able to understand her need to leave Neverland at the end of the novel so she can return home to accept adulthood. Nell Boulton tells us that Barrie wanted "to map out the mind of the child, which he envisaged in terms of the imaginative territory of Neverland."[7] In the novel Barrie discusses the zigzag lines imprinted on a child's mind, which he suggests are roads on Neverland, and therefore representative of the different paths we might choose in our lives as we develop emotionally and physically. By using the island as a metaphor for the child's imagination, Barrie illustrates how the act of maturing into early adulthood, and thus progressing through Erikson's various stages, can be a thrilling yet dangerous experience when we must hike across the unpredictable terrain of Neverland:

> Coral reefs and rakish-looking craft in the offing, and savages and lonely lairs, and gnomes who are mostly tailors, and caves through which a river runs, and princes with six elder brothers, and a hut fast going to decay, and one very small old lady with a hooked nose. It would be an easy map if that were all, but there is also first day at school, religion, fathers, the round pond, needlework, murders, hangings, verbs that take the dative, chocolate pudding day, getting into braces, say ninety-nine, threepence for pulling out your tooth yourself..., it is all rather confusing, especially as nothing will stand still.[8]

Barrie's description seems to portray Neverland as a fun, dangerous, and chaotic environment, a setting where energy runs high and there is no sense of structure or order. Indeed, Neverland is a collection of childhood fears and wonders, a melting pot of Gothicism (murders, hangings, and pirates) and paradise (coral reefs, chocolate pudding, and rivers). The word "confusing" is the perfect adjective to describe the way children often feel when they consider not only the adult world, but also the struggles they experience when trying to move beyond family relations so they can establish a new sense of identity with peer groups, teachers, and significant others who can assist them in practicing the art of intimacy and love.

We should not forget, however, that children do not search for Neverland. It searches for them, and that is the only way that "anyone may sight those magic shores."[9] This idea strengthens the argument that the numerous transitory phases necessary for each stage of our identity development are not just phases that we can simply plan out and organize. Certainly, many people want to grow quickly and rush through the entire maturation process, eager to hurry past all the confusions and frustrations that line each complicated stage. But the beauty of growing old and progressing through each of Erikson's stages is the subtle way in which they sneak up on us when we're not looking, as sudden and shocking as a strange boy flying into our bedroom in the middle of the night. As readers, we understand that the island of Neverland summons Wendy because she is now ready to explore her own feelings and begin that important journey toward early adulthood.

As exciting as Neverland seems, however, we must always remember the various dangers that lurk on the island. Neverland is a foil to the real world, and the gothic elements contained therein represent the pain and heartache through which we must suffer if we want to develop our identities and become mature adults. Fred Botting suggests, "Gothic shadows flicker among representations of cultural, familial and individual fragmentation, in uncanny disruptions of the boundaries between inner being, social values and concrete reality."[10] Put simply, because Neverland is a foil to the adult world, it must therefore contain the same sense of anger, hurt, and loneliness as the adult world; it must pulse with the same sense of pervading gloom and darkness that affects all of us throughout different moments in our lives, although certainly to a lesser extreme given its childlike atmosphere. Even Barrie alludes to this idea when he writes, "Odd things happen to all of us on our way through life without our noticing for a time that they have happened."[11] Thus, to navigate through the emotional and physical hazards of pirates, hangings, murders, and swordfights is also to learn about the various conflicts inherent in adult relationships. Encountering these dark moments might be painful and traumatic, but these experiences will help to show us the different ways we can solve conflicts and fix the instability that threatens to disrupt our own sense of identity, as well as our interactions with significant relations.

Wendy Darling

As a young girl on the verge of womanhood, Wendy is ready and eager to explore her sexual limitations. As a Victorian woman she is expected to become a dutiful wife, tend house, and raise many children. Inside a domestic setting is precisely where Wendy belongs, according to her society. Slightly, one of the Lost Boys, echoes this sentiment later in the novel when Wendy arrives on Neverland. When Curly says, "Let us carry [Wendy] down into the house," Slightly replies, "Aye, that is what one does with ladies."[12] Even on Neverland there are still gender boundaries and expectations, clearly delineated roles that suggest a lingering adult presence. However, it is while living in Neverland that Wendy is able to move past mere role-playing and actually become, at least temporarily, a wife and a mother. More importantly, she does so within an environment that is not associated with other adults who might interfere with her identity crises and personality development.

In fact, Peter appeals to Wendy's growing desire for independence, and also her motherly instincts, when he first lures her to Neverland. He says, "How we should all respect you.... You could tuck us into bed at night.... And you could darn our clothes, and make pockets for us. None of us has any pockets."[13] Peter Pan verbally seduces Wendy with promises of respect and authority, the two main values that children and adolescents covet because they see and envy these two values in the adults that surround them. From a child's standpoint, a trip to Neverland is captivating because children do not receive respect, whether from adults or even from other children. Also, they possess no authority, needing constant guidance from their parents and unable to live independently. It seems natural, then, that a child like Wendy would want to travel to an exotic location, far away from home, where she can indulge in the recognition of being a provider and a leader.

From a teenager's standpoint, the attention Wendy will receive in Neverland boosts her ego. She wants to be noticed, and this desire to be recognized is typical of teenagers, mostly because teenagers "are immediate and everything is *about* them. Egocentrism is necessary for them to develop into compassionate, empathic beings—the better you know yourself, the better you know yourself in relation to the world around you."[14] Wendy might fuss and complain, but she enjoys the Lost Boys' constant attention. She likes managing a household and tending to the daily needs of her "children." In assuming these more mature roles and responsibilities, Wendy also realizes more fully the challenges and difficulties we all must endure if we wish to move past adolescence by establishing a personal identity separate from that of our parents, peers, and partners.

Wendy assumes many different roles throughout the novel. At home, in London, she pretends to be her own mother, and even dances with joy when John, pretending to be the father, validates Wendy's role-playing by declaring that she is indeed a mother. These childish acts at home, and later in Neverland, help Wendy to understand the feelings and responsibilities that surface when we reach early adulthood and must therefore become independent and self-fulfilling. Erikson explains this psychosocial development in *The Life Cycle Completed*:

Young adults emerging from the adolescent search for a sense of identity can be eager and willing to fuse their identities in mutual intimacy and to share them with individuals who, in work, sexuality, and friendship promise to prove complementary. One can often be "in love" or engage in intimacies, but the intimacy now at stake is the capacity to commit oneself to concrete affiliations which may call for significant sacrifices and compromises.[15]

The first step in this process is Wendy's make-believe performance in London with her brother, John. While this performance lacks the sexual tension and energy that will eventually arise between Wendy and Peter Pan, the process of assuming a parental role nevertheless prepares Wendy for her soon to be job as both mother to the Lost Boys and husband to Peter Pan.

Once Peter arrives in Wendy's bedroom, the sexual tension skyrockets as the two children participate in a courting period that exists mainly on casting glances and engaging in flirtatious asides. Obviously attracted to Peter, Wendy offers to give him a kiss, and his bewilderment at her proposal reveals Peter's own innocence and inexperience. When Peter then offers to kiss Wendy, she replies, "If you please," and Barrie tells us that "she made herself rather cheap by inclining her face toward him."[16] Already we can see a natural desire in Wendy, and even in Peter, to form a partnership, to share stories and avoid the dangers inherent in becoming alone and isolated. Even though he does not wish to grow up, Peter's constant bragging about his adventures and his control over the Lost Boys reveals a desire to surround himself with other people whom he can impress on a daily basis. Whereas Peter's desire for intimacy centers on friendship and self-validation, Wendy's desire seems to center on her dream of establishing a rewarding marriage and then raising a happy family. Unlike Peter Pan, Wendy seeks an identity that she knows is part of her future: loving partner and caregiver. Practicing this role in a familiar and comfortable setting, namely her own "house," perhaps instills in her a sense of confidence that renders her performance on Neverland, which is unfamiliar territory, less awkward and stressful.

This idea makes sense when we consider that all during childhood and adolescence we tend to role-play in front of people, and within environments, that offer us a sense of security. These identity trials, often in front of parents and siblings, performed in cramped bedrooms or spacious backyards, provide us with the self-assurance we require to move beyond those familiar boundaries and instigate new identity trials with new radii of significant relations. As we mature into early adulthood and expand our own radii, much like Wendy does throughout *Peter and Wendy*, we tend to discover within ourselves new thoughts and dreams, additional hopes and fears, and a thriving desire for intimacy in which we gravitate toward a succession of lovers like planets revolving in orbit.

Wendy's initial flight to Neverland is an important step in her blossoming sexuality and identity development. Barrie describes the children's inability to navigate around the clouds, and how they constantly collide with them: "Indeed they were constantly bumping. They could now fly strongly, though they still kicked far too much; but if they saw a cloud in front of them, the more they tried to avoid it, the more certainly did they bump into it."[17] Their awkwardness at flying echoes the performance of a toddler who is learning how to walk and keeps crashing into the furniture; yet it also echoes the uncertain movements of a teenager who is trying to emulate the actions and behaviors of those around her so as to better understand her own identity.

The flight to Neverland becomes a transitory phase in which Wendy becomes comfortable with her own body through the act of flying. Soaring through the air, she experiences a sense of independence at leaving her parents for probably the first time in her life, and she also matures by having to fend for herself and her brothers. That Wendy and her brothers are high up in the atmosphere signifies an emotional, as well as a physical, rise from their lower positions in London as children who needed to be supervised and disciplined by adults. Now, flying through the night sky, Wendy is liberated from the constraints of her Victorian upbringing and is free to make her own decisions. This surge of confidence and self-esteem is what allows her to later navigate through those obstacles on Neverland that pose a threat to her survival and identity development.

The act of flying also suggests a sexual awakening in Wendy, as Nell Boulton explains Feud's idea that "dreams of flying represent wish-fulfillment phantasies of sexual pleasure. However, as Wendy discovers, flying can be dangerous. Her flight exposes her to the sexual jealousy of Tinkerbell, who encourages one of the lost boys, Tootles, to shoot her down."[18] Female jealousy from Tinkerbell thus results in attempted murder as Tinkerbell assumes the role of a jealous lover who obviously feels spurned and rejected by Peter's interest in Wendy. Barrie tells us how Tinkerbell "hated [Wendy] with the fierce hatred of a very woman."[19] Like many people involved in an intimate relationship, Tinkerbell feels both insecure and insignificant in the presence of Peter and Wendy. She feels pushed off to the side and forgotten, relegated to the outer limits of a circle through which she once wandered freely. The theme of jealousy is one to which we can all relate, and while most of us will at some point act on our own jealous feelings to varying degrees, we do not take it to the extreme by shooting arrows into people who vie for our lover's attention. This episode does remind us, though, that sexuality can be dangerous for either gender, and that to enter into an adult relationship is to take certain risks on both a physical and an emotional level. This idea offers yet another implicit argument in favor of gothic elements as teaching tools in both children's and young adult literature.

Then again, we might interpret Tootles' act of shooting down Wendy as a subconscious attempt by Tinkerbell to keep Neverland free of Victorian femininity and domesticity, both of which Wendy certainly represents. Each new boundary that we cross during our life presents new obstacles, and in literature these obstacles often take the shape of gothic elements, such as the ones that Wendy encounters on Neverland. Without these gothic elements intruding upon our daily lives we cannot hope to progress toward future stages of psychosocial and psychosexual development. These encounters with Gothicism are crucial in presenting us with a strong sense of reality that is sorely lacking in the various performances we act out playfully as children and adolescents. Gothic elements teach us how to handle miscommunication, jealousy, anger, or confusion. To overcome these obstacles can offer us a sense of accomplishment and pride, boosting our self-esteem and allowing us to feel more secure and open in our intimate relationships.

Tinkerbell fears isolation from Peter, yet by planning Wendy's death she isolates herself even further by angering him. We see here how isolation arises through a gradual withdrawal from love, as well as from an inability to deal adequately with issues of communication once we are involved in a relationship. Tinkerbell's malice toward Wendy symbolizes the anger and jealousy we often feel in intimate relationships, whether sexual or not. And yet such feelings are important because in struggling with our own conflicted emotions we can then understand more intensely the nature of commitment, as well as the values that shape and define each of our intimate relationships, however different each one of them might be. Of course, Tinkerbell herself never gains such an understanding, but her reaction at being banished by Peter, as well as Peter's own anger at the situation, provides an opportunity for each one of us to gain a deeper understanding of intimacy and commitment through our own personal observations of Tinkerbell's mistakes and the subsequent repercussions from which she suffers.

Wendy survives her near-death experience because the arrow strikes against the acorn button Peter gave her in the bedroom before they flew off to Neverland. Peter says, "It is the kiss I gave her. It has saved her life."[20]

Here, Barrie emphasizes the sexual bond that has developed between Peter and Wendy, although they both cannot define this bond because they understand it purely on a subconscious level. Wendy is still a child, as her graceless flight into Neverland illustrates. Her learning to fly, as well as her dangerous episode with Tinkerbell, reminds us that while newfound independence and sexuality may often be thrilling and exciting, these experiences also arrive with issues of competition, jealousy, and anger. In addition, Wendy's arrival on the island alerts her to the fact that she is no longer safe at home under the watchful eyes of her parents. The potential for danger exists and she must be aware of everything around her. She must learn to rely on herself.

Like Wendy weaving through the clouds, we must also learn how to avoid those gothic elements that can cripple communication and misplace our love. Had Peter not left Wendy all alone up in the sky, then perhaps she might have been safe and uninjured. The lesson seems to be that when we find ourselves in committed relationships, it's much better to navigate through gothic elements as a unified couple rather than as an isolated, solitary figure that bumps into them with such awkwardness and hesitancy that we betray our lack of confidence. The complication, of course, is that Peter cannot offer Wendy a commitment because he is too immature himself. Eventually, having interacted with Neverland's gothic elements, Wendy will realize this truth about Peter Pan, and this clarity will reveal to her the importance in using reason and emotion to choose a mature partner.

Once she arrives on Neverland, Wendy settles into a new domestic life that is reminiscent of the one she just left in London. She remains inside the house that Peter and the Lost Boys build for her, cooking and cleaning and telling the children stories. She enjoys living in the small cottage that has "gay windows all about, / With roses peeping in... / And babies peeping out."[21] Barrie tells us that Wendy spends most of her time underground, which implies that this domestic environment is stifling and constrictive, though Wendy does not realize this because she is still entranced by the beauty and newness of Neverland. For Wendy, the time spent on the island allows her to live an adult life while also allowing her the opportunity to revert back to childhood whenever she wishes. She can practice being a wife and a mother, and if she feels insecure or perhaps fails at a task, then she can simply claim that the game is imaginary in the first place. Such is the advantage of pretending, and in his introduction to *Peter and Wendy*, Peter Hollindale explains the importance of role-playing in the novel:

Wendy is the child playing adult roles and games, and in her the incipient adult and mother already control the child; Peter is the child playing adult roles also, but in him the child is inviolable, separate and free. For Peter being "father" is fun only if he knows that it is not and will not be true. The children are playing games, and the stories about them are also a game, played out in the no man's land between child and adult worlds.[22]

Unlike Peter, who is forgetful and often confuses reality with make-believe, Wendy understands, even when she doesn't want to, that life on Neverland is only a game. For instance, when Peter and the Lost Boys ask Wendy to be their mother, she replies, "I am only a little girl. I have no real experience."[23] Nevertheless, she treasures her new role and is content to spend her days acting a dutiful mother who watches over her boys.

For Wendy, Neverland provides her with experience. It is her first real relationship, albeit free of sexual activity, and it proves beneficial to her maturation process because she knows it is only temporary. The child in Wendy is beginning to diminish, fading away into a distant memory as the adult in her grows stronger, fueled by raging hormones and the natural desire to seek out new radii of significant relations. Because Peter separates his child persona from his adult persona, however, he can never make that same transition into early adulthood, nor does he want to make such a transition.

Unlike Wendy, Peter can never improve his future relationships because he is incapable of reflecting on his past ones. For Peter Pan, each relationship, whether it's with Wendy or one of the Lost Boys, is not a chance to grow and mature. Rather, each relationship is an opportunity to engage in a series of thrilling and daring adventures. These adventures yield material rewards instead of emotional ones, allowing Peter to maintain his cavalier attitude about growing up and falling in love. This attitude is an enormous shield Peter holds up to protect himself from being hurt. In pretending he doesn't care about adult feelings, Peter only strengthens the loneliness and isolation that stem from his firm decision to live in the present and refuse to learn from past experiences.

By watching Peter interact with the Lost Boys and the pirates, and by listening to all his wild adventures, Wendy realizes that Peter is not a person who can provide her with a lasting and fulfilling relationship. This is a hard, but important, lesson to learn. How many times are we attracted to someone that we wish we could change, either physically or emotionally? How many times do we try to mold someone to our own specific ideas and interests? It is only by entering into a series of relationships that we are then able to figure out those qualities and traits we desire in a potential partner. And we must anticipate that dark moments and tragedy will be sprinkled among all the love and happiness we experience. Those of us who repeatedly attempt to create a lover out of the spare parts of our past relationships only end up isolating ourselves from genuine intimacy, pretending we are truly happy when all we have done is just to shipwreck ourselves on our own private Neverland.

Although Wendy's near-death experience at the hands of the jealous Tinkerbell alerts her to the fact that Neverland can be a dangerous place, it is her first real threat of danger at Marooners' Rock that warns her of the seriousness and complexity with which one must approach and navigate an adult relationship. It is during this scene in the novel that Wendy almost drowns. Having rescued Princess Tiger Lily from Captain Hook, Peter and Wendy find themselves trapped on Marooners' Rock while the water rises around them. For a young Victorian woman, this episode seems particularly frightening, and Barrie even remarks that "Wendy was crying, for it was the first tragedy she had seen."[24] It is her relationship with Peter Pan that has landed Wendy in this predicament, and she no longer has her parents to aid and protect her. She is now an independent woman who must make her own choices and live with the consequences of her own decisions. When adults read this scene we cannot help but reflect on the fact that when we enter into an intimate relationship we must also endure our partner's struggles and hardships as well as our own.

Wendy seems to realize this idea when she voices her desire to remain with Peter on Marooners' Rock. True, the danger lies in the fact that they cannot flee, and for a moment they seem fated to drown together, but Wendy is still expressing a mature decision not to abandon Peter. We all know that sometimes it is much easier to walk away or to remain silent, but typically these selfish moments tend to isolate us even further from the people with whom we should be loving and intimate. Peter, acting the part of egotistical hero rather than concerned lover, ties the tail of a kite around Wendy and pushes her from the rock. He envisions himself as a gallant knight who can add yet another breathtaking story to his infamous collection of brave deeds. He completely misses the deeper meaning inherent in this tense yet tender moment with Wendy, namely that every relationship requires a certain amount of sacrifice and selflessness if it hopes to succeed.

To Peter, this scene on Marooners' Rock is just another adventure, but to Wendy, and also to adult readers, it is a shocking reminder of the intensity that can interrupt the calmness in our daily lives. It is also interesting that this scene occurs in a body of water, namely a lagoon, which, much like the ocean that surrounds Neverland, symbolizes a rebirth or an awakening. Given that this episode at Marooners' Rock is Wendy's first tragedy, we can see the connection between the gothic elements (darkness, pirates, and the threat of drowning) and Wendy's realization that she has strong feelings for Peter and does not wish to leave his side. Therefore, we can see how gothic moments in the novel help Wendy to realize more fully her own feelings, thus assuring that, unlike Peter, she does not become too dependent on the make-believe structure of Neverland.

The importance of this episode on Wendy's psychosocial and psychosexual development is evident in that after her escape from Marooners' Rock she begins to feel more intense feelings of jealousy toward Tinkerbell and Tiger Lily. This makes sense when we consider that often—usually after a stressful or traumatic event—two people sometimes find themselves growing closer together, their feelings intensifying because of a shared personal moment. When Peter tells Wendy, "There is something [Tiger Lily] wants to be to me, but she says it is not my mother," Wendy replies angrily, "No, indeed it is not."[25] Because Peter has not progressed past childhood he is not aware that Tiger Lily wants to be his girlfriend. His feelings toward women, Wendy included, are innocent and asexual. As adults, we can certainly understand Wendy's anger, which is directed not so much at Peter as at his ignorance and naivety. It is always frustrating when two people in different stages of psychosocial and psychosexual development attempt to communicate their feelings. For Wendy, her domestic life as wife to Peter and mother to the Lost Boys has not only allowed her to glimpse the nature of an adult relationship, but it has also provided her with a false sense of hope that Peter might one day progress through adolescence and then be able to reciprocate her feelings.

Wendy finally realizes she cannot free Peter Pan from the chains of eternal boyhood. In short, she cannot experience a true adult relationship while she remains at Neverland. And while the island, with all its gothic elements and tropical charms, has certainly contributed to Wendy's growing sense of identity by supplying her with various adult roles in which to practice being mature, it has also convinced her that remaining on the island would stunt her growth and development, rendering her as isolated from love as Peter Pan. We see this realization begin to take place in Wendy during the episode at Marooners' Rock (and it culminates during the novel's climax when she is held captive on the pirate ship). But another pivotal moment occurs during a conversation with Peter when she finally asks him to explain his feelings for her. This is the one question that Peter cannot answer, though he responds by telling her, "Those of a devoted son."[26] Of course, this is not the answer Wendy wants to hear, though it is probably the one she expects. She becomes withdrawn at Peter's reply and it is perhaps this honesty from him that spurs Wendy to announce, later that same night, that she and her brothers are leaving Neverland to return home to their parents. To continue progressing through adolescence, and eventually to move into early adulthood, Wendy must rely not only on parental guidance, but also on new radii of significant relations that she feels confident to seek out and explore in the real world.

Wendy's final adventure in Neverland, and her final mingling with the island's gothic elements, involves the kidnapping of herself and the Lost Boys, the demise of Captain Hook, and the eventual takeover of his pirate ship, *The Jolly Roger*. The novel's climax involves a smorgasbord of gothic elements: pirates, attempted murder, death, devourment, and a ravenous crocodile. The battle aboard the pirate ship is the final obstacle that Wendy must face before returning to London. That the children assume the role of pirates after the battle is over and won implies they have successfully navigated the island's gothic elements. For Wendy, this conquering signifies a new stage of psychosocial and psychosexual development in which she can now begin to construct meaningful adult relationships, which is expected of her by a Victorian society. For Peter, this conquering of his arch nemesis is yet another opportunity to boast, and it simply assures him of new adventures he will simply repeat over and over again until perhaps another woman enters Neverland and tries to push him toward the maturity and identity fulfillment he desperately needs, but refuses to acknowledge.

When the crocodile, with the ticking clock inside its stomach, finally eats Captain Hook, we sense that time has run out not only for Captain Hook, but also for Wendy. Her journey into Neverland now complete, she must return home to build upon the feelings and emotions she has cultivated with Peter Pan. Aboard the pirate ship, sailing toward her own future, Wendy is now more aware of such emotions as jealousy and hurt, of unrequited love and the numerous stresses that accompany every new relationship. While she might feel a certain amount of hesitancy at leaving behind Neverland and Peter Pan, that final tick tock that echoes across the ocean is a reminder that time will catch up to all of us if we refuse to grow up and discover our identities. Along with eventual death, the silence of the clock seems to symbolize the necessary end of childhood as well. When the crocodile swallows Captain Hook the make-believe game is over, and so is another stage in Wendy's life.

Perhaps Peter realizes this, for later that same night he has a bad dream. Wendy holds him while he cries in his sleep. This final intimate moment between the two of them, of which Peter is unaware, is also a tender goodbye between the two children. That Wendy holds Peter tight is a testament to how strong her feelings for him have grown. Perhaps her embrace also suggests a lingering curiosity about what might have been. This pause for reflection is an act most of us have experienced at some point in our lives, and while it can often be difficult and painful, it also helps us to see more clearly the true nature of our own relationships.

Admittedly, Wendy is a passive character throughout much of her time on Neverland. She remains underground most days, cooking and sewing and tending to the Lost Boys; and when she does encounter the island's gothic elements she does so as more of an observer than as an active participant. Yet by observing the ways in which the characters around her interact, and the various ways in which the gothic elements impact many of their relationships, she is able to learn from these experiences and to process her embryonic feelings. Still, Wendy can be quite the feisty girl, as her arguments with Peter illustrate, as well as her displays of courage and lack of fear when speaking to Captain Hook and his band of pirates. I agree with Diablo Cody's proclamation that "inside every well-mannered Wendy ... there's a hyperactive Peter Pan longing to escape."[27] Wendy might seem to be a dainty girl surrounded by a horde of rambunctious boys, but her decision to fly to Neverland reveals a craving for danger and adventure that we all share and pursue. Like most adults, Wendy will always retain elements of her childhood, and she will always indulge in fantasies and dreams, but she will also know when to separate them from reality. This ability stems from her being mostly an observer on Neverland. Unlike the participatory boys, she knows the fantasies are not real.

Wendy has witnessed firsthand the ways in which a refusal to grow up, and a blurring between fantasy and reality, can lead to isolation and asexual feelings. At the end of the story, Wendy watches her own daughter fly off to Neverland with Peter. Thus, the cycle repeats itself, generation after generation, thereby affirming that we must all take that flight to Neverland at some point in our lives. While beginning the trip can be exciting and scary, it takes maturity and responsibility to say goodbye to something that has become comfortable and familiar and then return home to an uncertain future.

Peter Pan

If Wendy is the character who develops the most throughout *Peter and Wendy*, then Peter Pan is certainly the antithesis, a character whose growth and identity remain unchanged because of his own anger, naivety, and self-centeredness. To children, Peter seems to be a role model. He is a young boy with no parents to order him about; he has no bedtime, he is the leader of a group of children who revere him, and every day, instead of going to school, he embarks on a series of countless adventures from which he always returns home safely. It makes sense, then, that most children would envy Peter and secretly wish they could live on Neverland where children always seem to win and there are no adults to spoil the fun.

To adults, however, Peter Pan is a pitiable figure. He can neither write nor spell, he has no memory, and he lacks the ability to learn from personal experience because he has no firm sense of identity on account of his adamant refusal to grow up and become a man. At one point in the novel Barrie writes of Peter, "I don't believe he ever thought."[28] Indeed, Peter is spontaneous and impulsive, only concerned with himself and the roles he creates and then expects others to play. While Wendy certainly panders to Peter's chosen role for her as a wife and a mother, she soon learns, as most adults will, that she cannot play the part forever and must eventually live it. Peter, however, will never experience this epiphany, as Humphrey Carpenter stresses: "Barrie seems to be saying that the childish imagination, splendid as it is, has the most terrible limitations, and can never (without growing up) come to terms with the real world. *Peter Pan* thus manages both to celebrate imagination and to give a rather chilling warning of its limitations."[29] Because Peter confuses reality and fantasy, he cannot function in the adult world where people share such important emotions as remorse, sympathy, and compassion.

At one point in the novel Barrie even remarks that Peter is more interested in his cunning and quickness than he is in protecting his friends from danger. Added to this fact is Barrie's admission that "Peter had seen many tragedies, but he had forgotten them all."[30] Not valuing his own life, how can he be expected to respect and appreciate someone else's life? How can he be expected to place someone else's needs before his own? Peter's imagination, which seems so wonderful and magical to a child, becomes a prison in which his adult identity struggles for freedom. As a result, he hinders himself from maturing into a responsible man who is able to give and accept intimacy. Clouded by his intolerance of the adult world, Peter does not realize that to engage in intimacy with a loving partner is perhaps the greatest adventure of them all.

As adults, we realize that Peter has not been nurtured by a family or a community. His lack of maturity stems from an absence of parental love and supervision. Parents are responsible for instilling in their children a sense of right and wrong, a set of values that will help carry them through each one of Erikson's stages of psychosocial development. In *Peter and Wendy*, Barrie writes a beautiful passage that emphasizes the impact a parent's proper care and attention can have on a child's state of mind and well-being:

> It is the nightly custom of every good mother after her children are asleep to rummage in their minds and put things straight for next morning, repacking into their proper places the many articles that have wandered during the day.... It is quite like tidying up drawers.... When you wake in the morning, the naughtiness and evil passions with which you went to bed have been folded up small and placed at the bottom of your mind and on the top, beautifully aired, are spread out your prettier thoughts, ready for you to put on.[31]

Because Peter does not have a mother to tidy up his mind, it makes sense that he confuses make-believe with reality. He has never had to suffer the consequences for mistakes and misbehavior, and so he cannot differentiate between good and bad etiquette. Without good examples to follow, Peter does not move forward in life, but repeats the same experiences over and over again.

Rather than progress naturally through the various stages of psychosocial and psychosexual development, and thus establish an identity and personality that will allow him to engage in intimacy, Peter chooses to stifle those circadian rhythms of growth and maturity, thereby creating a self-imposed exile to Neverland that he views as nothing more than an endless romp through his very own theme park. It is also interesting to note that while tending to view Peter Pan as symbolic of our own loss of innocence, we sometimes neglect to realize that Peter's tragic persona stems not from innocence lost, but from innocence retained.

Peter Pan retains his innocence because he does not allow the gothic elements on Neverland to impact his psychosocial and psychosexual development. Afraid of growing up and assuming adult responsibilities, he refuses to see the gothic elements as instructional and educational, relegating them to a fantasy world where he can control them and not vice versa. Those gothic elements on Neverland, which prove so important to Wendy's growth and development, are as useless to Peter as gaining an adult identity and forming an intimate relationship. Instead of allowing him rich experiences that he can process and reflect upon, the gothic elements simply supply him with the opportunity to tell more stories about himself and fuel his belief that the only real adventures in life involve pirates, mermaids, and redskins.

Because Peter Pan does not experience any major crises, and because he refuses to think about grown-up issues, he is unable to mature. He is proof, then, of the important role that Gothicism plays in helping to shape our identities. Without its influence, we are unable to understand the darker side of human nature. We cannot search out new ways of establishing our own identity, and so we become overwhelmed and intimidated by all the pain, anger, and hurt that are so vital to successful growth and development.

Admittedly, there are some adults who idolize Peter Pan. They envy his adventures and perpetual state of innocence. Many of these adults are often unhappy with intimacy in their own lives and unable to navigate through personal crises. In struggling to maintain adult relationships they tend to withdraw into their own fantasies, and their yearning for childhood simplicity is a detriment to their need for community and companionship. Such adults fear closeness, echoing Peter's own fear of being touched. The consequences of this emotional and physical seclusion can impact every aspect of their daily lives, including work, family, and community. Alison Lurie sums it up best when she writes, "The effort to remain young, if too long continued, is exhausting and demoralizing."[32] A person who spends all of his time worrying about affection, and also trying to recapture a youth that is gone forever, will one day find himself well into Erikson's eighth stage of psychosocial development, *ego integrity versus despair*, feeling regretful and angry at having worried incessantly about maturity during early adulthood, as well as now fearing the onset of death.

By successfully navigating through all of Erikson's stages of development, we can eventually arrive at a place in our lives where not only will we feel proud of our accomplishments, but feel knowledgeable about our failures. As C. George Boeree notes, "Someone who approaches death without fear has the strength Erikson calls wisdom. [Erikson] calls it a gift to children, because 'healthy children will not fear life if their elders have integrity enough not to fear death.'"[33] Since Peter Pan has no elders to emulate and respect, he is fearful and apprehensive of growing into a man and leaving behind his childhood. The lack of adult supervision in Peter's life, as well as his inability to interact with gothic elements, have not provided him with a set of codes and behaviors to which he can respond and from which he can learn. He has not suffered through a series of crises that spark self-reflection. True, he announces his famous line that "to die will be an awfully big adventure," but his courage in the face of death is not earned, and he says it with the full knowledge that he is simply embroiled in yet another adventure in which he will survive and become a hero.[34]

Throughout *Peter and Wendy*, Barrie emphasizes Peter's innocence and naivety by describing him in childlike terms and also linking his character with symbols of infancy. Barrie describes Peter as having all his baby teeth, and later, during the episode at Marooners' Rock, he places Peter inside the Never bird's nest, further implying that Peter Pan is in need of a caregiver who can lavish him with attention and who can nurture his development. Peter himself repeats this idea during his final battle with Captain Hook when he says, "I'm a little bird that has broken out of the egg."[35] That Peter has absolutely no understanding of his own identity is illustrated further when Barrie reveals Captain Hook's response to Peter's previous statement: "It was proof to the unhappy Hook that Peter did not know in the least who or what he was."[36] The ease with which Peter is able to switch identities throughout the novel, from loving husband to doting father to cheeky braggart, culminates at the end of the story with the wearing of a new suit that Wendy fashions out of Captain Hook's clothes. Barrie tells us that Wendy made this suit "against her will," which suggests that she, too, realizes Peter's propensity for adopting different identities, and that he does so because he lacks a concrete identity himself.[37]

While we do not assume that Peter will take on certain characteristics of Captain Hook, the effortlessness he displays in adopting the mannerisms of such a frightening and violent character nevertheless stresses a need for him to stop playing games and to grow up. It is this desire to assume different personas that creates an emotional distance between Peter and those who might wish to care for him. Part of the reason Peter enjoys role-playing is because he fears progressing through the various stages that will result in him changing into an adult. By concentrating on other identities, which he can wear and discard whenever he chooses, he is free to neglect his own identity and to live vicariously through manufactured dreams rather than through fulfilled reality. Peter enjoys the repetition of his life and the familiarity that such an existence affords him. His constant ridiculing of Captain Hook, and adult figures in general, betrays his own loss of identity, which, Erikson explains, "is often expressed in a scornful and snobbish hostility toward the roles offered as proper and desirable in one's family or immediate community."[38] People who tend to dismiss the importance of intimate relationships and family values often express their distaste of such values because they lack those values in their own lives. The hostility projected from their harsh actions or words, which they frequently try to disguise as callous or indifferent, clearly illustrate strong feelings of jealousy and resentment toward those of us who are fortunate enough to possess these values. What these lonely people do not understand, however (and this is Peter's dilemma, too), is that we experience these values as a result of having attained successful psychosocial and psychosexual development, and also because of the numerous crises that have helped to shape our personalities.

The one major crisis that Peter suffered through, and still remembers, is the feeling of abandonment when his mother shut the window and replaced him with another child. It seems that Peter's constant declarations of wanting to always be a boy and to have fun (as well as "No one is going to catch me and make me a man") are residual effects of being disowned.[39] As most of us do when we feel abandoned and unwanted, Peter tries to convince himself that he is happier without a mother, and that he does not wish to be an adult because eternal boyhood is more rewarding. Barrie even tells us that Peter thought mothers to be extremely glorified. Clearly, this attempt to distance himself emotionally from such a painful memory contributes to his hatred and distrust of authority. Erikson tells us that "the counterpart of intimacy is distantiation, the readiness to repudiate, ignore, or destroy those forces and people whose essence seems dangerous to one's own."[40] Peter exhibits this behavior throughout the novel, attempting to quell any opportunity in which he might be forced to admit feelings, such as when he seeks reassurance from Wendy that their roles as father and mother are just make-believe. That he seeks this reassurance only reaffirms his fear of growing older, as well as his apprehension of assuming adult responsibilities and having to provide care for other people in addition to watching out for just himself.

Likewise, at the end of the novel, Peter bars the window to Wendy's room so when she arrives back home she will believe her mother does not want her anymore. Although Peter does not view Wendy in a sexual context, he still harbors feelings for her that he cannot understand. He likes the attention Wendy showers upon him, but more importantly, he does not want to lose her to an adult world that he believes abandoned him so many years ago. As with everything else in Peter's life, human relationships are nothing more than a game to him. If Wendy chooses to leave Neverland and pursue her own adult life, then perhaps Peter will view that decision as an attack on his own character. None of us want to feel that our lives are insignificant, but Peter's own fear of abandonment and loneliness actually isolate him further by forcing him to establish a series of relationships that are as shallow and fake as some of the adventures he concocts on Neverland.

Although Peter's relationships are self-serving and asexual, they do allow him to express his own form of intimacy, namely through the act of flying. Earlier, I discussed Freud's idea that dreams of flying often symbolize our sexual fantasies. There are many times throughout the novel, whether bringing Wendy and her brothers to Neverland, or soaring high above Captain Hook's pirate ship, when Peter exhibits his flying skills so as to impress his audience and inflate his ego. Peter's flying routines, which often contain an assortment of tricks and stunts, parallel the intense showmanship that adults often mimic when we are trying to impress a lover with our romantic behavior or sexual stamina. For Peter, flying is the only way he can achieve what the rest of us develop naturally throughout our adolescence and early adulthood: an awareness of our own sexuality. In Peter's case, however, flying is still a fairy act, allowing him to approximate sexual fantasies without ever having to recognize or to face them.

Because he can neither feel nor share the necessary emotions that must accompany mature sexuality, Peter Pan remains alone and childish, even when surrounded by his friends. At the end of *Peter and Wendy* he remains unchanged, still content to circle his own private island, and still oblivious to the joys of intimacy. His outward happiness and exuberance only mask the hurt and anger he still harbors at being abandoned by his own mother. This painful memory distances Peter, both emotionally and physically, from the very people and stimuli that can provide him with an opportunity for growth and maturity. It is clear through Peter's words and actions that his embrace of Neverland is a selfish attempt to avoid the psychosocial and psychosexual development that is necessary for his identity formation. Unlike Wendy, Peter is unable to benefit from the island's gothic elements. He chooses to view them as projections of his own self-centered fantasies rather than as opportunities to explore his own actions and their effect on his limited personality. Without these gothic encounters, Peter will continue to remain naïve and immature, never realizing that many fulfilling adventures exist beyond the boundaries of Neverland.

Captain James Hook

If Peter Pan can be said to shun Gothicism, then surely Captain James Hook embraces it and embodies it. Even Hook's appearance is gloomy and menacing. He sports an iron hook instead of a right hand, and Barrie describes him as being "cadaverous and blackavised, and his hair was dressed in long curls.... His eyes were of the blue of the forget-me-not, and of a profound melancholy.... He was never more sinister than when he was most polite."[41] Hook's personality also mirrors his gothic appearance; he broods like a Byronic hero and constantly wanders through Neverland in a melancholy state. Captain Hook is envious of Peter Pan's youth and carefree nature. He is a lonely adult, and perhaps in Peter he sees a childhood to which he desperately wants to return, but cannot. While many adults experience similar pangs when reflecting upon their early days, most do not obsess over these reflections or allow them to consume their everyday lives. In his many attempts to kill Peter and the Lost Boys, Captain Hook is also attempting to erase any symbols that might remind him of his youth, as well as the terrifying figure he has since become.

Captain Hook hates Peter because of the young boy's arrogance. While Peter's cockiness stems from his bravery and constant survival, it also reflects a subconscious attempt by Peter to mask the pain and anger he feels at being abandoned by his mother, as well as his determination to crowd lots of energy and excitement into a repetitive life that lacks any form of commitment. Hook does not know that Peter Pan's life is devoid of intimacy. On the contrary, he believes Peter to be living every child's fantasy. Erikson elaborates on Hook's obsession with Peter by revealing that "the greatest danger of isolation is a regressive and hostile reliving of the identity conflict and, in the case of a readiness for regression, a fixation on the earliest conflict with the primal Other."[42] Clearly, Peter Pan represents the Other, an ever present symbol of the childhood that Hook has lost. Hoping to dispel his own feelings of isolation, Hook constantly uses his anger to lash out at Peter, believing that to murder Peter's identity will somehow improve his own identity and allow him to progress onward through adulthood on his way to securing an intimate relationship.

Many of us experience these moments of displaced anger, especially during the stage of early adulthood when we are trying to juggle the end of our adolescence with the newfound responsibilities and expectations of being a mature grownup. Often, in our failure to achieve intimacy, we become envious of a past that was typically free of such pressures. When this happens, we often revert back to exhibiting childish behavior in our language and actions. In attempting to adopt the persona and characteristics of a former identity, we sometimes attack, both verbally and physically, any object or person that might remind us of our own personal crises. Like Peter Pan and Captain Hook, we exhibit such behavior to numb the difficulties that occur during specific stages of our growth and development. Ironically, these role reversals only accentuate the great distance between childhood and adulthood, isolating us even further from the very crises that warrant our complete attention.

Surrounded by his band of pirates, Captain Hook endures such a life without intimacy. He is "terribly alone. This inscrutable man never felt more alone than when he was surrounded by his [men]. They were so socially inferior to him."[43] Perhaps Hook represents those of us too scared to pursue a loving partner. Or perhaps he represents those of us wanting to progress through early adulthood, but hesitant to leave behind our glorious childhood. In quoting Daphne du Maurier, Janet Dunbar refers to Captain Hook as "a tragic and rather grisly creation who knew no peace, and whose soul was in torment; a dark shadow; a sinister dream; a bogey of fear who lives in the gray recesses of every small boy's mind ... a lonely spirit that was terror and inspiration in one."[44] Captain Hook seems to symbolize a child's fear of what he might become if he is unable to grow and mature during the natural stages of psychosocial and psychosexual development. To a child, Captain Hook might represent the true nature of adulthood; to an adult, he might represent someone who is unable to create intimacy because he continues reflecting upon a lost childhood rather than focusing his mind and needs on the future.

Both Peter Pan and Captain Hook are surrounded by friends, yet they do not develop intimate relationships with any of them. Neither character learns from his radius of significant relations. Instead, they each abuse these relations in an effort to achieve their own means. Certainly, Erikson would agree that to resolve our crises at any given stage involves learning from a radius of significant relations that we can view as equals, and not merely as expendable objects. But whereas Peter is ignorant of this lack of intimacy, as illustrated by his ability to remain happy and naïve, Hook is fully aware of its presence and laments his solitude. If Peter is angry at the thought of growing up to become a man, Hook is angry that he has already done so. Hook cannot benefit from Neverland's gothic elements because, like Peter Pan, he does not interact with them. In many ways, they are extensions of Hook's own identity, and throughout *Peter and Wendy* he employs them not as educational tools that might provide self-reflection and aid him in gaining intimacy, but as weapons to be used in his mission to destroy Peter Pan and the Lost Boys.

In his mishandling of these gothic elements, as illustrated in his failure to poison, stab, and drown his enemies, Hook only becomes more fixated on childhood and thus isolates himself further from any chance of attaining intimacy. While Peter's dismissal of the island's gothic elements is proof of his enduring innocence and youth, Hook's absorption of those same elements only emphasizes his own intense loneliness and his fear of growing old, a trepidation he also shares with Peter Pan. Hook becomes a gothic figure because he lets negative emotions corrupt his character. While Peter has not yet reached early adulthood, the stage during which we typically gain a sense of our own mortality, Hook abhors being an adult and wishes to trade responsibility and dependability for simplicity and naivety.

Captain Hook's fear of death is symbolized by the crocodile that stalks him throughout Neverland, a ticking alarm clock inside its belly that alerts him of its presence. Clearly, time is stalking Hook as well. Because Hook has reached adulthood, he fully understands the concept of time and is powerless to stop its influence. The fact that he shies away at the sight of his own blood also seems to illustrate a fear of death, one that contributes to Hook's fixation on Peter Pan's dominance of childhood and his command of eternal youth. Unlike Peter, however, Hook knows that death is imminent, and Smee reinforces this truth when he tells him, "Some day the clock will run down, and then he'll get you."[45] It is interesting, however, that the first time Barrie refers to the crocodile he refers to the animal as "she." This suggests that the crocodile symbolizes a feminine presence. Like most of us, Hook harbors apprehensions about entering into a mature relationship, and from this standpoint the feminine crocodile could indicate his fear of adult intimacy. And yet the feminine crocodile also suggests that Hook is being stalked by the idea of what he needs most: a loving relationship. But he cannot consummate a rewarding relationship because he spends his days pursuing Peter instead of pursuing intimacy.

Captain Hook's quests for intimacy, and his constant attempts to murder Peter Pan (who accepts a life without intimacy in a lackadaisical way that Hook can only envy) reach a new level when Wendy arrives on Neverland. Both Hook and Peter desire Wendy for a female companion, although both characters desire her in purely asexual terms. We must remember that, unlike Peter, Captain Hook has achieved adulthood and is therefore capable of sexual activity. Jackie Wullschlager explains that Captain Hook is a "sexually mature male villain over whom the child Peter and the Lost Boys triumph. Hook, characterized by phallic symbolism from the start—the iron hook which twitches involuntarily, the big cigar—is a powerfully sexual creature who tries to seduce Wendy away from the boys. She finds him fascinating as well as frightening."[46] In observing Hook's efforts to lure Wendy to the *Jolly Roger*, we understand that he craves quiet conversation and female company rather than a sexual partner. He wants Wendy to tell stories to the pirates and also to cook and clean for them. Like Peter Pan, Captain Hook wants Wendy to be more of a mother than a wife.

Barrie emphasizes this idea when, during the episode at Marooners' Rock, Hook moans, "The game is up. Those boys have found a mother."[47] Hook's interest in securing Wendy as a surrogate mother reinforces Erikson's idea that during periods of isolation a person might revert back to his childhood wants and behaviors. Clearly, Captain Hook should be old enough to exist without a mother, but the fact that he wants a mother certainly reveals not only his need for attention, but also the fierce competition that exists between the pirates and the Lost Boys. Wendy, who is progressing through her own stage of development, is attracted to the masculine prowess of Hook, a trait that Peter clearly lacks. Yet she is also attracted to those boyish qualities of Peter that are certainly not aspects of Hook's somber demeanor. Neither Peter nor Hook is a suitable match for Wendy, but each one of them contains characteristics that appeal to her femininity. This love triangle intensifies throughout *Peter and Wendy* and also fuels the actions of Captain Hook and Peter Pan, both of whom wish to claim Wendy as their own mother.

In all of our adult relationships we crave love and acceptance, and Hook illustrates this craving toward the end of the novel when he says, "No little children love me."[48] This statement might seem odd coming from a man who spends the better part of the novel trying to hunt down and kill a group of children, but this statement also suggests that perhaps Hook pursues the children because he feels unloved by them. And this is certainly a childish behavior. Sometimes when we feel worthless and unwanted we tend to lash out at those we believe have slighted us or made us feel insignificant. Perhaps Hook believes that by instilling fear into the Lost Boys he can command their respect and feel important. This same idea applies to Hook's interest in obtaining Wendy as a surrogate mother. In his melancholy state, isolated and unable to express his own adult feelings, Hook desires Wendy because he believes that her presence will make him feel needed, thus validating his role as both a leader and a man.

Barrie makes it clear, however, that as sinister and vicious as Captain Hook seems to be, he is not entirely evil since he loves flowers and music. Also, he prides himself on maintaining good form, and Barrie writes that "however much he may have degenerated, he still knew that this is all that really matters."[49] These descriptions suggest that Hook's character does contain positive attributes, and there are moments when he displays common decency and acts like a gentleman. We might assume that Hook has become morose and despondent because he is not involved in an intimate relationship. He does not have a partner to woo and impress, a woman who can unlock that touch of the feminine that exists within his dark nature and sometimes gives him intuitions.[50] It is evident that within Captain Hook there live two identities that battle against each other, which might be why he sometimes refers to himself in the third person. This duality illustrates that Hook is not confident with his own identity, and, in a way, this detail also links him with Peter Pan, who still struggles with being abandoned by his own mother. Like many of us, Hook questions his own decisions and longs for someone with whom he can establish intimacy and form a strong commitment, whether it's of a sexual nature or not.

Hook's constant struggles with his own identity tend to peak during moments in which he wishes to perform brutal acts, such as tying Princess Tiger Lily to Marooners' Rock, putting poison into Peter's medicine, or dueling with Peter aboard the *Jolly Roger* at the end of the novel. These gothic moments seem to clash with his feminine nature, such as during the episode at Marooners' Rock. In response to Peter's assertion that Hook is nothing more than a codfish, we learn that "against such fearful evidence it was not their belief in [Hook] that he needed, it was his own. [Hook] felt his ego slipping from him. 'Don't desert me, bully,' he whispered hoarsely to it."[51] Through this exchange we sense that Hook's ego represents the gothic side of his personality. His ego gives him strength and infuses him with the menacing presence for which he is infamous. Yet perhaps Hook fears that in order to attain intimacy and indulge in the strengths that are characteristic of early adulthood, he must relinquish that part of his ego which affords him this threatening demeanor and well-known fearlessness. Erikson emphasizes that "the avoidance of such experiences because of a fear of ego loss may lead to a deep sense of isolation and consequent self-absorption."[52] Certainly, Hook is in the midst of an identity crisis brought about by his struggles to enjoy intimacy and to share parts of his personality with another person, yet also to remain the murderous pirate who instills fear and awe in all who behold him. Many of us undergo similar conflicts in wanting to form a commitment, yet also wanting to assert our independence.

Throughout the novel, Captain Hook experiences moments of hesitation, but he is unable to correctly interpret these feelings because he is too focused on pursuing Peter and the Lost Boys. By the time Hook arrives at his last moment, prepared to perish in the belly of the crocodile, we are fully aware that his jealousy and anger have not only fostered self-absorption and a subsequent identity complex, but they have also hindered him from solving his own personal crises concerning intimacy.

Hook's story is an important lesson in not being afraid to share our emotions. While most of us are able to progress through early adulthood, some adults are not able to make the journey, a point John Marsden illustrates:

> They find all kinds of ways to avoid such a scary experience, notably by staying child-like all their lives, retaining many of the characteristics of children. We can reasonably expect that part of the profile of such adults will be an ide-

alization of childhood: an attitude that childhood is where it's at, not a real childhood of course, but a grossly distorted one, best defined by that useful word "nice."[53]

Hook's final thoughts are of his own childhood, and I would like to think that in those last few seconds he finally realized the futility in trying to continuously regain a period of his life that had slipped away forever. For those of us trudging through early adulthood, Hook's death is a bitter reminder that sooner or later time will catch up to us all, and that during this short interim called life it is always best to celebrate intimacy rather than to lament isolation.

An Awfully Big Commitment

J.M. Barrie's *Peter and Wendy* is a commemoration of childhood, a novel that forces us to remember our younger days when time seemed to stretch on forever and the future seemed incomprehensible. All children want to grow up, but they want to live in an adult world that is dictated by childhood rules. They want to act like adults, but they do not want to accept responsibility for their actions. Like Peter Pan, they want to always remain young and innocent, unburdened by finances, employment, or relationships. J.A. Hammerton highlights one of the lasting truths about childhood:

> Childhood has many illusions, but seldom or never is the hope or desire to remain forever young one of these. No one who has watched children at play need be told that the consuming desire of childhood as it is of youth is to move onward in age, to play at being grown-up. The universal urge to develop, to grow, is implicit in every human thing, and only when the shock of the shortness of life comes upon one does the wish arise to mark time or to put back the clock.[54]

It is only when we realize that time is finite do we attempt to slow it down. Really, though, time moves no faster whether we are children or adults. We simply become busier and more focused, more preoccupied with adult responsibilities and those important issues that command our attention span for longer than thirty seconds.

For those of us navigating through Erikson's stage six of psychosocial development, that period known as early adulthood, there is much to be learned from Barrie's *Peter and Wendy*. While the three main characters are two children and one adult, the crises they undergo together are reflective of the same problems and difficulties that typically surface in our personal adult relationships. Having worked so hard toward an identity during our adolescence, we then feel confused and pressured when we are expected not only to share that identity with another person but to alter it, as well. Many of us want to believe that once we reach adulthood our identities will be solidified, etched into granite and untouchable. But adulthood is composed of many stages, and within each stage we interact with new radii of significant relations. We discover more aspects of our personalities, and we continuously enrich our identities. Our identities, then, are constantly evolving, constantly being molded and shaped by our life experiences and the variety of people with whom we interact on a daily basis.

In *Peter and Wendy*, each of the three main characters harbors some form of fear concerning growth and maturity. Their interactions with each other are reminders of how intimacy can often break down when two people have not yet reached the same stage of psychosocial and psychosexual development. All three characters are sympathetic because we can all see aspects of ourselves inside each one of them. We understand Wendy's desire to grow up and raise a family, yet continue to embark on grand adventures; we relate to Peter's apprehension of someday having to mature and assume adult responsibilities; and we acknowledge Captain Hook's fear of death, and his constant attempts to establish intimacy through abused power and a menacing demeanor. Although Peter and Wendy have not yet reached the stage of early adulthood, their words and behavior parallel many of the same thoughts and actions that define early adulthood. It seems clear, then, after reading *Peter and Wendy* that many of us in early adulthood still cling to traces of our adolescence and childhood, and it is only through careful consideration and self-reflection that we are able to solve our individual crises and move successfully to the next stage of development. For without doing so, how can we expect to engage in intimate relationships and to immerse ourselves in commitment? If we do not know ourselves, then how can we expect someone else to know us?

All of these questions are addressed in *Peter and Wendy*, which on one level is a brilliant combination of the fairy tale and the adventure story, but is also a perceptive case study for adult relationships. Jacqueline Rose pushes this idea further with her belief that "the most crucial aspect of psychoanalysis for discussing children's fiction is its insistence that childhood is something in which we continue to be implicated and which is never simply left behind."[55] The older we become, the more we realize that every new relationship is an entirely new experience in which we must relearn everything we thought we knew. To enter into a commitment is to feel young and hesitant, excited and nervous, almost as if we were retaking our first emotional steps.

We must remember that childhood is not something to be cut loose or waved away; it cannot be tucked into a drawer like an old photograph, forgotten for years until it is suddenly needed. Childhood is always lurking in the shadows, creeping along behind us throughout our entire lives; it constantly illuminates our past actions, and it constantly affects our future decisions. There will always be that moment, whether during our adolescence or early adulthood, when we suddenly realize we cannot remain on Neverland forever. Eventually we must ignore the steady ticking of the alarm clock. We must be bold and courageous, ready to seek out new relations, and eager to embark upon new adventures. We must discover our own identity and wear it like a cape. And then we must fly away.

Epilogue:
One Last Gasp

Sometimes, when I'm feeling nostalgic, I'll pull out my horror story from Miss Lawton's English class, remembering my classmates' reactions when I read it aloud. I'll remember their shocked expressions at the mention of a psychotic Santa Clause, their guilty smiles at the thought of nasty elves dishing out extreme punishments. They were entranced by the dark side of humanity, captivated by the communal joy of sharing stories. On that October day I brought my friends with me into the woods, and we talked about monsters and mayhem, entertained by our overactive imaginations and endless shouts of "What if!"

Sooner or later, at various times during our lives, we must all leave home to journey into the woods. Like Hansel and Gretel following a trail of breadcrumbs, we follow our nightmares into the gloomy underbrush, sometimes unsure which direction to travel or what dangers might await us. Our fears, whatever they might be, are integral to our growth and development, and the stories we share and tell can help us to understand those fears, as well as what it means to be human. Stories, as Maria Tatar explains, "ignite not just the imagination but also the intellectual curiosity, tugging at us and drawing us into symbolic other worlds, where we all become wide-eyed tourists, eager to take in the sights."[1] For children, Gothicism can provide these life-changing experiences; it is integral to their growth and development precisely because it terrifies and excites them. It nurtures their desire for change and autonomy.

Darkness is necessary and cathartic, but like all medicine it must be administered in small doses. Parents must be responsible for knowing their child's current stage of development. They must talk to their child and be prepared to guide the child when he stumbles or loses his way. Parents need to acknowledge whatever stage their child is going through and supply him with the necessary support and freedom to resolve individual crises on his own terms, and also at his own pace. Often, parents give their child this assistance in the form of literature. They buy books and share stories; they let their child experience other characters' joys and regrets, pains and sorrows. By diving into the pages of a book, children can wander endlessly through real and fantastic landscapes, becoming those wide-eyed travelers who return home with a greater sense of initiative and self-confidence.

While many parents might wish to shield their children from negative feelings and scary stories, it is this introduction to natural and supernatural fears that helps to guide children toward resolving those distressing emotions within themselves such as anger, jealousy, or disappointment. The reason fear is so effective—as presented in the gothic—in helping children come to terms with their anxieties is because children are vulnerable and helpless, already experiencing intense fear at the thoughts of being abandoned or overpowered. These scary moments, whether experienced in books or reality, have lasting impressions on a child's psyche and can assist him in not only understanding his limits, both emotionally and physically, but also the methods that others employ (and these "others" can be the child's own parents or the characters in a book) to overcome fear and apprehension. Only after we are able to control our fears can we then use those experiences to help resolve certain crises and progress toward future stages of psychosocial development.

Parents who wish to help their children navigate through Erikson's stages would do well to promote the reading of children's literature, especially those texts containing gothic elements. Certainly, the gothic journey that children will undertake is terrifying and exciting, but ultimately it is also encouraging and educational. Gothic elements are helpful as long as children are attempting to resolve their own personal crises within a given stage. If they've come to terms with their emotions, and if they've sensed positive growth in their identities and personalities, then those gothic elements can be left behind until they are needed later during another stage of development.

Children should receive the benefit of the doubt because more often than not they are able to handle much more than adults typically allow them. They might be highly emotional, but they are also tough and resilient. Instead of viewing the gothic as a barrier or a burden, we should view it as a vital component in the formation of our identities, mainly through strong, violent imagery, as well as its psychosocial and psychosexual influences. Learning experiences are a natural and routine part of everyone's life, regardless of age, and it's hard to be grateful for the good times if we haven't fought our way through the bad.

Children are just as susceptible to gothic influences as adults, and so it is crucial to their maturation process that they interact with such elements. We should not advocate that adults embrace Gothicism and that children hide from it. We should not celebrate children's literature as suitable material for children, and then ridicule those adults that wish to participate in its stories and lessons. Let's not forget that adults are the ones who write, edit, publish, market, and sell children's literature. All those monsters and ghouls and slimy creatures that creep from between the pages of a book are adult creations. Besides, don't adults embrace their inner child? Don't they read the Harry Potter series and fairy tales? How many adults act childish by attributing a specific gender to their personal belongings? How many adults talk to their pets as if they're human beings?

Unfortunately, many adults believe that books for children are beneath them, arguing that such literature lacks depth and uses a simple vocabulary. Nothing could be further from the truth. Author Philip Pullman once proclaimed, "There are some themes, some subjects, too large for adult fiction; they can only be dealt with adequately in a children's book."[2] Pullman's comment illustrates the idea that children's literature is for all ages, and that children have important ideas and lessons to offer, if only adults would pay them more attention and respect. If adults claim they have no use for fantasy or imaginary worlds, if they scoff at magical powers and faraway kingdoms, it's only because they've forgotten how to dream and wonder.

The popularity and success of children's literature has not only made these imaginary worlds more accessible to children and their parents, but has also inspired countless films, adaptations, poems, novelizations, and pop culture references too many to count. The story of Little Red Riding Hood, for example, exists in hundreds of versions worldwide, each one echoing the values and beliefs of a particular culture. The story has also served as the inspiration for such films as the violent R-rated *Freeway*, the animated *Hoodwinked*, and the teen romance *Red Riding Hood*; picture books such as *Lon Po Po: A Red Riding Hood Story from China* and *The Tale of Jemima Puddle-Duck*; poems such as "Little Red Riding Hood and the Wolf" and "The Waiting Wolf"; and short stories such as "Wolf," "Riding the Red," and "The Company of Wolves."

Besides being adapted into the classic 1940 Disney film, *Pinocchio* has been adapted into a live-action film, *The Adventures of Pinocchio*, and a horror film, *Pinocchio's Revenge*. The wooden puppet has also been a recurring character in the *Shrek* series. *Coraline* was adapted into a 2009 stop-motion film. And Peter Pan has not only been a dominating presence on the stage since its premiere in 1904, but it has inspired such film adaptations as Steven Spielberg's *Hook*, Disney's 1953 version, *Peter Pan,* and its 2002 sequel, *Return to Never Land,* and the 2003 *Peter Pan* that really amps up the adolescent attraction between Peter and Wendy.

All of these adaptations and spin-offs can be helpful additions when discussing the primary text with children. While most adaptations deviate from the source material, sometimes adding and removing characters and plot points, or even changing the tone and mood, each one still retains the original text's main themes and ideas. Those children who do not have access to Ellen Raskin's picture book *Goblin Market,* for instance, can still read Christina Rossetti's poem and understand how the story plays out against Erikson's theories on psychosocial development. Likewise, a child who watches Disney's *Pinocchio* or *Peter Pan* is still able to grasp the conflicts and crises the characters undergo as they struggle to assert their independence and to mature.

Introducing children to different versions of these classic texts can deepen their knowledge of the original material, foster further discussions with their radii of significant relations, and teach them that multiple perspectives and opinions are valid. These different versions allow children to experience various creative forms: novels, poems, short stories, plays, picture books, and films. The more children interact with a wide range of artistic expressions, the more likely they will better understand a given text, which will then lead to reflection and analysis. This emotional process not only enhances a child's reading, writing, and speaking skills, but contributes to the formation of the child's self-identity.

We must remember, too, that our identities are constantly evolving. They are never truly defined or discovered. Our childhoods are comprised of a series of interconnected stages, each one like a building block that rests atop the one before it. To remove even one block might cause the entire structure to collapse. In this way, childhood is more than just a stepping stone to adulthood. Jacqueline Rose offers the opinion that "childhood persists as something which we endlessly rework in our attempt to build an image of our own history."[3] This idea implies that each stage of our psychosocial development does not dead end into a brick wall. Rather, they all blend together seamlessly, folded together like a chain of hands that leads us through endless cycles of pain and happiness, supplying us with a maturation process that will last our entire lives.

Everything we do in our lives is directly influenced by certain choices we made as children, by decisions we formulated as we searched bravely for an identity and struggled to advance through each stage of our psychosocial development. As children, everything we did was based on an increasing need to grow up and become an important part of the adult world. Even as adults, we still cling to those characters and stories that have left an indelible print on our childhoods.

When we examine characters like Coraline and Little Red Riding Hood, Peter and Wendy, a puppet named Pinocchio, or even Laura and Lizzie, we are looking into a mirror, viewing remnants of ourselves at an earlier age: scared and lonely, unsure of our place in the world, and needing to make mistakes so we can gain the confidence required to ensure our maturity. In many ways, traces of these characters still linger inside all of us, influencing our daily decisions and affecting how we communicate with our radii of significant relations. When I feel bossed around I tend to identify with Pinocchio; when I feel stressed out and inadequate I am heartened by Coraline's productivity. Relationship issues drag me into the woods where I think of Little Red Riding Hood and her rendezvous with the wolf; Laura and Lizzie help me reflect on the importance of family; and whenever I tire of paying all those monthly bills, I long for the safety and solace that only Neverland can provide.

If these complex characters can immerse themselves in gothic landscapes and then return home once more as refined individuals, then shouldn't we allow children to participate in similar experiences? Shouldn't children be given the freedom to set out on their own journeys, making their own choices and learning from the consequences? Reading gothic literature affords children the comfort in knowing they are not alone in their fears and anxieties, that there are others out there suffering the same doubts and frustrations, and dreaming the same hopes for positive growth and development.

We all have a desire to be heroic and victorious, to slay giants and to unearth secrets. We want to feel hints of danger lurking in the background. We want to shiver as the hairs stand up on the backs of our necks. We read stories about ghouls and werewolves and vampires, about potions and spells, and we want them to be true. We want to see the gothic and to feel it. Gothic literature entices us and teaches us; it provides us with those opportunities to conquer our fears and to stand proud. Every child should have an opportunity to wrench open that creaky door and tiptoe down old wooden stairs, breath held tight as he disappears into the musty darkness. It's no wonder Dr. Pellinore Warthrop appeals to our dark sides at the end of *The Monstrumologist* when he says, "Yes, my dear child, monsters are real. I happen to have one hanging in my basement."[4]

Notes

Preface

1. Highlights of my story included bloody entrails strung around a Christmas tree like garland, severed heads wrapped in gift boxes, and stockings stuffed with organs. I was overjoyed at my creative descriptions, but my teacher, Miss Lawton, was not impressed with my warped view of Christmas. I failed the assignment and was ordered to stop writing gory, disgusting stories that might cause my classmates to faint, vomit, or have terrifying nightmares.

2. Fred Botting, *Gothic* (London: Routledge, 1996), 18.

3. Carlos Ruiz Zafon, *The Shadow of the Wind* (New York: Penguin, 2004), 35.

4. Eino Railo, *Haunted Castle: A Study of the Elements of English Romanticism* (New York: E.P. Dutton, 1927), 299.

5. Erik Erikson, *Identity: Youth and Crisis* (New York: W.W. Norton, 1968), 82.

6. *The Gothic in Children's Literature* is a significant contribution to children's literature. Published in 2008, it examines how Gothicism helps to shape a child's identity. The text, composed of thirteen essays, does a fine job covering subjects like cyber-fiction, gothic comics, and the uncanny, as well as incorporating literature from England, New Zealand, and the West Indies.

7. Carrie Hintz and Eric Tribunella, *Reading Children's Literature: A Critical Introduction* (New York: Bedford St. Martin's, 2013), 11.

Introduction: *Lurking in the Shadows*

1. Anna Jackson, Karen Coats, and Roderick McGillis, introduction to *The Gothic in Children's Literature: Haunting the Borders* (New York: Routledge, 2009), 4.

2. Erikson, *Identity*, 96.

3. Ibid., 22.

4. Ibid., 95.

5. Erik Erikson, *The Life Cycle Completed* (New York: W.W. Norton 1997), 36.

6. Erikson, *Identity*, 158.

7. Maria Tatar, *Enchanted Hunters: The Power of Stories in Childhood* (New York: W.W. Norton, 2009), 22.

8. Bruno Bettelheim, *The Uses of Enchantment* (New York: Vintage, 1989), 3.

Chapter 1: *Behavior and Boundaries*

1. Erikson, *Identity*, 107.

2. Children often exhibit this tendency to collect and discard when they first learn to

walk. They wander around the house grabbing random objects like coasters, magazines, and picture frames. They examine them for a minute or two, and then drop them somewhere when they become bored. Many children will collect a bunch of items and lug them around the house, sometimes hiding them to assert their control. These actions illustrate the child's attempt to make sense of the world around them.

3. Erikson, *The Life Cycle Completed*, 107.

4. Erikson, *Identity*, 272.

5. Ellen Raskin, afterword to *Goblin Market* (New York: E.P. Dutton, 1970), 32.

6. Ibid.

7. Bette B. Robert, *The Gothic Romance* (New York: Arno Press, 1980), 43.

8. Botting, *Gothic*, 32.

9. Suzy Waldman, "O Wanton Eyes Run Over: Repetition and Fantasy in Christina Rossetti," *Victorian Poetry* 38 (2000): 547.

10. Raskin, *Goblin Market*, 1.

11. Leonard Wolf, *Horror: A Connoisseur's Guide to Literature and Film* (New York: Facts on File, 1989), 94.

12. Antony H. Harrison, *Christina Rossetti in Context* (Chapel Hill: University of North Carolina Press, 1988), 114.

13. Raskin, *Goblin Market*, 26.

14. Ibid., 6.

15. Raskin, afterword to *Goblin Market*, 32.

16. Raskin, *Goblin Market*, 13.

17. Ibid., 17.

18. Ibid., 6.

19. Edna Kotin Charles, *Christina Rossetti: Critical Perspectives, 1862–1982* (London: Associated University Presses, 1985), 129.

20. Raskin, *Goblin Market*, 22.

21. Ibid., 6.

22. Ibid., 24.

23. Ibid., 22.

24. Ibid., 26.

25. Ibid.

26. Peter Merchant, "'Like a Beacon Left Alone': The Position of Christina Rossetti's Goblin Market," *Children's Literature in Education* 25 (1994): 77.

27. Tatar, *Enchanted Hunters*, 12.

Chapter 2: *Fools' Trap*

1. Terry Castle, *The Female Thermometer: Eighteenth-Century Culture and the Invention of the Uncanny*, (New York: Oxford University Press, 1995), 10.

2. Claudia Card, "Pinocchio," in *From Mouse to Mermaid: The Politics of Film, Gender, and Culture*, eds. Elizabeth Bell, Lynda Haas, and Laura Sells (Indianapolis: Indiana University Press, 1995), 63.

3. Erikson, *Identity*, 115.

4. A child's physical and mental development does not happen at the same rate, which often leads to frustration with the child. For example, if you throw a ball to a toddler, he will put up his hands a few seconds too late and become upset when he misses the ball or it hits him. The child knows he must put up his hands, but the message from his brain is not synced with his arm movement, which causes the delay in his actions.

5. Richard Wunderlich and Thomas J. Morrissey, *Pinocchio Goes Postmodern: Perils of a Puppet in the United States* (New York: Routledge, 2002), 2.

6. Erikson, *The Life Cycle Completed*, 108.

7. Erik Erikson, *Childhood and Society* (New York: W.W. Norton, 1950), 224.

8. Carlo Collodi, *Pinocchio* (New York: Puffin, 1996), 113.

9. Erikson, *Identity*, 171.

10. Collodi, *Pinocchio*, 51.

11. Ibid., 61.

12. Ibid., 81.

13. Ibid., 93.

14. Ibid., 95.

15. Ibid., 94.

16. Ibid., 187.

17. Erikson, *Identity*, 121.

18. Jack Zipes, *Happily Ever After: Fairy Tales, Children, and the Culture Industry* (New York: Routledge, 1997), 76.

19. Collodi, *Pinocchio*, 138.

20. Ibid., 150.

21. Ibid., 86.

22. Erikson, *Identity*, 122.

23. Collodi, *Pinocchio*, 140.

24. Ibid., 147.

25. Ibid., 189

26. Card, "Pinocchio," 66.

27. Collodi, *Pinocchio*, 206.

28. Ibid., 258.

29. Erikson, *Identity*, 119.

30. Collodi, *Pinocchio*, 21.

31. Ibid., 24.

32. Robert D. Feild, *The Art of Walt Disney* (New York: Macmillan, 1942), 138.

33. Collodi, *Pinocchio*, 43.

34. Wunderlich, *Pinocchio Goes Postmodern*, 13.

Chapter 3: *Games and Challenges*

1. Hugh Haughton, introduction to *Alice's Adventures in Wonderland*, by Lewis Carroll (New York: Penguin, 1998), xiii.

2. Karen Coats, "Between Horror, Humor, and Hope: Neil Gaiman and the Psychic Work of the Gothic," in *The Gothic in Children's Literature: Haunting the Borders*, eds. Anna Jackson, Karen Coats, and Roderick McGillis (New York: Routledge, 2009), 77.

3. Erikson, *Identity*, 123.

4. Ibid., 124.

5. Erikson, *Childhood and Society*, 227.

6. Erikson, *The Life Cycle Completed*, 75.

7. Donna Heiland, *Gothic and Gender: An Introduction* (Malden, MA: Blackwell, 2004), 3.

8. Botting, *Gothic*, 157.

9. Neil Gaiman, *Coraline* (New York: Harper Trophy, 2002), 124.

10. Ibid., 161.

11. Ibid., 30.

12. Sandra M. Gilbert and Susan Gubar, *The Madwoman in the Attic: The Woman Writer and Nineteenth-Century Literary Imagination* (New Haven: Yale University Press, 1979), 83.

13. Gaiman, *Coraline*, 84.

14. Coats, *The Gothic in Children's Literature*, 84.

15. Gaiman, *Coraline*, 37.

16. Castle, *The Female Thermometer*, 9.

17. Gaiman, *Coraline*, 27–28.

18. Ibid., 29.

19. Ibid., 67.

20. Ibid., 119.

21. Ibid., 65.

22. Ibid., 60.

23. Linda Bayer-Berenbaum, *The Gothic Imagination: Expansion in Gothic Literature and Art* (London: Associated University Presses, 1982), 16.

24. Gaiman, *Coraline*, 65.

25. Elena Gianini Belotti, *What Are Little Girls Made Of? The Roots of Feminine Stereotypes* (New York: Schocken Books, 1976), 86.

26. Gaiman, *Coraline*, 21.

27. Ibid., 26.

28. William Patrick Day, *In the Circles of Fear and Desire: A Study of Gothic Fantasy* (Chicago: University of Chicago Press, 1985), 23.

29. Gaiman, *Coraline*, 154.

Chapter 4: *Genital Dystopia*

1. Erikson, *Identity*, 166.

2. Ibid., 110.

3. Julian Fleenor, introduction to *The Female Gothic* (London: Eden Press, 1983), 10.

4. Erikson, *Identity*, 110.

5. Peter and Iona Opie, *The Classic Fairy Tales* (New York: Oxford University Press, 1980), 13.

6. Seth Lerer, *Children's Literature: A Reader's History from Aesop to Harry Potter* (Chicago: University of Chicago Press, 2008), 231.

7. Jack Zipes, *The Trials and Tribulations of Little Red Riding Hood: Versions of the Tale in Sociocultural Context* (Westport, CT: Bergin & Garvey, 1983), 7.

8. Jack Zipes et al., *The Norton Anthology of Children's Literature* (New York: W.W. Norton, 2005), 340.

9. Martin Hallett and Barbara Karasek, eds., *Folk and Fairy Tales* (Ontario: Broadview Press, 2002), 5.

10. Erikson, *Identity*, 132.

11. Charles Perrault's "Little Red Riding Hood" appeared in his 1697 collection of children's stories titled *Histoires et contes du temps passé, avec des moralités. Contes de ma mère l'Oye* (*Stories or Tales from Times Past, with Morals: Tales of Mother Goose* (1697). Other tales in this collection include "Bluebeard," "Puss in Boots," and "Sleeping Beauty."

12. Zipes, *The Trials and Tribulations of Little Red Riding Hood*, 54.

13. Bettelheim, *The Uses of Enchantment*, 173.

14. Ibid., 169.

15. Charles Perrault, "Little Red Riding Hood," in *Folk and Fairy Tales*, eds. Martin Hallett and Barbara Karasek (Ontario: Broadview Press, 2002), 8.

16. Charles Perrault's tales were not written for children, but for the French aristocracy at the court of Versailles. Perrault himself was a member of the court under the reign of King Louis XIV, and his tales emphasize the proper codes of behavior that women were expected to display. Women in Perrault's time were viewed as helpless and innocent, and so his tales reflect the bourgeois-aristocratic values embraced by the royal court. His version of "Little Red Riding Hood" provides strict moral instruction for young girls, and it reinforces the need for feminine submission.

17. The Grimms' "Little Red Cap" was included in the first edition of their 1812 collec-

tion of tales titled *Kinder- und Hausmärchen (Children's and Household Tales)*. They revised "Little Red Cap" for future editions of the collection, and the most well-known version of the tale appeared in the 1857 edition, which is also the basis for many of the most popular versions of the Grimms' fairy tales.

18. Jacob and Wilhelm Grimm, "Little Red Cap," in *Folk and Fairy Tales*, eds. Martin Hallett and Barbara Karasek (Ontario: Broadview Press, 2002), 9.

19. Maria Tatar, *The Hard Fact of the Grimms' Fairy Tales* (Princeton: Princeton University Press, 2003), 43.

20. Bettelheim, *The Uses of Enchantment*, 172.

21. Grimm, "Little Red Cap," 9.

22. Ibid., 10.

23. Erikson, *Identity*, 129.

24. Grimm, "Little Red Cap," 11.

25. Cristina Bacchilega, *Postmodern Fairy Tales: Gender and Narrative Strategies* (Philadelphia: University of Pennsylvania Press, 1997), 56.

26. Bettelheim, *The Uses of Enchantment*, 175.

Chapter 5: *An Awfully Big Adventure*

1. Alison Lurie, *Don't Tell the Grown-Ups: The Subversive Power of Children's Literature* (New York: Little, Brown, 1990), 128.

2. Erikson, *Identity*, 88.

3. Ibid., 92.

4. Ibid., 137.

5. Peter Hollindale, introduction to *Peter Pan and Other Plays*, by J.M. Barrie (Oxford: Oxford University Press, 1995), xxi.

6. "The Angel in the House," written in 1854, was a popular Victorian poem by Coventry Patmore. The title alluded to women who embodied those Victorian feminine ideals expected in a mother or a wife: purity, passivity, devotion to her family, and submission to her husband. Patmore wrote the poem for his wife, Emily, whom he idolized and touted as a model for all Victorian women.

7. Nell Boulton, "Peter Pan and the Flight from Reality: A Tale of Narcissism, Nostalgia, and Narrative Trespass," *Psychodynamic Practice* 12.3 (2006): 308.

8. J.M. Barrie, *Peter Pan in Kensington Gardens & Peter and Wendy*, ed. Peter Hollindale (Oxford: Oxford University Press, 1991), 73.

9. Ibid., 105.

10. Botting, *Gothic*, 156.

11. Barrie, *Peter and Wendy*, 195.

12. Ibid., 127.

13. Ibid., 97.

14. Pam B. Cole, *Young Adult Literature in the 21st Century* (New York: McGraw Hill, 2009), 1.

15. Erikson, *The Life Cycle Completed*, 70.

16. Barrie, *Peter and Wendy*, 92.

17. Ibid., 104.

18. Boulton, "Peter Pan and the Flight from Reality," 309.

19. Barrie, *Peter and Wendy*, 111.

20. Ibid., 126.

21. Ibid., 130.

22. Hollindale, introduction to *Peter Pan and Other Plays*, xiv.

23. Barrie, *Peter and Wendy*, 131.

24. Ibid., 143.

25. Ibid., 162.

26. Ibid.

27. Diablo Cody, "Screw Wendy, I'm Peter," *Jane* 11.4 (2007): 128.

28. Barrie, *Peter and Wendy*, 89.

29. Humphrey Carpenter, *Secret Gardens: A Study of the Golden Age of Children's Literature* (Boston: Houghton, 1985), 179.

30. Barrie, *Peter and Wendy*, 143.

31. Ibid., 73.

32. Lurie, *Don't Tell the Grown-Ups*, 135.

33. C. George Boeree, "Personality Theories Erik Erikson," Psychology Dept., Shippensburg University, http://www.social-psychology.de/do/pt_erikson.pdf. Last modified 2006.

34. Barrie, *Peter and Wendy*, 152.

35. Ibid., 203.

36. Ibid.

37. Ibid., 207.

38. Erikson, *Identity*, 172.

39. Barrie, *Peter and Wendy*, 217.

40. Erikson, *Identity*, 168.

41. Barrie, *Peter and Wendy*, 115.

42. Erikson, *The Life Cycle Completed*, 71.

43. Barrie, *Peter and Wendy*, 88.

44. Janet Dunbar, *J.M. Barrie: The Man Behind the Image* (Boston: Houghton, 1970), 168.

45. Barrie, *Peter and Wendy*, 120.

46. Jackie Wullschlager, *Inventing Wonderland: The Lives and Fantasies of Lewis Carroll, Edward Lear, J.M. Barrie, Kenneth Grahame, and A.A. Milne* (New York: The Free Press, 1995), 128.

47. Barrie, *Peter and Wendy*, 145.

48. Ibid., 189.

49. Ibid., 188.

50. Ibid., 147.

51. Ibid.

52. Erikson, *Childhood and Society*, 229.

53. John Marsden, "Speech to the Sixth National Conference of the Children's Book Council of Australia," Perth, May 2002, quoted in Andrea Schwenke Wyile and Teya Rosenberg, *Considering Children's Literature: A Reader* (Toronto: Broadview Press, 2008), 201.

54. J. A. Hammerton, *Barrie: The Story of a Genius* (Chapel Hill: University of North Carolina Press, 1988), 365.

55. Jacqueline Rose, *The Case of Peter Pan: Or the Impossibility of Children's Fiction* (Philadelphia: University of Pennsylvania, 1984), 12.

Epilogue: *One Last Gasp*

1. Tatar, *Enchanted Hunters*, 199.

2. Philip Pullman "Carnegie Medal Acceptance Speech," Random House LLC, www.randomhouse.com/features/pullman/author/carnegie.php. Accessed August 31, 2013.

3. Rose, *The Case of Peter Pan*, 12.

4. Rick Yancey, *The Monstrumologist* (New York: Simon & Schuster, 2009), 434.

Bibliography

Adler, Gerhard, ed. *Selected Letters of C.G. Jung, 1909–1961*. Princeton: Princeton University Press, 1984.

Bacchilega, Cristina. *Postmodern Fairy Tales: Gender and Narrative Strategies*. Philadelphia: University of Pennsylvania Press, 1997.

Barrie, J.M. *Peter Pan and Other Plays*. Edited by Peter Hollindale. Oxford: Oxford University Press, 1995.

_____. *Peter Pan in Kensington Gardens & Peter and Wendy*. Edited by Peter Hollindale. Oxford: Oxford University Press, 1991.

Bayer-Berenbaum, Linda. *The Gothic Imagination: Expansion in Gothic Literature and Art*. London: Associated University Presses, 1982.

Belotti, Elena Gianini. *What Are Little Girls Made Of? The Roots of Feminine Stereotypes*. New York: Schocken Books, 1976.

Bettelheim, Bruno. *The Uses of Enchantment*. New York: Vintage, 1989.

Birkin, Andrew. *J.M. Barrie & The Lost Boys: The Love Story that Gave Birth to Peter Pan*. New York: Clarkson N. Potter, 1979.

Boeree, C. George. "Personality Theories Erik Erikson," Psychology Dept., Shippensburg University. http://www.social-psychology.de/do/pt_erikson.pdf. Last modified 2006.

Botting, Fred. *Gothic*. London: Routledge, 1996.

Boulton, Nell. "Peter Pan and the Flight from Reality: A Tale of Narcissism, Nostalgia, And Narrative Trespass." *Psychodynamic Practice* 12.3 (2006): 307–17.

Brown, Marshall. "A Philosophical View of the Gothic Novel." *Studies in Romanticism* 26 (Summer 1987): 275–304.

Burke, Edmund. *A Philosophical Enquiry into the Origin of our Ideas of the Sublime and Beautiful*. New York: Oxford University Press, 1998.

Burnett, Frances Hodgson. *The Secret Garden*. New York: Penguin, 1999.

Card, Claudia. "Pinocchio." In *From Mouse to Mermaid: The Politics of Film, Gender, and Culture*, edited by Elizabeth Bell, Lynda Haas, and Laura Sells, 62–71. Indianapolis: Indiana University Press, 1995.

Carpenter, Humphrey. *Secret Gardens: A Study of the Golden Age of Children's Literature*. Boston: Houghton Mifflin, 1985.

Carroll, Lewis. *Alice's Adventures in Wonderland*. Edited by Hugh Haughton. New York: Penguin, 1998.

Castle, Terry. *The Female Thermometer: Eighteenth-Century Culture and the Invention of the Uncanny*. New York: Oxford University Press, 1995.

Charles, Edna Kotin. *Christina Rossetti: Critical Perspectives, 1862–1982*. London: Associated University Presses, 1985.

Coats, Karen. "Between Horror, Humor, and Hope: Neil Gaiman and the Psychic Work of the Gothic." In *The Gothic in Children's Literature: Haunting the Borders*, edited by Anna Jackson, Karen Coats, and Roderick McGillis. New York: Routledge, 2009.

Cody, Diablo. "Screw Wendy, I'm Peter." *Jane* 11.4 (2007): 128.

Cole, Pam B. *Young Adult Literature in the 21st Century*. New York: McGraw Hill, 2009.

Collodi, Carlo. *Pinocchio*. New York: Puffin, 1996.

Day, William Patrick. *In the Circles of Fear and Desire: A Study of Gothic Fantasy*. Chicago: University of Chicago Press, 1985.

Dunbar, Janet. *J. M. Barrie: The Man Behind the Image*. Boston: Houghton, 1970.

Ellis, Markman. *The History of the Gothic Novel*. Edinburgh: Edinburgh University Press, 2001.

Erikson, Erik. *Childhood and Society*. New York: W.W. Norton, 1950.

_____. *Identity: Youth and Crisis*. New York: W.W. Norton, 1968.

_____. *The Life Cycle Completed*. New York: W.W. Norton, 1982.

Feild, Robert D. *The Art of Walt Disney*. New York: Macmillan, 1942.

Freud, Sigmund. *The Interpretation of Dreams*. Translated by Joyce Crick. Oxford: Oxford University Press, 1999.

_____. *Introductory Lectures on Psychoanalysis*. Translated by James Strachey. New York: W.W. Norton, 1989.

_____. *Three Essays on the Theory of Sexuality*. Translated by James Strachey. London: The Hogarth Press, 1962.

_____. *The Uncanny*. Translated by David McLintock. New York: Penguin, 2003.

Gaiman, Neil. *Coraline*. New York: Harper Trophy, 2002.

Gilbert, Sandra M., and Susan Gubar. *The Madwoman in the Attic: The Woman Writer and Nineteenth-Century Literary Imagination*. New Haven: Yale University Press, 1979.

"Goblin Market: A Ribald Classic." *Playboy*, Sept. 1973: 117.

Gohlke, Madelon S. "Re-reading The Secret Garden." *College English* 41 (1980): 894–902.

Grimm, Jacob, and Wilhelm Grimm. "Little Red Cap." In *Folk and Fairy Tales*, edited by Martin Hallett and Barbara Karasek, 9–12. Ontario: Broadview Press, 2002.

Griswold, Jerry. *Audacious Kids: Coming of Age in America's Classic Children's Books*. Oxford: Oxford University Press, 1992.

Hallett, Martin, and Barbara Karasek, eds. *Folk and Fairy Tales*. Ontario: Broadview Press, 2002.

Hammerton, J. A. *Barrie: The Story of a Genius*. New York: Dodd, Mead, 1930.

Harrison, Antony H. *Christina Rossetti in Context*. Chapel Hill: University of North Carolina Press, 1988.

Heiland, Donna. *Gothic & Gender: An Introduction*. Malden, MA: Blackwell, 2004.

Hintz, Carrie, and Eric Tribunella, eds. *Reading Children's Literature: A Critical Introduction*. New York: Bedford St. Martin's, 2013.

Hurley, Kelly. *The Gothic Body: Sexuality, Materialism, and Degeneration at the Fin de Siècle*. New York: Cambridge University Press, 1997.

Jackson, Anna, Karen Coats, and Roderick McGillis, eds. *The Gothic in Children's Literature*. New York: Routledge, 2007.

James, Susan E. "Wuthering Heights for Children: Frances Hodgson Burnett's The Secret Garden." *Connotations: A Journal for Critical Debate* 10.1 (2000–01): 59–76.

Kilgour, Maggie. *The Rise of the Gothic Novel*. London: Routledge, 1995.

Lacan, Jacques. "The Mirror Stage as Formative of the Function of the I as Revealed in Psychoanalytic Experience." In *Ecrits: A Selection*, 1–2, 4–5. Translated by Alan Sheridan. New York: W.W. Norton, 1977.

Lerer, Seth. *Children's Literature: A Reader's History from Aesop to Harry Potter.* Chicago: University of Chicago Press, 2008.

Lindahl, Carl, John McNamara and John Lindow, eds. *Medieval Folklore: A Guide to Myths, Legends, Tales, Beliefs, and Customs.* Oxford: Oxford University Press, 2002.

Lurie, Alison. *Boys and Girls Forever: Children's Classics from Cinderella to Harry Potter.* New York: Penguin, 2003.

_____. *Don't Tell the Grown-Ups: The Subversive Power of Children's Literature.* New York: Little, Brown, 1990.

McGillis, Roderick. "Christina Rossetti: The Patience of Style." *Children's Literature Association Quarterly* 31.2 (2006): 211–16.

Merchant, Peter. "'Like a Beacon Left Alone': The Position of Christina Rossetti's Goblin Market." *Children's Literature in Education* 25 (1994): 67–80.

Monk, Samuel. *The Sublime: A Study of Critical Theories in XVIII-Century England.* Ann Arbor: University of Michigan Press, 1960.

Mussell, Kay J. "But Why Do They Read Those Things? The Female Audience and the Gothic Novel." In *The Female Gothic*, edited by Juliann E. Fleenor. London: Eden Press, 1983.

Opie, Peter, and Iona Opie, eds. *The Classic Fairy Tales.* New York: Oxford University Press, 1980.

Orenstein, Catherine. *Little Red Riding Hood Uncloaked: Sex, Morality, and the Evolution of a Fairy Tale.* New York: Basic, 2003.

Perrault, Charles. "Little Red Riding Hood." In *Folk and Fairy Tales*, edited by Martin Hallett and Barbara Karasek, 6–8. Ontario: Broadview Press, 2002.

Pullman, Philip. "Carnegie Melon Acceptance Speech," Random House LLC. www.randomhouse.com/features/pullman/author/carnegie.php. Accessed August 31, 2013.

Potter, Beatrix. *The Giant Treasury of Peter Rabbit.* New York: Derrydale, 1980.

Railo, Eino. *Haunted Castle: A Study of the Elements of English Romanticism.* New York: E.P. Dutton, 1927.

Raskin, Ellen. *Goblin Market.* New York: E.P. Dutton, 1970.

Roberts, Bette B. *The Gothic Romance.* New York: Arno Press, 1980.

Rose, Carol. *Spirits, Fairies, Gnomes, and Goblins: An Encyclopedia of the Little People.* Oxford: ABC-CLIO, 1996.

Rose, Jacqueline. *The Case of Peter Pan: Or The Impossibility of Children's Fiction.* Philadelphia: University of Pennsylvania Press, 1984.

Rossetti, Christina. *Goblin Market.* Illustrated and adapted by Ellen Raskin. New York: E.P. Dutton, 1970.

Schilder, Paul M. *The Image and Appearance of the Human Body: Studies in the Constructive Energies of the Psyche.* New York: John Wiley, 1964.

Schwenke, Wyile, and Teya Rosenberg. *Considering Children's Literature: A Reader.* Toronto: Broadview Press, 2008.

Shove, Fredegond. *Christina Rossetti: A Study.* New York: Octagon Books, 1969.

Stone, Kay. "Fairy Tales for Adults: Walt Disney's Americanization of the Märchen." In *Folklore on Two Continents: Essays in Honor of Linda Degh*, edited by Nikolai Burlakoff and Carl Lindahl. Bloomington, IN: Trickster Press, 1980.

"The Story of Grandmother." In *Folk and Fairy Tales*, edited by Martin Hallett and Barbara Karasek, 4–6. Ontario: Broadview Press, 2002.

Tatar, Maria. *Enchanted Hunters: The Power of Stories in Childhood.* New York: W.W. Norton, 2009.

_____. *The Hard Facts of the Grimms' Fairy Tales.* Princeton: Princeton University Press, 2003.

Varma, Devendra P. *The Gothic Flame.* New York: Russell & Russell, 1966.

Waldman, Suzy. "O Wanton Eyes Run Over: Repetition and Fantasy in Christina Rossetti." *Victorian Poetry* 38 (2000): 533–53.

Wallerstein, Robert S. *Ideas and Identities: The Life and Work of Erik Erikson.* Madison, CT: International Universities Press, 1999.

Welchman, Kit. *Erik Erikson.* Berkshire: Open University Press, 2000.

Wolf, Leonard. *Horror: A Connoisseur's Guide to Literature and Film.* New York: Facts on File, 1989.

Wullschlager, Jackie. *Inventing Wonderland: The Lives and Fantasies of Lewis Carroll, Edward Lear, J. M. Barrie, Kenneth Grahame and A.A. Milne.* New York: The Free Press, 1995.

Wunderlich, Richard, and Thomas J. Morrissey. *Pinocchio Goes Postmodern: Perils of a Puppet in the United States.* New York: Routledge, 2002.

Yancey, Rick. *The Monstrumologist.* New York: Simon & Schuster, 2009.

Zafon, Carlos Ruiz. *The Shadow of the Wind.* New York: Penguin, 2004.

Zaturenska, Marya. *Christina Rossetti: A Portrait with Background.* New York: Macmillan, 1949.

Zipes, Jack. *Happily Ever After: Fairy Tales, Children, and the Culture Industry.* New York: Routledge, 1997.

_____. *The Trials and Tribulations of Little Red Riding Hood: Versions of the Tale in Sociocultural Context.* Westport, CT: Bergin & Garvey, 1983.

Zipes, Jack, Lissa Paul, Lynne Vallone, Peter Hunt, and Gillian Avery, eds. *The Norton Anthology of Children's Literature.* New York: W.W. Norton, 2005.

Index